MW01377986

RONALD ROLHEISER

MODERN SPIRITUAL MASTERS SERIES

RONALD ROLHEISER

Essential Writings

Selected with an Introduction by

ALICIA VON STAMWITZ

ORBIS BOOKS
Maryknoll, New York 10545

ORBIS BOOKS
Maryknoll, New York 10545

Fathers and Brothers
MARYKNOLL

Founded in 1970, Orbis Books endeavors to publish works that enlighten the mind, nourish the spirit, and challenge the conscience. The publishing arm of the Maryknoll Fathers and Brothers, Orbis seeks to explore the global dimensions of the Christian faith and mission, to invite dialogue with diverse cultures and religious traditions, and to serve the cause of reconciliation and peace. The books published reflect the views of their authors and do not represent the official position of the Maryknoll Society. To learn more about Maryknoll and Orbis Books, please visit our website at www.orbisbooks.com

---

Published by Orbis Books, Box 302, Maryknoll, NY 10545-0302.

Manufactured in the United States of America

Library of Congress Cataloging-in-Publication Data

Names: Rolheiser, Ronald, author. | Stamwitz, Alicia von, editor, writer of introduction.
Title: Ronald Rolheiser : essential writings / selected with an introduction by Alicia von Stamwitz.
Description: Maryknoll, NY : Orbis Books, [2021] | Series: Modern spiritual masters series | Includes bibliographical references. | Summary: "Essential writings by leading Catholic spiritual writer, Ronald Rolheiser"-- Provided by publisher.
Identifiers: LCCN 2021013416 (print) | LCCN 2021013417 (ebook) | ISBN 9781626984400 (trade paperback) | ISBN 9781608339037 (epub)
Subjects: LCSH: Spirituality--Catholic Church. | Spiritual life--Catholic Church.
Classification: LCC BX2350.65 .R66 2021 (print) | LCC BX2350.65 (ebook) | DDC 248--dc23
LC record available at https://lccn.loc.gov/2021013416
LC ebook record available at https://lccn.loc.gov/2021013417

Contents

Sources and Acknowledgments ix

INTRODUCTION xi
Growing Up on the Canada Prairies xiii
University Studies and Priesthood xvi
From Theology to Spirituality xvii

PART ONE: HOLY LONGING

1. WHAT IS SPIRITUALITY? 3
The Fire Within 3
Eros: The Basis of the Spiritual Life 9
The Image of God inside Us 11
Our Grandiosity and Our Wounds 13
The Flavor of God's Energy 15
Different Challenges in Different Seasons 17
The Spiritual Life and the Stages of Christian Discipleship 19
The Major Imperatives within Mature Discipleship 23

2. OUR RESTLESS SELVES 26
Desire, Our Fundamental Dis-Ease 26
Struggling inside Our Own Skin 28
Loneliness In Youth And Old Age 30
The Reality Of Loneliness 31
The Incurable Pull toward God 38
Some Christian Theologians on Loneliness 40
The Purpose Of Restlessness 50

3. SEXUALITY AS SACRED FIRE 52
Healthy Sexuality 52
The Goddess Artemis 56
The Sacrament of Marriage 58
Accepting Disappointment in Love 65
Understanding Chastity 68

Celibacy as Solidarity with the Poor 70
A Mature Sexuality 72
Mourning Our Virginity 74

PART TWO: GUIDELINES FOR A GENERATIVE SPIRITUALITY

4. **THE INCARNATION AT THE ROOT OF ALL CHRISTIAN SPIRITUALITY** 79
Our Misconception of the Incarnation 79
Ordinary Goodness and Our Spiritual Journey 81
In Praise of Skin 83
The Earthiness of Christmas 85
Born into the Ordinary 88
Christmas as Shattering the Containers of Our Expectations 90
Touching Our Loved Ones inside the Body of Christ 92
Holy Thursday and the Eucharist 94
Incarnation—Another Meaning of Christmas 96

5. **PRAYER AND THE PERENNIAL INVITATION TO ALWAYS GO DEEPER** 99
We Are Made for Love 99
Prayer as Lifting Mind and Heart to God 101
Affective Prayer 103
Priestly Prayer—Prayer for the World 105
Contemplation and Meditation 108
The Value of Ritual in Sustaining Prayer 111
Deeper Things under the Surface 113
Prayer as Seeking Depth 115
Turning Our Eyes toward Heaven 117
Paralysis, Exasperation, and Helplessness as Prayer 119
Longing for Solitude 122
A Prayer for Stillness 124

6. **ENTERING THE MYSTERY OF PASSIVITY—ON AGING AND DYING** 127
The Intelligence inside of the Aging Process 127
A Lesson in Aging 129
The Route to Depth and Wisdom 130
Flowers and the Rich Young Man 133

Growing to Our Deepest Center 134
The Last Temptation 136
The Lessons of the Passion 138
The Summer of My Discontent 139
Undergoing Our Own Passion 141
The Grace within Passivity 143
"Blood and Water Poured Out" 144
Leaving Peace behind as Our Farewell Gift 146
Faith, Doubt, and Dying 149
Redemption for All 151
Giving Our Deaths to Our Loved Ones 152

7. **FAITH, DOUBT, AND DARK NIGHTS WITHIN THE SPIRITUAL JOURNEY** 155
Dark Nights and Maturity 155
Mother Teresa's Faith 158
God's Quiet Presence in Our Lives 160
Why Dark Nights of the Soul? 163
To Whom Can We Go? 164
Self-Abandonment and Obedience unto Death 167
The Desert—The Place of God's Closeness 174
God's Mercy and Peace 176
On The Road to Emmaus 178

8. **THE PROMINENT PLACE OF JUSTICE AND CHARITY** 181
Social Justice—New Knowledge/New Responsibility 181
What Is Love Asking of Us Now? 184
The Importance of the Interior and Private 186
But Where Are the Others? 188
Prophetic Balance 190
The Importance of Mellowness of Heart 192
Systemic Injustice 194
Our Need to Share Our Riches with the Poor 196
Prophetic Mantra about the Poor 199
Kissing the Leper 201
Can the Ground Cry Out? 203
Everything Is Interconnected 206
A Lord's Prayer for Justice 208

9. THE PASSION AND THE CROSS 211
The Cross of Jesus 211
The Tearing of the Temple Veil 213
The Meaning of Jesus' Death 216
The Cross as Revealing the Non-Violence of Christ 218
God as Redeemer, Not as Rescuer 220
The Cross as Revealing God's Presence in the Poor 223
How Jesus Takes Away the Sin of the World 224
Jesus' Last Words 227
Standing with Mary Under the Cross 229
Dying into Safe Hands 232
Facing Our Tough Hours 233
Carrying Tension 235

Sources and Acknowledgments

Selections from the following are reprinted in this volume:

In Exile. A series of columns written by Ron Rolheiser beginning in 1982 and continuing to this day. The individual columns can be found at ronrolheiser.com in the archives section.

The Holy Longing: The Search for a Christian Spirituality by Ronald Rolheiser, © 1999. Used by permission of Doubleday, an imprint of the Knopf Doubleday Publishing Group, a division of Penguin Random House LLC. All rights reserved.

Against an Infinite Horizon: The Finger of God in Our Everyday Lives by Ronald Rolheiser, © 2002. Used by permission of The Crossroad Publishing Company, www.crossroadpublishing.com. All rights reserved.

The Restless Heart: Finding Our Spiritual Home in Times of Loneliness by Ronald Rolheiser, copyright © 2004. Used by permission of Doubleday, an imprint of the Knopf Doubleday Publishing Group, a division of Penguin Random House LLC. All rights reserved.

The Shattered Lantern: Rediscovering a Felt Presence of God by Ronald Rolheiser, © 2005. Used by permission of The Crossroad Publishing Company, www.crossroadpublishing.com. All rights reserved.

Prayer: Our Deepest Longing by Ronald Rolheiser, © 2013. Used by permission of Franciscan Media, www.franciscanmedia.org. All rights reserved.

Introduction

In the summer of 1961, Ron Rolheiser was worrying about the kinds of things most fourteen-year-old boys worry about. His physical appearance. His popularity at school. Whether girls liked him. Whether he would make the high school softball team.

Then something happened that shattered his world:

> Our nearest neighbor, twenty-one years old—a gentle person, someone I looked up to and even envied for his athletic body—hung himself in a barn. His brother was in the same grade as me and we did everything together.
>
> When you're fourteen you can't really talk to anybody about something like that. You try to hide it. You try to bury yourself in work. But you don't have the tools to handle it, to process the death. I went through three years of depression after that. Three years—right through high school.
>
> Nothing in my life, including my parents' death and other suicides since, has ever rocked me to the core the way this suicide did. It's just—it's been the deepest dark night of my life. I'm a priest because of that summer.

Ron told this story in February 2020, near the end of a conference in San Antonio, Texas, where he's lived since 2005, serving for fifteen of those years as the President of Oblate School of Theology. Along with his academic work and several leadership roles in his religious community, he's a highly sought-after speaker and an award-winning spiritual writer. In his first "In Exile" column, published in 1982 in the *Western Catholic Reporter*, Ron quoted a line by the Canadian novelist Margaret Atwood: "What touches you is what you touch." Two thousand columns and sixteen books later, that's still his maxim. He's spent a lifetime mining literature, scripture, theology, philosophy, contemporary stories, and his own experience to touch the deepest places in the human heart—a place he first visited when his own inner world collapsed.

While the crisis left its scars, it also left him with a profound gift. "As all that pain, disillusionment, and loss of self-confidence was seeping into my life, something else was seeping in too," he later wrote, "a deeper faith, a deeper vision of things, an acceptance of my vulnerability and mortality, and a sense of my vocation." He now describes it as the period of his deepest growth and transformation. Solid theology grounds Ron's writings, but it's his vulnerability that lends his work a disarming, gentle power. Even casual readers are taken by his personal stories and his candor. No wonder he's found such a large audience: like great works of art, Ron's writings connect deeply with millions of people.

You'll get to know Ron in these pages: an affable man with a brilliant mind, a self-described sports nut, a good storyteller, a loyal friend, a faithful priest. His writings reflect both a mature Christian faith and moral character. As longtime friend Gerry Weinkauf puts it, "Ron is completely transparent. What you see is what you get." That matches my own experience. I've known Ron for almost twenty years, since meeting him in Rome at his religious order's international headquarters. I've read nearly everything he's written, and I've listened to him speak on several dozen occasions. Whether he's speaking to thousands of people in an auditorium or one person on a retreat, he radiates empathy, sincerity, and optimism. One thing you won't get in these pages, unfortunately, is his sense of humor. That's more evident in person, whether he is speaking publicly (he nearly always starts his talks with a sound check and a joke) or relaxing with good friends. For that side of him, I encourage you to watch one of the many available recordings of his live talks and retreats.

In an interview in his San Antonio office in 2019, I asked Ron how he hoped to be remembered after his death. He hesitated a long moment before answering. "I guess I want to be remembered as somebody who's trustworthy, as someone who didn't betray anybody's faith, as someone who never hurt anyone. Someone who was kind and who dispensed mercy in God's name, rather than any kind of judgment." That's as good a preface as any to this brief biography. If you are seeking a trustworthy and merciful spiritual guide, you have come to the right place.

GROWING UP ON THE CANADA PRAIRIES

Ron was born on October 13, 1947, in Macklin, Saskatchewan, a rural, immigrant community in the heart of the Canadian prairies. He was the twelfth of sixteen children—eight boys and eight girls—born to George and Mathilda Rolheiser between 1932 and 1955. His parents and grandparents, of German and Russian stock, were homesteaders who eked out a living on the semiarid land.

In the 1940s, according to Ron's older brother George, prairie life was fragile. The family farm survived the Dust Bowl (1930–1940) and the economic impact of the Second World War (1939–1945), but modern comforts were scarce. The Rolheiser home lacked indoor plumbing and electricity. Wood and coal stoves provided their only heat, and oil lamps their light. The work was hard, and daily chores were endless on the family's mixed farm. Before and after school, Ron and his siblings milked the cows, fed the pigs and chickens, looked after the horses, mucked out stalls, hoed the garden, and so on. They also worked in the fields, planting and harvesting oats, wheat, and barley.

When I ask George in a phone conversation if Ron stood out in any way in his youth, he tells me a story. At fifteen, Ron was driving the family's grain truck and hauling loads of wheat. He did not yet have a license, but it was common practice on prairie farms for children to drive early. "We had a really good crop in 1963 and we didn't have a lot of bins," George said. "So when the bins were filled up, we had to put piles of grain on the ground and in our yard. We set two big posts to mark the path, and my dad marveled at Ron's ability to back the grain truck between the posts without hitting them. He had less than six inches on either side, but he was careful and efficient and never hit the posts." (The story is telling on a metaphorical level for anyone familiar with Ron's public persona: he has a remarkable ability to steer clear of opposing ideological poles, never, for example, bashing either conservatives or liberals.)

George also talks about Ron's intelligence and scholarship with obvious pride. Despite the high value Ron's parents placed on education, the older siblings had to quit school early. George himself never got beyond the eighth grade. "It was a matter of economics," he says simply. "We just couldn't afford to stay in school. We were scraping along, you know, with a big family and no money. It was rather amazing that my parents were able to keep the land and keep the farm running." Fortunately, by the time Ron entered school, the family's financial situation had improved. Ron and all his younger siblings were able to finish high school and go on to college. Ron's love of stories and literature emerged in these years and never abated. "As a child, I loved storybooks, mysteries and adventures," he wrote in a 2017 column. "In grade school, I was made to memorize poetry and loved the exercise. High School introduced me to more serious literature: Shakespeare, Kipling, Keats, Wordsworth, Browning. But on the side, I still would read cowboy tales from the old West, taken from my dad's bookshelf."

As for other leisure activities, the Rolheiser children were active and competitive. In the warmer months, they'd divide up and form baseball teams. In the winter, they played hockey on frozen ponds. If inclement weather forced them inside, they'd play board games, cards, or ping pong. Ron's father later managed a local baseball team.

Ron has written several columns about his father, describing him as the moral compass of the family; a dependable father and faithful citizen who participated in local politics and served on various hospital and school boards. Of his mother, Ron writes that she was naturally warm and kindhearted. She was, understandably, stretched thin and occasionally overwhelmed by the demands on her time as the mother of such a large brood. "But she gave us, and in spades, the most important thing that a home is really asked to give, safety and security." George too talks about his parents, saying their great legacy is the love and loyalty they instilled in their children. The Rolheiser clan, now spanning four generations and hundreds of family members, gets together at least twice a year in Canada.

Ron's traditional Roman Catholic upbringing was typical for children raised in the 1950s and 1960s. The family attended daily Mass whenever possible at St. Donatus Church near Cactus Lake, where Ron was an altar server, and Ron recalls daily recitation of the rosary. "We had statues and holy pictures everywhere in our house; wore blessed medals around our necks; prayed litanies to Mary, Joseph, and the Sacred Heart; and practiced a warm devotion to the saints. It was wonderful. I will forever be grateful for that religious foundation."

Had it not been for such a solid foundation, the depression Ron experienced in high school surely would have left deeper scars. Even so, Ron remembers feeling restless and unsettled in his teenage years. He longed for a bigger, more exciting and significant life than his rural community could offer.

> I tormented myself by comparing my life, my body, and my anonymity to the grace, attractiveness, and fame of the professional athletes, movie stars, and other celebrities I admired and whose names were household words. For me, they had real lives, ones I could only envy. Moreover, I felt a deeper restlessness that had to do with my soul. I ached for a singular, erotic intimacy with a soulmate.

Despite his longing for romance and intimacy, Ron began asking himself whether he might have a call to the priesthood. An older brother had gone to the seminary, but Ron vacillated.

> The answer came to me, not in a flashing insight, or in some generous movement of heart, or in an attraction

> to a certain way of life. None of these. The answer came to me as hook in my conscience, as something that was being asked of me, as something I couldn't morally or religiously turn away from. It came to me as an obligation, a responsibility. And initially I fought against and resisted that answer. This wasn't what I wanted. But it was what I felt called to. This was something that was being asked of me beyond my own dreams for my life.

At age seventeen, Ron entered a religious congregation, the Missionary Oblates of Mary Immaculate, and began to train for the Catholic priesthood.

UNIVERSITY STUDIES AND PRIESTHOOD

Ron entered the novitiate of the Missionary Oblates in 1965, near the close of the Second Vatican Council (1962–1965), professing first vows two years later. It was a heady time in the Roman Catholic Church, a period of major reform and renewal. He caught the beginning of this worldwide wave and relished his studies, first at the University of Ottawa where he majored in philosophy, and then at Newman Theological College in Edmonton where he studied theology. He was a natural student, curious and bright. Challenged by his professors, he started to read literature differently, taking special note of the social and religious commentary embedded in their stories. He was struck by the beauty, power and form of written words. "While the catechism held my faith," he wrote, "literature held my theology."

Gerry Weinkauf has known Ron since their seminary days together. In a phone interview, he describes Ron as loyal and humble—"the salt of the earth." But that doesn't mean Gerry thinks Ron is ordinary. "His intellectual prowess was obvious early on. While the rest of us seminarians would be studying and memorizing information, he would very quickly grasp things, and then he'd internalize and synthesize lessons in such a way that, later, if we were struggling to understand something, we could ask Ron to explain it. He'd break it down and explain it to us in a new way that we could actually absorb."

Ron's intellectual appetite was insatiable in those years. He was smitten, first, by philosophy; then systematic theology; then by the writings of Christian mystics like St. John of the Cross and St. Thérèse of Lisieux. After receiving bachelor's degrees from the University of Ottawa and from Newman Theological College, he was ordained to the priesthood. Within a year he had picked up a master's degree at the University of San Francisco and started teaching Graduate Theology courses at Newman College. At age twenty-six, he was the youngest member on the faculty.

Still, Ron had some lessons to learn. Asked to prepare a vocation talk for a high school class, he prepared a fine lecture—or so he thought. Upon finishing his erudite presentation, a student raised his hand to ask his burning questions. "Do you have horses at the seminary? What are their names? Can you ride them? Do women ever come out there?" Ron laughs at the memory. He credits his years in youth ministry with bringing him back to earth and reminding him to use everyday language and stories in his public talks and writings. He also learned the importance of keeping up with popular culture and the arts—songs, movies, poetry, television shows, new fiction and nonfiction by emerging writers in North America and abroad. (He is still an avid reader with eclectic tastes. For a sampling of his recommendations, you can check his annual "In Exile" column listing his "Top Ten" books of the year.)

FROM THEOLOGY TO SPIRITUALITY

In the early 1980s, Ron's religious superiors encouraged him to continue his theological studies. He started looking into doctoral programs at the University of Chicago, the Berkeley School of Theology, and Yale Divinity School. He was unsure where to go, until the day a colleague commented, "You're going to be North American your whole life. Go to Europe so you can have a different experience." That made sense to Ron: he ended up choosing the University of Louvain in Belgium, where he received a second master's degree and completed his doctorate.

His dissertation on the philosophical proof of the existence of God later would become the basis of an award-winning book: *The Shattered Lantern: Rediscovering a Felt Presence of God*.

Although his specialty was systematic theology, Ron found himself increasingly attracted to spirituality. "So much so," he later wrote, "that after a few years I could no longer justify calling some of my former courses in systematic theology by their old catalog titles. Honesty now compelled me to name them courses in spirituality." In a 2017 column, he explains the difference between theology and spirituality—a distinction that helps to describe his niche as a writer:

> At one level, there's no difference. Spirituality is, in effect, applied theology. They are of one and the same piece, either ends of the same sock. But here's a difference: Theology defines the playing field, defines the doctrines, distinguishes truth from falsehood, and seeks to enflame the intellectual imagination. It is what it classically claims itself to be: Faith seeking understanding.
>
> But, rich and important as that is, it's not the game. Theology makes up the rules for the game, but it doesn't do the playing nor decide the outcome. That's the role of spirituality, even as it needs to be obedient to theology. Without sound theology, spirituality always falls into unbridled piety, unhealthy individualism, and self-serving fundamentalism. Only good, rigorous, academic theology saves us from these.
>
> But without spirituality, theology too easily becomes only an intellectual aesthetics, however beautiful. It's one thing to have coherent truth and sound doctrine; it's another thing to give that actual human flesh, on the streets, in our homes, and inside our own restless questioning and doubt. Theology needs to give us truth; spirituality needs to break open that truth.

By the mid-1980s, Ron was giving talks and leading retreats in Canada, the United States, and Europe. He'd published one small book with New Jersey publisher Dimension books, *The Loneliness Factor* (1979), and his column "In Exile" had been picked up by three more Catholic newspapers: two national papers in Canada, and a diocesan newspaper in the United States. Still, Ron was relatively unknown in 1987 when he traveled to Dublin to teach a summer theology course. One of the students in his class was a famous British chef, television personality, and author named Delia Smith, whom Ron describes as having "a wonderfully deep, Catholic spiritual mind." She was so taken by Ron's lectures that upon her return to London she pitched his small U.S. book to Hodder and Stoughton, a notable UK book publisher, and she showed Ron's columns to the editor of a leading Catholic newspaper, the *Catholic Herald*.

Hodder and Stoughton published a new edition of *The Loneliness Factor* the following year, retitling it *The Restless Heart*. Not only did it win a major award in the United Kingdom for best spiritual writing, it led to other contracts and books and, eventually, to Ron's bestseller with Doubleday in New York, *The Holy Longing*. The column, too, took off. In the decades that followed, "In Exile" would appear in more than ninety newspapers worldwide, reaching well over one million readers every week. Not bad for a guy who's never had an agent or much time to promote his writing!

When the Family Needs You (Leadership)

Despite juggling two careers in the early 1990s—as a theology professor and as a rising spiritual writer and speaker—Ron was destined for yet more responsibility. In 1991, he was selected by his confreres to serve as the Superior of St. Mary's Province in Western Canada. After two terms as Superior, he was elected Regional Councilor representing all the Canadian Provinces in the Congregation's General Administration. He moved to Rome in 1998 and spent the next six years traveling the world as he helped to lead the international missionary community. Ron hoped for a change from administration after twelve consecutive years in leadership roles, but that was not to be. In 2005, he was named President of the Oblate School of Theology (OST) in San Antonio, Texas.

Nobody enters religious life with a zeal for administrative positions, and Ron is no exception. Still, he understood that it was important to be available to his community. "I'm like a stay-at-home parent," he said cheerfully in a 2010 interview for the *National Catholic Reporter*. "I'd like to have my career going on a different track, but right now the family needs me." Throughout his nearly thirty years in administration, he has managed to write his weekly column every single Sunday.

Gerry Weinkauf remembers traveling with Ron from Saskatoon to San Antonio one particular Sunday. Boarding the plane, they both were frazzled. They'd nearly missed their international flight after bumping into a professional hockey player at the airport terminal and getting so caught up in conversation with him that they lost track of time. But as soon as they were settled in their seats on the plane, Ron opened his laptop, turned to Gerry and said, "I need a little quiet to write up a column." He seemed perfectly relaxed and focused as he tapped away at the keyboard, finishing the column in what seemed to Gerry record time. That discipline and concentration, Gerry says, helps explains how Ron handles so many responsibilities with enviable composure.

Ron admits that the hectic pace of his life overwhelms him at times. Mostly, he blames himself. "I have been driving my engines hard for a long time, dodging bullets as I overwork and am over-extended" he wrote in 2011. "So many times in the past years, in a trance of overwork, I promised God that I would slow my life down, just as soon as this particular task was finished. Indeed, often, explicitly in prayer, I asked God to let me do this slowdown willfully, and not have some health breakdown force it on me. Like the young Augustine, I was praying: 'Slow me down, but not yet!'"

That year, at age sixty-three, a health breakdown did force him to slow down. During a routine colonoscopy, Ron's doctor discovered a cancerous tumor. Ron had already beat the family odds and outlived his father, who died of pancreatic cancer at age sixty-two, and his mother, who died a few months later at age fifty-eight of pancreatitis and kidney failure. Seven siblings have died of cancer too, two of them in their fifties. Fortunately, Ron's cancer was discovered relatively early, and surgery to remove the tumor and affected lymph nodes went well. But even with chemotherapy, the cancer has returned twice—most recently in July 2020.

As I write this, in spring 2021, Ron is doing well. "I've had two scans since July and both indicate that the cancer is in check," he wrote in his December 2020 Christmas letter. "I work with full energy, enjoy good health, and exercise regularly. I've had to give up swimming (my 'go-to' exercise) because of COVID-19, but our school has a small gym where I can work out regularly. Also, the campus here is some fifty acres and so there is ample space to walk. My classes and lectures and workshops have continued as before, except all of it is on Zoom. Ironically, I have been busier on the speaking circuit this year than last. I have learned that sometimes you can draw a bigger audience for a virtual event than you can for an in-person event."

Ron plans to continue speaking and teaching in the near future. He is a full-time faculty member at OST, teaching in all three levels of the Institute for the Study of Contemporary Spirituality that he helped found, and he advises doctoral students. He also has begun work on the final book of his long-planned trilogy, which includes *The Holy Longing* (1999) and *Sacred Fire* (2014). Tentatively entitled "Insane for the Light"—a line from the poem by Johann Wolfgang von Goethe that inspired Ron's first title in the set—the third book will treat "what is asked of us in our autumn years and how, in the end, we are asked 'to give our deaths away.'" Finally, Ron has taken an active part in the development of the book you are reading now, drawing up the outline and selecting the texts that reflect his core themes.

Writing for a New Generation

Ron had known at an early age—by his late teens—that he wanted to be a writer. But beyond a few popular articles for an Oblate magazine called *Our Family* when he was a seminarian, he did not have a regular outlet for his creative work until age thirty-five. That's when he pitched his column "In Exile" to the editor of the *Western Catholic Reporter*. From the start, his columns addressed what he would later call "our pathological complexity" and our need to integrate eros and soul. "Everyone, absolutely everyone, must live a spiritual life," he wrote in a December 1982 column. "What we do with the eros inside of us, be it heroic or perverse, is our spiritual life. The tragedy is that so many persons, full of riches and bursting with life, see this drive as something that is essentially irreligious, as something that sets them against what is spiritual. Nothing could be further from the truth. Our erotic pulses are God's lure in us. They are our spirit!"

He also tried to write simply and clearly in order to be accessible to the widest possible audience. In this, his model and inspiration was another twentieth-century spiritual master—the Dutch writer and Catholic priest Henri Nouwen. "Few writers, religious or secular, have influenced me as deeply as Henri Nouwen," Ron wrote in a tribute. "I know better than to try to imitate him, recognizing that what is imitative is never creative and what is creative is never imitative. Where I do try to emulate him is in his simplicity, in his rewriting things over and over in order to make them simpler, without being simplistic. Like him, I believe that there's a language of the heart (that each generation has to create anew) that bypasses the divide between academics and the street and which has the power to speak directly to everyone, regardless of background and training."

Like Henri, Ron would try to meet people with their questions and their heartaches—their loneliness, restlessness, fears, and disappointments. He also tried to address their frustrations with religion. "I grew up with a strong trust and belief in the church, but the church has wounded a lot of people," he said in our 2019 interview. "Not everybody's met the church the way I did. That's one reason I've morphed more and more from theology to spirituality. I'm more worried about people's pain and questions than I am about defending the church. We need apologists for the faith, but my questions are more along the lines of, *Why aren't people coming to church? Where are the women and children? Why are people angry at the church?*"

Ron was intrigued when Eric Major, the Religion Editor at Hodder and Stoughton, invited Ron to "write a book that I can give to my adult children to explain why I still believe in God and why I still go to church—and that I can read on days when I am no longer sure why I believe or go to church." First published in the United Kingdom under the title *Seeking Spirituality* (retitled *The Holy Longing* by Doubleday), and intended "for anyone who is struggling spiritually," it offered a roadmap for a healthy Christian spirituality and struck a chord not only with Catholics, but with readers from different Christian denominations.

How is it that the writings of a Catholic priest from Canada appeal to such a broad audience—even to people who no longer identify with any religious tradition? In part, the answer is because Ron is "an unapologetic eclectic." Granted, his spirituality has been most deeply shaped by Catholic giants like St. Augustine, Thomas Aquinas, John of the Cross, and Karl Rahner; but Ron consciously integrates insights from myriad sources. For example, in *Sacred Fire*, his follow-up to *The Holy Longing*, he draws key insights from anthropology, scripture, literature, and John of the Cross to explore the human stages of growth and the essential challenge of Jesus.

Moreover, he is a member of a missionary congregation that was founded to work with the poor and with those who are on the margins of society. For Ron, that includes anyone without spiritual moorings, anyone who is lost or searching for a deeper human maturity. Once, when asked by a bishop in the Roman Catholic Church why he wasn't more focused on basic catechesis in his writings, Ron explained that as a missionary, his call is to reach out to those who are outside the church and its programs. For that, something other than catechesis is needed.

Ultimately, what Ron hopes to do through his ministry and his writing is to help people see that spirituality is in fact connected to "everything that is moving most deeply inside of us, our desires, our aching, our ambitions, our sexuality, even our most pagan and irreverent feelings, our 'holy longing.'"

Pressing on toward the Goal

Eventually, God willing, Ron will return to Canada. There, family and friends will welcome him with great joy. Their love and admiration for Ron is difficult to describe without seeming maudlin. Let me just say that people who know Ron well routinely tear up when they talk about what Ron means to them and how his work has changed their lives. As for his legacy, Gerry Weinkauf puts it well:

> There is no doubt in my mind that he is one of the great theologians of our time. Some might be intimidated by his spirituality and theology, but many of us crave it. His insights and explanations often blow you out of the water, they are so original and exactly what we need today.
>
> I suspect that people will be studying him and reading his books well into the next century. For many of us who went to the seminary, Aquinas was required reading. For future seminarians, it will be Rolheiser—especially because what he's given us is still at the gestation stage. I think we'll see his particular school of thought mature and grow. And I know the church is going to be better off for it, for what he's done and brought forward for us.

Gerry's words remind me of a line in the Italian film *Il Postino:* "Poetry does not belong to those who write it. It belongs to those who need it." Something similar can be said for this book. It does not belong to Ron: it belongs to you and to all those who may need it.

PART ONE

Holy Longing

The Sacred Fire Undergirding All Spirituality

1

What Is Spirituality?

We begin this chapter with a passage from The Holy Longing *that treats common misconceptions about the spiritual life. Spirituality is not for the few; it's for everyone. It's not so much about how often we go to church as it is about how we channel our eros—the "sacred fire" that burns within us. What we do with that fire, how we channel that energy, defines our spirituality. Ron puts skin on his thesis in a modern parable about three famous women who channeled their erotic energy in different ways: Mother Teresa, Janis Joplin, and Princess Diana.*

Ron then considers what it means to be made "in the image and likeness" of God. His own ideas and images of God have evolved over the years, and he traces that journey. Toward the end of the chapter, in a passage drawn from Sacred Fire, *he describes the three stages of Christian discipleship: the struggle to get our lives together, the struggle to give our lives away, and the struggle to give our deaths away.*

THE FIRE WITHIN

Today there are books on spirituality everywhere. However, despite the virtual explosion of literature in the area, in the Western world today, especially in the secular world, there are still some major misunderstandings about the concept. Chief among these is the idea that spirituality is, somehow, exotic, esoteric, and not something that issues forth from the bread and butter of ordinary life. Thus, for many people, the term spirituality conjures up images of something paranormal, mystical, churchy, holy, pious, otherworldly, New Age, something on the fringes and something optional. Rarely is spirituality understood as referring to something vital and nonnegotiable lying at the heart of our lives.

This is a tragic misunderstanding. Spirituality is not something on the fringes, an option for those with a particular bent. None of us has a choice. Everyone has to have a spirituality and everyone does have one, either a life-giving one or a destructive one. No one has the luxury of choosing here because all of us are precisely fired into life with a certain madness that comes from the gods and we have to do something with that. We do not wake up in this world calm and serene, having the luxury of choosing to act or not act. We wake up crying, on fire with desire, with madness. What we do with that madness is our spirituality.

Hence, spirituality is not about serenely picking or rationally choosing certain spiritual activities like going to church, praying or meditating, reading spiritual books, or setting off on some explicit spiritual quest. It is far more basic than that. Long before we do anything explicitly religious at all, we have to do something about the fire that burns within us. What we do with that fire, how we channel it, is our spirituality. Thus, we all have a spirituality whether we want one or not, whether we are religious or not. Spirituality is more about whether or not we can sleep at night than about whether or not we go to church. It is about being integrated or falling apart, about being within community or being lonely, about being in harmony with Mother Earth or being alienated from her. Irrespective of whether or not we let ourselves be consciously shaped by any explicit religious idea, we act in ways that leave us either healthy or unhealthy, loving or bitter. What shapes our actions is our spirituality.

And what shapes our actions is basically what shapes our desire. Desire makes us act, and when we act what we do will either lead to a greater integration or disintegration within our personalities, minds, and bodies—and to the strengthening or deterioration of our relationship to God, others, and the cosmic world. The habits and disciplines we use to shape our desire form the basis for a spirituality, regardless of whether these have an explicit religious dimension to them or even whether they are consciously expressed at all.

Spirituality concerns what we do with desire. It takes its root in the eros inside of us and it is all about how we shape and discipline that eros. John of the Cross, the great Spanish mystic, begins his famous treatment of the soul's journey with the words: "One dark night, fired by love's urgent longings." For him, it is urgent longings, eros, that are the starting point of the spiritual life and, in his view, spirituality, essentially defined, is how we handle that eros.

Thus, to offer a striking example of how spirituality is about how one handles his or her eros, let us compare the lives of three famous women: Mother Teresa, Janis Joplin, and Princess Diana.

Mother Teresa

We begin with Mother Teresa. Few of us would, I suspect, consider Mother Teresa an erotic woman. We think of her rather as a spiritual woman. Yet she was a very erotic woman, though not necessarily in the narrow Freudian sense of that word. She was erotic because she was a dynamo of energy. She may have looked frail and meek, but just ask anyone who ever stood in her way whether that impression is correct. She was a human bulldozer, an erotically driven woman. She was, however, a very disciplined woman, dedicated to God and the poor. Everyone considered her a saint. Why?

A saint is someone who can, precisely, channel powerful eros in a creative, life-giving way. Søren Kierkegaard once defined a saint as someone who *can will the one thing*. Nobody disputes that Mother Teresa did just that, willed the one thing—God and the poor. She had a powerful energy, but it was a very disciplined one. Her fiery eros was poured out for God and the poor. That—total dedication of everything to God and poor—was her signature, her spirituality. It made her what she was.

Janis Joplin

Looking at Janis Joplin, the rock star who died from an overdose of life at age twenty-seven, few would consider her a very spiritual woman. Yet she was one. People think of her as the opposite of Mother Teresa, erotic, but not spiritual. Yet Janis Joplin was not so different from Mother Teresa, at least not in raw makeup and character. She was also an exceptional woman, a person of fiery eros, a great lover, a person with a rare energy. Unlike Mother Teresa, however, Janis Joplin could not will the one thing. She willed many things. Her great energy went out in all directions and eventually created an excess and a tiredness that led to an early death. But those activities—a total giving over to creativity, performance, drugs, booze, sex, coupled with the neglect of normal rest—were her spirituality. This was her signature. It was how she channeled her eros. In her case, as is tragically often the case in gifted artists, the end result, at least in this life, was not a healthy integration but a dissipation. She, at a point, simply lost the things that normally glue a human person together and broke apart under too much pressure.

Looking at Joplin's life, and at our own lives, there is an interesting reflection to be made on Kierkegaard's definition of being a saint—someone who can will the one thing. Most of us are quite like Mother Teresa in that we want to will God and the poor. We do will them. The problem is we will everything else as well. Thus, we want to be a saint, but we also want to feel every sensation experienced by sinners; we want to be innocent and pure, but we also want to be experienced and taste all of life; we want to serve the poor and have a simple lifestyle, but we also want all the comforts of the rich; we want to have the depth afforded by solitude, but we also do not want to miss anything; we want to pray, but we also want to watch television, read, talk to friends, and go out. Small wonder life is often a trying enterprise and we are often tired and pathologically overextended.

Medieval philosophy had a dictum that said: Every choice is a renunciation. Indeed. Every choice is a thousand renunciations.

To choose one thing is to turn one's back on many others. To marry one person is to not marry all the others, to have a baby means to give up certain other things; and to pray may mean to miss watching television or visiting with friends. This makes choosing hard. No wonder we struggle so much with commitment. It is not that we do not want certain things, it is just that we know that if we choose them we close off so many other things. It is not easy to be a saint, to will the one thing, to have the discipline of a Mother Teresa. The danger is that we end up more like Janis Joplin; good-hearted, highly energized, driven to try to drink in all of life, but in danger of falling apart and dying from lack of rest.

Janis Joplin is perhaps an extreme example. Most of us do not die from lack of rest at age twenty-seven. Most of us, I suspect, are a bit more like Princess Diana—half-Mother Teresa, half Janis Joplin.

Princess Diana

Princess Diana is worth a reflection here, not just because her death stopped the world in a way that, up to now, few others ever have, but because it is interesting to note that in looking at her, unlike either Mother Teresa or Janis Joplin, people do spontaneously put together the two elements of erotic and spiritual. Princess Diana is held up as a person who is both, erotic and spiritual. That is rare, given how spirituality is commonly understood. Usually we see a person as one or the other, but not as both, erotic and spiritual. Moreover, she deserves that designation for she does reflect, fairly clearly, both of these dimensions.

The erotic in her was obvious, though not always in the way many people first understand that term. On the surface, the judgment is easy: She was the most photographed woman in the world, widely admired for her physical beauty, who spent millions of dollars on clothing, and was clearly no celibate nun. She had affairs, vacationed with playboys on yachts in the Mediterranean, ate in the best restaurants in London, Paris and New York, and had a lifestyle that hardly fits the mode of the classic saint. But that itself is superficial, not necessarily indicative of a person with a powerful eros. Many people do those things and are quite ordinary. More important was her energy. Here she was a Mother Teresa and Janis Joplin, someone who obviously had a great fire, that madness the Greeks spoke of, within her. Partly this was an intangible thing, but partly it could be seen in her every move, in her every decision, and in every line of her face. It is not for nothing, nor simply because of her physical beauty or because of her causes, that people were drawn so powerfully toward her. Her energy, more so than her beauty or her causes, is what made her exceptional.

The spiritual part of her was also obvious, long before she became friends with Mother Teresa and took up seriously trying to help the poor. It was this dimension that her brother spoke of when he eulogized her—her causes, yes, but more important, something else inside of her, a depth, a moral ambiguity that never allowed her to be comfortable simply with being a jetsetter, a habitual effacement, an anxious desire to please, a person under a discipline, albeit often a conscriptive one, a person who, however imperfectly, willed what Kierkegaard spoke of, God and the poor, even if she still willed many other things too.

Spirituality is about how we channel our eros. In Princess Diana's attempts to do this, we see something most of us can identify with, a tremendous complexity, a painful struggle for choice and commitment, and an oh-so-human combination of sins and virtues. Spirituality is what we do with the spirit that is within us. So, for Princess Diana, her spirituality was both the commitment to the poor and the Mediterranean vacations . . . and all the pain and questions in between. Hers, as we can see, was a mixed road. She went neither fully the route of Mother Teresa nor of Janis Joplin. She chose some things that left her more integrated in body and soul and others which tore at her body and soul. Such is spirituality. It is about integration and disintegration, about making the choices that Princess Diana had to make and living with what that does to us.

What Is Spirituality?

Thus, we can define spirituality this way: Spirituality is about what we do with the fire inside of us, about how we channel our eros. And how we do channel it, the disciplines and habits we choose to live by, will either lead to a greater integration or disintegration within our bodies, minds, and souls, and to a greater integration or disintegration in the way we are related to God, others, and the cosmic world. We see this lived out one way in Mother Teresa, another in Janis Joplin, and still in a different manner in Princess Diana.

We can see from all of this that spirituality is about what we do with our spirits, our souls. And can we see too from all of this that a healthy spirit or a healthy soul must do dual jobs: It has to give us energy and fire, so that we do not lose our vitality, and all sense of the beauty and joy of living. Thus, the opposite of a spiritual person is not a person who rejects the idea of God and lives as a pagan. The opposite of being spiritual is to have no energy, is to have lost all zest for living—lying on a couch, watching football or sit-coms, taking beer intravenously! Its other task, and a very vital one it is, is to keep us glued together, integrated, so that we do not fall apart and die. Under this aspect, the opposite of a spiritual person would be someone who has lost his or her identity, namely, the person who at a certain point does not know who he or she is anymore. A healthy soul keeps us both energized and glued together. —*The Holy Longing*, 6–12

EROS: THE BASIS OF THE SPIRITUAL LIFE

In the past several years I have been more than a little hurt when, on more than a few occasions, friends of mine would leave the priesthood, the convent or even the church itself because they felt that they were too full of the zest for life, too sensual, too sexual and generally too human and complicated to live the spiritual life. Most often the complaint sounds something like this: "I can never be a real spiritual person. I am just too restless! I want to live too much! I am too full of life! I feel like Zorba the Greek! I want to experience things more! I am just too unspiritual!" Such an attitude, while extremely common, is extremely dangerous for it is either a grave rationalization or a very serious mistake. It is deadly in either case. When in fact someone in all sincerity believes that they are too full of life and eros, restlessness and complexity, to live the spiritual life they are being sucked in by a viral heresy which would have us believe that eros, the drive for life, is fundamentally irreligious. That is always a serious and costly mistake because eros is the very basis of the spiritual life and everyone, absolutely everyone, must live a spiritual life.

What we do with the eros inside of us, be it heroic or perverse, is our spiritual life. The tragedy is that so many persons, full of riches and bursting with life, see this drive as something that is essentially irreligious, as something that sets them against what is spiritual. Nothing could be further from the truth. Our erotic pulses are God's lure in us. They are our spirit! We experience them precisely as "spirit," as that which makes us more than mere mammals. However, again and again, in my ministry and in my friendships I am confronted with persons who sincerely believe that they are unspiritual when, in fact, they are deeply spiritual persons. Unable to form a vision within which they can integrate their drive for life, celebration and sexuality, into a commitment which includes church-going, Christian sexual morality, prayer and involvement in a Eucharistic community, they are forced into a false dilemma: They must choose between a Christian commitment (which appears as erotic suicide) and a life partially away from Christian community, sacraments, prayer and morality, but within which they feel they can be fully human, sensual, sexual and celebrating. This dilemma, within which the church is seen as a parasite, sucking life's pulse out of its subjects, then allows society's amorality to parade itself as being ultimately life-giving and the true defender of eros.

This is a plea: If you are the type of person who, precisely, understand yourself as too complicated, too bursting with eros, too driven in the pursuit of life, too sensual and too sexual, to be a real spiritual person then don't, please don't, see this drive as something irreligious. Nobody is more qualified than you, nor more called, to live the spiritual life. —*In Exile,* December 6, 1982

THE IMAGE OF GOD INSIDE US

Inside each of us, beyond what we can name, we have a dark memory of having once been touched and caressed by hands far gentler than our own. That caress has left a permanent mark, the imprint of a love so tender and good that its memory becomes a prism through which we see everything else. This brand lies beyond conscious memory but forms the center of the heart and soul.

This is not an easy concept to explain without sounding sentimental. Perhaps the old myths and legends capture it best when they say that, before being born, each soul is kissed by God and then goes through life always, in some dark way, remembering that kiss and measuring everything it experiences in relation to that original sweetness. To be in touch with your heart is to be in touch with this primordial kiss, with both its preciousness and its meaning.

What exactly is being said here?

Within each of us, at that place where all that is most precious within us takes its root, there is the inchoate sense of having once been touched, caressed, loved, and valued in a way that is beyond anything we have ever consciously experienced. In fact, all the goodness, love, value, and tenderness we experience in life fall short precisely because we already know something deeper. When we feel frustrated, angry, betrayed, violated, or enraged it is in fact because our outside experience is so different from what we already hold dear inside.

We all have this place; a place in the heart, where we hold all that is most precious and sacred to us. From that place our own kisses issue forth, as do our tears. It is the place we most guard from others, but the place where we would most want others to come into; the place where we are the most deeply alone and the place of intimacy; the place of innocence and the place where we are violated; the place of our compassion and the place of our rage. In that place we are holy. There we are temples of God, sacred churches of truth and love. It is there too that we bear God's image.

But this must be understood: The image of God inside of us is not to be thought of as some beautiful icon stamped inside of the soul. No. The image of God in us is energy, fire, memory; especially the memory of a touch so tender and loving that its goodness and truth become the energy and prism through which we see everything. Thus we recognize goodness and truth outside of us precisely because they resonate with something that is already inside of us. Things "touch our hearts" when they touch us here and it is because we have already been touched and caressed that we seek for a soul mate, for someone to join us in this tender space.

And we measure everything in life by how it touches this place: Why do certain experiences touch us so deeply? Do not our hearts burn within us in the presence of any truth, love, goodness, or tenderness that is genuine and deep? Is not all knowledge simply a waking up to something we already know? Is not all love simply a question of being respected for something we already are? Are not the touch and tenderness that bring ecstasy nothing other than the stirring of deep memory? Are not the ideals that inspire hope only the reminder of words somebody has already spoken to us? Does not our desire for innocence (and innocent means "not wounded") mirror some primal unwounded place deep within us? And when we feel violated, is it not because someone has irreverently entered the sacred inside us?

When we are in touch with this memory and respect its sensitivities then we are feeling our souls. At those times, faith, hope, and love will be spring up in us and joy and tears will both flow through us pretty freely. We will be constantly stabbed by the innocence and beauty of children and pain and gratitude will, alternately, bring us to our knees. That is what it means to be recollected, to inchoately remember, to feel the memory of God in us. That memory is what is both firing our energy and providing us a prism through which to see and understand.

Today, too often, a wounded, calloused, cynical, over-sophisticated, overly adult world invites us to forget, to move beyond this childishness (which is really child-likeness). It invites us to forget God's kiss in the soul. But, unless we lie to ourselves and harden ourselves against ourselves, the most dangerous of all activities, we always remember, dimly, darkly, the caress of God.

—*In Exile*, October 16, 1997

OUR GRANDIOSITY AND OUR WOUNDS

We wake up into life with the incurable sense that we're special, that we're the center of the universe. And, subjectively, we are! In our awareness we're the center of the universe and life does revolve around us. Our own being is what's most massively real to us. As Descartes famously said, the only thing that we know for sure is real is our own selves; *I think, therefore, I am.* We may be dreaming everything else.

Spirituality has perennially judged this negatively. Egocentricity, feelings of grandiosity, self-centeredness, and pride were seen as the result of the corruption of human nature through original sin. We called it, The Fall. Our first parents attempted to overreach, to be more than God intended them to be, and this irrevocably corrupted their nature and we, their children, inherit this. So we, adult children of Adam and Eve, too instinctually tend to overreach, to puff up in self-importance, to fill with pride, and think first about ourselves.

That doctrine of original sin has something important to say, but it isn't first of all to shame us in our natural pride and sense of specialness. The real reason why pride and grandiosity are incurably ingrained inside us is because God built us that way, and that, of itself, is not a fault or a corruption but instead constitutes what's highest and most precious inside us. But with that too comes (as part of the same package) pride and grandiosity.

Simply put, we can't have Godliness inside us and not feel ourselves as special.

And that makes for a less-than-serene situation for the planet. We're now seven and half billion people on this earth, each one with the same innate sense that he or she is the center of the universe and that his or her own reality is what's most real. That's the real cause behind what you see happening on the world news each night, for worse and for better. Grandiosity is the source of human strife, but equally the source of human greatness.

Important in our understanding of this is that our innate sense of godliness is also the place where we suffer our deepest wounds. What most wounds the image and likeness of God inside us? These things: humiliation, lack of adequate self-expression, the perennial frustration of bumping up against the limits of life, and the martyrdom of obscurity.

Each of us, by our nature, possesses a divinely-given uniqueness and dignity and thus nothing wounds us more than being humiliated and shamed in our struggle to live this out. A shameful humiliation, even as a very young child, can scar us for the rest of our lives. It's one of the reasons why we have mass killings. Likewise, as Iris Murdoch once said, the greatest human pain is the pain of inadequate self-expression. There's a great artist, composer, teacher, athlete, and performer inside each of us, but few people can ever give that satisfying expression. The rest of us have to live with perennial frustration because what's deepest in us lies unexpressed. As well, we're forever bumping up against the real limits of our own lives and limits of life itself. In the end, all of us die with a life that was never fully consummated. And that isn't easily accepted! Everything inside us militates against this. Finally, almost all of us live a certain martyrdom of obscurity, recognized and famous only inside our own daydreams, our greatness hidden from the world. That too isn't easily accepted.

What's to be taken away from this? Since we secretly nurse thoughts of specialness should we also nurse a secret shame? Is our innate pride something that sets us against holiness? Is our grandiosity a bad thing? Is our frustration with the limits and inadequacy of our lives something that displeases God? Are our daydreams of uniqueness and greatness something which taints our contemplation and prayer? Is our nature, of itself, somehow corrupt? Must we somehow step outside of our own skin to be saints?

Each of these questions can be answered in two ways. Grandiosity, pride, shame, frustration, and daydreams of greatness, can indeed be our downfall and turn us into awful persons, selfish, jealous, spiteful, and murderous. But they can also be the source of greatness, of nobility of soul, of generosity, of selflessness, of generativity, of true prayer, and can turn us into selfless martyrs of faith, hope, and charity. Our godliness is a very mixed blessing; but it is, no doubt, our greatest blessing.

—*In Exile*, July 29, 2019

THE FLAVOR OF GOD'S ENERGY

All things considered, I believe that I grew up with a relatively healthy concept of God. The God of my youth, the God that I was catechized into, was not unduly punishing, arbitrary, or judgmental. He was omnipresent, so that all of our sins were noticed and noted, but, at the end of the day, he was fair, loving, personally concerned for each of us, and wonderfully protective, to the point of providing each of us with a personal guardian angel. That God gave me permission to live without too much fear and without any particularly crippling religious neuroses.

But that only gets you so far in life. Not having an unhealthy notion of God doesn't necessarily mean that you have a particularly healthy one. The God whom I was raised on was not overly stern and judgmental, but neither was he very joyous, playful, witty, or humorous. Especially, he wasn't sexual, and had a particularly vigilant and uncompromising eye in that area. Essentially he was grey, a bit dour, and not very joyous to be around. Around him, you had to be solemn and reverent. I remember the

Assistant Director at our Oblate novitiate telling us that there is no recorded incident, ever, of Jesus having laughed.

Under such a God you had permission to be essentially healthy, but, to the extent that you took him seriously, you still walked through life less than fully robust and your relationship with him could only be solemn and reverent.

Then, already a generation ago, there was a strong reaction in many churches and in the culture at large to this concept of God. Popular theology and spirituality set out to correct this, sometimes with an undue vigor. What they presented instead was a laughing Jesus and a dancing God and while this was not without its value it still left us begging for a deeper literature about the nature of God and what that might mean for us in terms of a health and relationships.

That literature won't be easy to write, not just because God is ineffable, but because God's energy is also ineffable. What, indeed, is energy? We rarely ask this question because we take energy as something so primal that it cannot be defined but only taken as a given, as self-evident. We see energy as the primal force that lies at the heart of everything that exists, animate and inanimate. Moreover, we feel energy, powerfully, within ourselves. We know energy, we feel energy, but what we rarely recognize its origins, its prodigiousness, its joy, its goodness, its effervescence, and its exuberance. We rarely recognize what it tells us about God. What does it tell us?

The first quality of energy is its prodigiousness. It is prodigal beyond our imagination and this speaks something about God. What kind of creator makes billions of throwaway universes? What kind of creator makes trillions upon trillions of species of life, millions of them never to be seen by the human eye? What kind of father or mother has billions of children?

And what does the exuberance in the energy of young children say about our creator? What does their playfulness suggest about what must also lie inside of sacred energy? What does the energy of a young puppy tell us about what's sacred? What do laughter, wit, and irony tell us about the God?

No doubt the energy we see around us and feel irrepressibly within us tells us that, underneath, before and below everything else, there flows a sacred force, both physical and spiritual, which is at its root, joyous, happy, playful, exuberant, effervescent, and deeply personal and loving. That energy is God. That energy speaks of God and that energy tells us why God made us and what kind of permissions God is giving us for living out our lives.

When we try to imagine the heart of reality, we might picture things this way: At the very center of everything there sit two thrones, on one sits a King and on the other sits a Queen, and from these two thrones issues forth all energy, all creativity, all power, all love, all nourishment, all joy, all playfulness, all humor, and all beauty. All images of God are inadequate, but this image hopefully can help us understand that God is perfect masculinity and perfect femininity making perfect love all the time and that from this union issues forth all energy and all creation. Moreover that energy, at its sacred root, is not just creative, intelligent, personal, and loving, it's also joyous, colorful, witty, playful, humorous, erotic, and exuberant at it very core. To feel it is an invitation to gratitude.

The challenge of our lives is to live inside that energy in a way that honors it and its origins. That means keeping our shoes off before the burning bush as we respect its sacredness, even as we take from it permission to be more robust, free, joyous, humorous, and playful—and especially more grateful.

—*In Exile*, March 6, 2017

DIFFERENT CHALLENGES IN DIFFERENT SEASONS

One size doesn't fit everyone. This isn't just true for clothing, it's also true for spirituality. Our challenges in life change as we age. Spirituality hasn't always been fully sensitive to this. True, we've always had tailored instruction and activities for children, young people, and for people who are raising children, carrying a job, and paying a mortgage, but we've never developed a spirituality for what happens when those years are over.

Why is one needed? Jesus seemingly didn't have one. He didn't have one set of teachings for the young, another for those in mid-life, and still another for the elderly. He just taught. The Sermon on the Mount, the parables, and his invitation to take up his cross are intended in the same way for everyone, irrespective of age. But we hear those teaching at very different times in our lives; and it's one thing to hear the Sermon the Mount when you're seven years old, another when you're twenty-seven, and quite another when you're eighty-seven. Jesus' teachings don't change, but we do, and they offer very specific challenges at different times of our lives.

Christian spirituality has generally kept this in mind, with one exception. Except for Jesus and an occasional mystic, it has failed to develop an explicit spirituality for our later years, for how we are meant to be generative in our senior years and how we are to die in a life-giving way. But there's a good reason for this lacuna. Simply put, it wasn't needed because up until this last century most people never lived into old age. For example, in Palestine, in Jesus' time, the average life expectancy was thirty to thirty-five years. A century ago in the United States, it was still less than fifty years. When most people in the world died before they reached the age of fifty, there was no real need for a spirituality of aging.

There is such a spirituality inside the Gospels. Even though he died at thirty-three, Jesus left us a paradigm of how to age and die. But that paradigm, while healthily infusing and undergirding Christian spirituality in general, was never developed more specifically into a spirituality of aging (with the exception of some of the great Christian mystics).

In essence, here's the issue: today, we're living longer and healthier late into life. It's common today to retire sometime in our early sixties after having raised our children, superannuated from our jobs, and paid our mortgages. So what's next, given that we probably have twenty or thirty more years of health and energy left? What are these years for? What are we called to now, beyond loving our grandkids? Abraham and Sarah, in their old age, were invited to set out for a new land and conceive a child long after this was biologically impossible for them. That's our call too. What "Isaac" are we called to give birth to in our later years? We need guidance. —*In Exile*, October 5, 2020

THE SPIRITUAL LIFE AND THE STAGES OF CHRISTIAN DISCIPLESHIP

Life has its stages and so too does Christian discipleship. The key is to properly identify both and then interface them. Happily, this is happening more and more. Today there is a rich literature growing within the field of spirituality that speaks of the different stages of our lives and tries to name the appropriate spiritual and human challenges that meet us there. While the language inside this literature is often new, the concept of stages within discipleship is not. Stages of discipleship are implicit in the Gospels and were made explicit throughout history in a bevy of categories within Christian theology and spirituality. Sadly, sometimes these attempts to define the various levels of discipleship were sloppy and inaccurate, biblically and theologically. For instance, to highlight perhaps the worst example, for long periods of time in Christianity there were schools of thought, sometimes nearly universal in influence, which believed that only certain people, like monks and nuns, were called to radical discipleship and full holiness, while the rest of us could be content to walk a less-demanding road.

There were many other categorizations of this kind that were unhelpful and sometimes positively harmful. Unfortunately, we are still not completely free of false understandings of both the spiritual life and the stages of discipleship within it. However, that being admitted, it is also true to say that, happily, there is a better understanding today in virtually all the Christian churches apposite Christ's universal call to full discipleship. The problem is more that we are not always as clear as to all that is involved in that and what its particular stages are. What is involved? What are the stages of Christian discipleship? Or, to ask the question more widely, what are the stages of the spiritual life? . . .

Essential Discipleship and the Struggle to Get Our Lives Together

Our first real struggle in life is the struggle to get our lives together. From our first breath onward we begin to struggle to find our own identity and find fulfillment and peace there. But this struggle takes on its real poignancy only at puberty. Prior to puberty, unless our lives have been unnaturally traumatized or we have suffered serious neglect, our lives are essentially together. We are born in a hospital and soon taken home to a place where we have parents, elders, a family of some kind that is our own, and a place that is ours. This period of our lives, childhood, is intended by God and by nature to be a secure time. We are home, secure, safe! Our huge anthropological and spiritual struggles have not yet begun. But that will change, and change dramatically, at puberty.

Simply put, puberty is designed by God and nature to drive us out of our homes. And puberty generally does its job, sometimes too well! It hits us with a tumult and violence that overthrows our childhood and sends us out, restless, sexually driven, full of grandiose dreams, but confused and insecure, in search of a new home, one that we build for ourselves. And this is a time of much longing and searching: searching for an identity, searching for acceptance, searching for a circle of friends, searching for intimacy, searching for someone to marry, searching for a vocation, searching for a career, searching for the right place to live, searching for financial security, and searching for something to give us substance and meaning—in a word, searching for a home. Expressions of this longing and search are what make up the meat of popular music, literature, and movies. Invariably the motifs and refrains that abound there will revolve around questions like: Who am I? Where do I find meaning? Who will love me? How do I find love in a world full of infidelity and false promises? Countless expressions of longing, of heartache, of searching; but, in the end, one focus: a burning desire for a home we once had, somehow lost, and are looking for again.

The struggle from being restlessly driven out of our first home to finding a state and a place to call home again is the journey of Essential Discipleship.

And normally we do find our way home again. It might take ten, fifteen, twenty, or more years, but, at a certain point, we land. We find ourselves "at home" again, namely, with a place to live that is our own, a job, a career, a spouse, a vocation, perhaps children, a mortgage, a series of responsibilities, and a certain status and identity. At that point, the fundamental struggle in our life changes, even though it may take years for us to consciously realize and accept this. Our question then is no longer: How do I get my life together? Rather, it becomes: How do I give my life away more deeply, more generously, and more meaningfully? At that stage, we enter the second phase of discipleship.

Mature Discipleship and the Struggle to Give Our Lives Away

Most people reach this second stage sometime during their twenties or thirties, though some of us might be in our forties, fifties, or even sixties before we cross the threshold between struggling to get our lives together as opposed to struggling to give our lives away. Moreover, for all of us, the crossover is never pure and complete. The struggle for self-identity and private fulfillment never completely goes away; we are always somewhat haunted by the restlessness of our youth and our own idiosyncratic needs, but the essential default line shifts. At a certain point, we are more fundamentally concerned with life beyond us than with ourselves.

Mature Discipleship begins, whether we are explicitly conscious of this or not, when we begin living more for others than for ourselves. For most of us this will constitute the longest period of our lives, the adult years. Imagine, for instance, someone, at age thirty, having established a career, gotten married or made a commitment to a religious or humanitarian vocation, perhaps having children, having acquired a house, and having taken on a whole series of family, community, and religious responsibilities. For him, whatever the burden, the next forty to fifty years will be fairly clear; that is, the duties and responsibilities he has taken on will pretty much dictate his life. His anthropological and spiritual task will be clear: How do I give my life away more purely and more generously? Living out that struggle is what constitutes Mature Discipleship.

But this stage of raising and teaching children, running our communities and churches, and being generous adults is still not the final stage of our lives. We still have to die, and that is not a minor anthropological or spiritual task. It is the most daunting task of all. And none of us are exempt. Thus, our default line must shift yet one more time, and radically so. Henri Nouwen suggests that at a certain point of our lives, the real question is no longer: What can I still do so that my life makes a contribution? Rather, the question becomes: How can I now live so that my death will be an optimal blessing for my family, my church, and the world? We must leave home a second time, and this time we face a much larger unknown.

Radical Discipleship and the Struggle to Give Our Deaths Away

As Christians, we believe that Jesus lived for us and that he died for us, that he gave us both his life and his death. What we often fail to distinguish in this, however, is that there are two clear and separate movements here: Jesus gave his life for us in one movement, and he gave his death for us in another movement. In essence, he gave his life for us through his activity, through his generous actions for us; and he gave his death through his passivity, through absorbing in love the helplessness, diminutions, humiliations, and ultimate loneliness of dying.

Like Jesus, we too are meant to give our lives away in generosity and selflessness, but we are also meant to give our deaths away, not just at the moment of our deaths, but in a whole process of leaving this planet in such a way that our diminishment and death is our final, and perhaps greatest, gift to the world. Needless to say, this is not easy. Walking in discipleship behind the master will require that we too sweat blood and feel "a stone's throw" from everybody. This struggle, to give our deaths away, constitutes Radical Discipleship.

—*Sacred Fire*, 12–13, 15–20

THE MAJOR IMPERATIVES WITHIN MATURE DISCIPLESHIP

In his autobiography, Morris West suggests that at a certain age our lives simplify and we need have only three phrases left in our spiritual vocabulary: Thank you! Thank you! Thank you! He is right, if we understand fully what is implied in living out gratitude. Gratitude is the ultimate virtue, undergirding everything else, even love. It is synonymous with holiness.

Gratitude not only defines sanctity, it also defines maturity. We are mature to the degree that we are grateful. But what brings us there? What makes for a deeper human maturity? I would like to suggest ten major demands that reside inside both human and Christian maturity:

1. Be willing to carry more and more of life's complexities with empathy: Few things in life, including our own hearts and motives, are black or white, either-or, simply good or simply bad. Maturity invites us to see, understand, and accept this complexity with empathy so that, like Jesus, we cry tears of understanding over our own troubled cities and our own complex hearts.
2. Transform jealousy, anger, bitterness, and hatred rather than give them back in kind: Any pain or tension that we do not transform we will retransmit. In the face of jealousy, anger, bitterness, and hatred we must be like water purifiers, holding the poisons and toxins inside of us and giving back just the pure water, rather than being like

electrical cords that simply pass on the energy that flows through them.

3. Let suffering soften rather than harden our souls: Suffering and humiliation find us all, in full measure, but how we respond to them, with forgiveness or bitterness, will determine the level of our maturity and the color of our person. This is perhaps our ultimate moral test: Will my humiliations soften or harden my soul?
4. Forgive: In the end there is only one condition for entering heaven (and living inside human community), namely, forgiveness. Perhaps the greatest struggle we have in the second-half of our lives is to forgive: forgive those who have hurt us, forgive ourselves for our own shortcomings, and forgive God for seemingly hanging us out unfairly to dry in this world. The greatest moral imperative of all is not to die with a bitter, unforgiving heart.
5. Live in gratitude: To be a saint is to be fueled by gratitude, nothing more and nothing less. Let no one deceive you with the notion that a passion for truth, for church, or even for God can trump or bracket the non-negotiable imperative to be gracious always. Holiness is gratitude. Outside of gratitude we find ourselves doing many of the right things for the wrong reasons.
6. Bless more and curse less: We are mature when we define ourselves by what we are for rather than by what we are against and especially when, like Jesus, we are looking out at others and seeing them as blessed ("Blessed are you!") rather than as cursed ("Who do you think you are!"). The capacity to praise more than to criticize defines maturity.
7. Live in an ever-greater transparency and honesty: We are as sick as our sickest secret, but we are also as healthy as we are honest. We need, as Martin Luther once put it, "to sin bravely and honestly." Maturity does not mean that we are perfect or faultless, but that we are honest.
8. Pray both affectively and liturgically: The fuel we need to resource ourselves for gratitude and forgiveness does

not lie in the strength of our own willpower, but in grace and community. We access that through prayer. We are mature to the degree that we open our own helplessness and invite in God's strength and to the degree that we pray with others that the whole world will do the same thing.

9. Become ever-wider in your embrace: We grow in maturity to the degree that we define family (Who is my brother or sister?) in way that is ever-more ecumenical, interfaith, post-ideological, and non-discriminatory. We are mature only when we are compassionate as God is compassionate, namely, when our sun too shines those we like and those we do not. There comes a time when it is time to turn in our cherished moral placards for a basin and a towel.
10. Stand where you stand and let God protect you: In the end, we are all vulnerable, contingent, and helpless both to protect our loved ones and ourselves. We cannot guarantee life, safety, salvation, or forgiveness for ourselves or for those we love. Maturity depends upon accepting this with trust rather than anxiety. We can only do our best, whatever our place in life, wherever we stand, whatever our limits, whatever our shortcoming, and trust that this is enough, that if we die at our post, honest, doing our duty, God will do the rest.

God is a prodigiously-loving, fully-understanding, completely-empathic parent. We are mature and free of false anxiety to the degree that we grasp that and trust that truth.

—*In Exile,* March 10, 2013

2

Our Restless Selves

Ron's words have an uncanny ability to touch readers and listeners deeply, pulling back a curtain on their private anxieties, fantasies, and fears. At the level of soul, Ron explains, we are each "a bundle of untamed eros, of wild desire, longing, restlessness, loneliness, dissatisfaction, sexuality, and insatiability." What's more, this bundle of emotions is not a sign that something is wrong with us—it's a sign of something right.

In this chapter, Ron examines restlessness and loneliness from both a secular and a religious perspective. Included here are two passages from his first book, The Restless Heart *(originally entitled* The Loneliness Factor*), which Ron wrote while he was still in his twenties and for which he won the Winnifred Sanford Award in the United Kingdom. The final excerpt from* The Holy Longing *offers four steps that can help us move from restlessness to peace and acceptance.*

DESIRE, OUR FUNDAMENTAL DIS-EASE

It is no easy task to walk this earth and find peace. Inside of us, it would seem, something is at odds with the very rhythm of things and we are forever restless, dissatisfied, frustrated, and aching. We are so overcharged with desire that it is hard to come to simple rest. Desire is always stronger than satisfaction.

Put more simply, there is within us a fundamental dis-ease, an unquenchable fire that renders us incapable, in this life, of ever coming to full peace. This desire lies at the center of our lives, in the marrow of our bones, and in the deep recesses of the soul. We are not easeful human beings who occasionally get restless, serene persons who once in a while are obsessed by desire. The reverse is true. We are driven persons, forever obsessed, congenitally dis-eased, living lives, as Thoreau once suggested, of quiet desperation, only occasionally experiencing peace. Desire is the straw that stirs the drink.

At the heart of all great literature, poetry, art, philosophy, psychology, and religion lies the naming and analyzing of this desire. Thus, the diary of Anne Frank haunts us, as do the journals of Thérèse of Lisieux and Etty Hillesum. Desire intrigues us, stirs the soul. We love stories about desire—tales of love, sex, wanderlust, haunting nostalgia, boundless ambition, and tragic loss. Many of the great secular thinkers of our time have made this fire, this force that so haunts us, the centerpiece of their thinking.

Sigmund Freud, for example, talks about a fire without a focus that burns at the center of our lives and pushes us out in a relentless and unquenchable pursuit of pleasure. For Freud, everyone is hopelessly overcharged for life. Carl Jung talks about deep, unalterable, archetypal energies which structure our very souls and imperialistically demand our every attention. Energy, Jung warns, is not friendly. Every time we are too restless to sleep at night we understand something of what he is saying. Doris Lessing speaks of a certain voltage within us, a thousand volts of energy for love, sex, hatred, art, politics. James Hillman speaks of a blue fire within us and of being so haunted and obsessed by daimons from beyond that neither nature nor nurture, but daimons, restless demanding spirits from beyond, are really the determinative factors in our behavior. Both women's and men's groups are constantly speaking of a certain wild energy that we need to access and understand more fully. Thus, women's groups talk about the importance of running with wolves and men's groups speak of wild men's journeys and of having fire in the belly. New Age gurus chart the movement of the planets and ask us to get ourselves under the correct planets or we will have no peace.

Whatever the expression, everyone is ultimately talking about the same thing—an unquenchable fire, a restlessness, a longing, a disquiet, a hunger, a loneliness, a gnawing nostalgia, a wildness that cannot be tamed, a congenital all-embracing ache that lies at the center of human experience and is the ultimate force that drives everything else. This dis-ease is universal. Desire gives no exemptions.

It does however admit of different moods and faces. Sometimes it hits us as pain—dissatisfaction, frustration, and aching.

At other times its grip is not felt as painful at all, but as a deep energy, as something beautiful, as an inexorable pull, more important than anything else inside us, toward love, beauty, creativity, and a future beyond our limited present. Desire can show itself as aching pain or delicious hope.

Spirituality is, ultimately, about what we do with that desire.

—*The Holy Longing,* 3–5

STRUGGLING INSIDE OUR OWN SKIN

I've been both blessed and cursed by a congenital restlessness that hasn't always made my life easy. I remember as a young boy restlessly wandering the house, the yard, and then the open pastures of my family's farm on the prairies. Our family was close, my life was protected and secure, and I was raised in a solid religious faith. That should have made for a peaceful and stable childhood and, for the most part, it did. I count myself lucky.

But all of this stability, at least for me, didn't preclude an unsettling restlessness. More superficially, I felt this in the isolation of growing up in a rural community that seemed far removed from life in the big cities. The lives I saw on television and read about in the newspapers and magazines appeared to me to be much bigger, more exciting, and more significant than my own. My life, by comparison, paled, seemed small, insignificant, and second-best. I longed to live in a big city, away from what I felt to be the deprivations of rural life. My life, it seemed, was always away from everything that was important.

Beyond that, I tormented myself by comparing my life, my body, and my anonymity to the grace, attractiveness, and fame of the professional athletes, movie stars, and other celebrities I admired and whose names were household words. For me, they had real lives, ones I could only envy. Moreover, I felt a deeper restlessness that had to do with my soul. Despite the genuine intimacy of a close family and a close-knit community within which I had dozens of friends and relatives, I ached for a singular, erotic intimacy with a soulmate. Finally, I lived with an inchoate anxiety that I didn't understand and which mostly translated itself into fear, fear of not measuring up and fear of how I was living life in face of the eternal.

That was the cursed part, but all of this also brought a blessing. Inside the cauldron of that disquiet I discerned (heard) a call to religious life which I fought for a long time because it seemed the antithesis of everything I longed for. How can a burning restlessness, filled with eros, be a call to celibacy? How can an egotistical desire for fame, fortune, and recognition be an invitation to join a religious order whose charism is to live with the poor? It didn't make sense, and, paradoxically, that's why, finally, it was the only thing that did made sense. I gave in to its nudging and it was right for me.

It landed me inside religious life and what I've lived and learned there has helped me, slowly through the years, to process my own restlessness and begin to live inside my own skin.

The particular restlessness that I experienced in my youth is today in fact a near-universal disease. Virtually all of us believe that the good life is had only by those who live elsewhere, away from our own limited, ordinary, insignificant, and small-town lives. Our culture has colonized us to believe that wealth, celebrity, and comfort are the adequate object of the human intellect and will. They are, for us, "Being as such." In our culture's current perception, we look at the beautiful bodies, celebrity status, and wealth of our athletes, movie stars, television hosts, and successful entrepreneurs and believe that they have the good life and we don't. We're on the outside, looking in. We're now, in effect, all farm kids in the outback envying life in the big city, a life accessible only to a highly select few, while we're crucified by the false belief that life is only exciting elsewhere, not where we live. —*In Exile,* February 25, 2019

LONELINESS IN YOUTH AND OLD AGE

Loneliness haunts you in a very particular way when you're young. It comes turbo-charged with a restlessness that can beat you up like the playground bully, especially on a Friday or a Saturday night when it seems like the whole world is doing something exciting and you have been left out. When you're young it always feels like you're missing out on something. You ache to drink in the whole world and make love to it, but are stuck in a very confining situation where your life always seems too small. You want a larger connection to the world, more sex, deeper intimacy, and a soulmate that you have not yet found. At that time of life, you're also overly-romantic, driven by fantasies of finding perfect love, perfect sex, and a one-in-four-billion soulmate who will finally fill in every lonely spot inside you. When you're young it's easy to be besotted by Romeo and Juliet: Find perfect love, make perfect love, and then die together. Surely the most noble exit off the planet!

None of this really changes as you get older, but a new kind of loneliness begins to break through inside. This kind doesn't hit you broadside, like the turbulent restlessness of youth. It comes on more like a painful, bitter realization that, at first, you try to block out and deny. What is this loneliness?

It's the realization that, at some level, there will always be a distance between yourself and others, even from those nearest and dearest to you. This hits as part of the realization of your own mortality. To realize that you are mortal doesn't just mean that you more realistically accept the fact that some day, perhaps even soon, you will die. The brute fact of mortality also brings with it the realization that there will always be some areas of life where you will be all alone, alienated from others, separated by differences that seem, as the classical divorce formula puts it, irreconcilable. The ache in this kind of loneliness dwarfs the pain of youthful restlessness and often leads to bitterness of soul. It is helpful to understand this, precisely so as not to become bitter.

Where do you feel this kind of loneliness? You feel it in those silent areas that exist between you and your spouse, your families, your friends, and your community. There are always things that can't be spoken, can't be understood, can't be harmonized, even in your most intimate relationships and especially inside of family and community life. This is the loneliness you feel when you drive away from the family gathering, finish that long talk with your spouse, stand trying to explain something to your own child, or are left muttering to yourself after that church or civic meeting. At those moments you can feel like a minority-of-one, unanimity-minus-one, alone morally with most of what's deepest in you. —*In Exile,* February 3, 2002

THE REALITY OF LONELINESS

Loneliness is an experiential reality. Like other experiential realities such as joy, sorrow, and freedom, it affects not just our intellects, but our emotions and even our bodies. Thus, it is first and foremost an experience of our whole person.

What is this experience? At a certain level it is little more than a dark feeling, an undifferentiated sensation that speaks of alienation, exclusion, rejection, longing, discontent, restlessness, emptiness, frustration, dissatisfaction, incompleteness, insatiability, nostalgia, and death. At this state, too, these feelings are often not yet clearly directed toward any specific object. *We just feel lonely.* However, all these feelings do have an object. For example, we always long for something or someone; we are frustrated about something; or we are incomplete for some reason.

What is the object of our various feelings of loneliness? To attempt any type of exhaustive listing would be impossible, since nearly every human feeling we have has some dimension of loneliness to it. Only in a concrete experience, when we are confronted with this or that particular feeling of loneliness, can we sometimes pinpoint a precise object toward which our loneliness is directed. Since there can be no complete list of all the various feelings of loneliness with their corresponding objects, we can only look at a certain sampling.

What are we lonely for? We are lonely for many things: We are lonely for more love and communication, more unity and understanding, than we have at present. We are longing and restless for a wholeness we do not yet possess. We are tormented by feelings of insatiability, thirsting constantly, wanting to know more people, wanting to be known by more people, wanting to be more places, and wanting to be "where it is at," in every sense of that cliché. We are frustrated because our relationships are too frequently fraught with ambiguity and misunderstanding, with pettiness and betrayal. We feel empty and incomplete because we are missing out on so much of life, constantly living at the fringes, as behind a glass, darkly, away from the action, unable to completely sort through the riddle of life, at the door without a key, unable to fully enter. We feel nostalgia and death as precious friends and precious moments leave us, never to return, as youth and fullness slowly leave our bodies, as the clock ticks away and we lose so much of what we have had. We feel both agony and ecstasy in our loneliness as we experience both the tension that makes for life and the loss that makes for death.

Specific Types of Loneliness

Beyond this general definition, loneliness can be divided into various kinds. For purposes of analysis in general, and theological analysis in particular, I have divided loneliness into five distinct types, which I call: *Alienation, Restlessness, Fantasy, Rootlessness, and Psychological Depression.* Since they are types, they are therefore not always and everywhere separate from each other. There is some overlapping but there is a clear distinction among them, one that can be drawn on the basis of their cause, their meaning, and their resolution.

(1) *Alienation.* Alienation is the easiest type of loneliness to understand. It is what most people mean when they use the word

lonely. It refers simply to the experience of feeling alienated or estranged from others. It is the feeling we have when we are not able to love and understand, and be loved and understood, as fully as we would like, or as fully as we should as human beings. When our relationships are inadequate to the point of being painful and frustrating to us, we suffer alienation.

Many factors cause alienation; for example, fear, shame, lack of self-esteem, paranoia, ideological differences with others, selfishness, fear of rejection by others, positive rejection by others, physical handicaps, emotional handicaps, physical separation from others, or anything else that hinders us from relating as closely and intimately to others as we would like. . . .

We are social beings, meant to live in love and intimacy with others. Our nature demands this. When, for whatever reasons, we cannot achieve this and communicate the love as we should, then something is missing inside of us—and we feel it! We feel estranged and alienated.

(2) *Restlessness.* Restlessness is another type of loneliness. It refers not so directly to the experience of alienation or estrangement from others, but to the constant dissatisfaction and restlessness within us that perpetually keeps us frustrated and in a state of unrest. As we shall see, this type of loneliness is not caused directly by our alienation from others, but from the very way our hearts are built, from our structure as human persons.

All of us experience within ourselves a certain restlessness and insatiability. Our hearts and minds are so fashioned that they are never satisfied, always restless; never quiet, always wanting more of everything. Throughout history various persons have given different names to this restlessness. Religious thinkers have often called it "the spark of the divine to us"; philosophers sometimes referred to it as "the desire of the part to return to the whole"; the Greeks had two names for it, *Nostos*, a certain homesickness within the human heart, and *Eros*, a relentless erotic pull toward whatever we perceive as good; the Vikings called it "wanderlust," the constant urge to explore beyond all known horizons;

the biblical writer Qoheleth called it "timelessness" (*Ha Olam*), the congenital inability to bring ourselves into peaceful harmony with the world around us; St. Augustine called it "restlessness": "You have made us for Yourself, Lord, and our hearts are restless until they rest in you." Most of us simply call it "loneliness."

Whatever name we assign this feeling, the experience is universal. None of us is exempt. Abstracting from more direct feelings of alienation and estrangement, all of us still experience within ourselves a certain lonely thirst. At the center of our being an insatiable burning pushes us outward in wanderlust and eros, in restlessness and desire, to pursue some unknown timelessness, infinity, and wholeness. . . .

A classic example of this is "Richard Cory," the tragic hero of Edwin Arlington Robinson's poem of that name. Richard is indeed "the man with everything," material wealth, fame and prestige, culture and good friends. Yet for a reason that is total mystery to all except to the complexities of the human heart, he goes home one night and puts a bullet through his head. We are all potentially "Richard Corys" because all of us possess his insatiable heart. The more we have, the more we want! . . .

(3) *Fantasy.* The third type of loneliness might aptly be called Fantasy. It is the loneliness that is caused by our failure to be completely in contact with the truth, reality as it is in itself.

Scholastic philosophers defined truth as the "correspondence between what is in the mind, with reality the way it is outside of the mind" *("Adequatio intellectus et rei")*. They believed that we attain truth, and live in truth, when our thoughts correspond to the way reality is in itself. Conversely, when there is a discrepancy between the two, mind and reality, we suffer illusion, fantasy, or error. For instance, persons seeing a mirage might sincerely believe that they are seeing a lake in the distance, but since there is no correspondence between their thoughts and the actual reality, they are said to be in error. Conversely, if they believe in their minds that trees have roots beneath the ground, albeit not visible, they are said to have attained truth. The idea in their minds corresponds to reality.

Now all of us, according to degree, live in fantasy and illusion, not quite fully in tune with reality. We live with certain fantasies and illusions of who we are and where we fit into reality. We daydream and, after a while, get part of our dreams and fantasies mixed into how we see and interpret reality. Sometimes our assessment of ourselves and our place in life is close to reality; at other times it is fraught with illusion and unreality. To the degree that we are not truly and totally in touch with reality as it is, we are alienated and lonely.

For instance, we all live out various fantasies of ourselves. In our minds we see ourselves as an "intellectual," a "mystic," a "searcher," a "poet," a "holy person," and "indispensable executive," a "crucial member of the organization," or "your basic nice guy," to name just a few of the more common types. Usually there is a certain amount of truth to it, and we actually possess some of the qualities that we see in our ideal or fantasy of ourselves. However, generally there is also a discrepancy, at times painfully obvious to others, between our fantasy of ourselves and our true selves. . . .

(4) *Rootlessness.* A fourth type of loneliness can be called Rootlessness. In brief, it is the type of loneliness we feel when we experience ourselves without roots, without absolutes, without anchors, adrift without a harbor in which to feel secure, without stability zones, without a meaningful grounding in tradition, and without something that anchors us, however little, within the flow of evolution, time, and history.

There is a real loneliness in being without firm roots. It is the loneliness of ultimately having no place to lay your head. Jesus once complained that "the son of man has no place to lay his head." I cannot help thinking that, were he walking on earth today, his complaint would be different. In all likelihood he would have a place to lay his head, but the place would be flimsily constructed, of disposal plastic (good for one year or two hundred naps), and, worst of all, every time he would try to lay his head down, the place would shift!

And our world and everything in it appears to be shifting. There is a real loneliness and pain in this. It is the loneliness and pain of being caught in a storm with no "cleft in the rocks" to shelter us and give us some warmth and security against the cold and tempest. We can enjoy a storm, but only when we have a secure space from which we, warm and secure, can watch it and can venture in and out of it somewhat on our own conditions. If, however, we are simply caught in it, without shelter, ill-prepared and without proper dress, the storm can be a very painful experience. The storm of life is no different. If, at times at least, we can slip into a cleft in the rocks and root ourselves onto certain things that can protect us against its full brunt, we can cope with the storm. If, however, that cleft is never to be found, the storm is a cold, lonely experience.

Today fewer and fewer of us are able to find that secure cleft in the rocks. Many of the things in which we used to root ourselves—family ties, religious and moral values, ideals and heroes, unshakable truths and trusted institutions—are constantly being wrested from our grasp. For the most part, we grow up in a small nuclear family (which itself has an even chance of breaking up before we reach adulthood), with no meaningful connection with any extended family and its specific roots and traditions. We do not really know or care whether our ancestors came from Italy, Africa, Russia, or Ireland—or whether they ate pizza, sauerkraut, or pierogi! We move from place to place, eating whatever is there, forgetting our history, and letting go of many of our former religious ties and moral values. At the same time, society is debunking remains our moral absolutes, demythologizing our former trusted institutions, and showing many of our heroes, to whom we looked for ideals and inspiration, to be morally bankrupt. Besides that, we are finding out that many of the so-called facts we learned in high school and college, including mathematical facts (and what can be surer than mathematics?) are no longer valid. All our roots are constantly being cut, and, as they are, we become like a boat without an anchor, set adrift, at the mercy of the winds, wanting something to clutch onto, but having nothing solid without our reach: neither a history nor a tradition; neither a timeless cult nor a trusted institution; neither an absolute moral imperative nor an anchor in something sacred, beyond history; indeed, not even a physical universe and a positivistic mathematics that is not relative. We are rootless! There is a loneliness that comes from being set adrift in this way. . . .

(5) *Psychological Depression.* The last type of loneliness can simply be called psychological depression or the blues. As its name suggests, this is more or less "the blues," pure and simple.

This type of loneliness is distinguishable from the other types essentially by one feature, that is, it is an ephemeral experience as opposed to one that is constant and abiding. The other types of loneliness are, for those who suffer from them, constant underlying concerns. The blues, on the other hand, are something we normally experience only on a random or sporadic basis.

The blues are really psychological depression that people often call "loneliness." The blues are a form of loneliness that though generally short-lived can pass through us at times, causing very intense pain, and relativizing our whole life and everything that seems positive and worthwhile to us.

Often it is impossible to pinpoint with any exactitude what causes these blues and what makes up the feelings contained in them. They are usually a combination of the other types of loneliness with additional depression and nostalgia. A wide range of factors can trigger the "blues" within us: anything ranging from the season of the year, to the season of our life, or the death of a loved one, or the wedding of a son or daughter, or the position of the moon, or the chemical balances within our bodies. We talk, for instance, of "getting over a death," "middle-age crisis," "getting over something"; and less significantly, about "spring fever," "end-of-semester blues," "rainy days and Mondays," and so on. As these clichés suggest, the blues can be caused by a variety of things. However, as these expressions also suggest, they are generally an ephemeral experience, linked to some definite event, season, or happening in our lives. They can be pesky and painful at times, but for most normal people they do not constitute a major problem, except perhaps at certain times in life when specific crises such as the death of a loved one, onset of middle age, and other such happenings can render us particularly vulnerable. However, for some people who are prone to depression, this type of loneliness can constitute a major threat.

—*The Restless Heart*, 40–43, 48–49, 57–58, 62–64, 66–67

THE INCURABLE PULL TOWARD GOD

God is erotically charged and the world is achingly amorous, hence they caress each other in mutual attraction and filiation.

Jewish philosopher Martin Buber made that assertion, and while it seems to perfectly echo the opening line of St. Augustine's autobiography *("You have made us for yourself, Lord, and our hearts are restless until they rest in you.")* it hints at something more. St. Augustine was talking about an insatiable ache inside the human heart which keeps us restless and forever aware that everything we experience is not enough because the finite unceasingly aches for the infinite, and the infinite unceasingly lures the finite. But St. Augustine was speaking of the human heart, about the restlessness and pull towards God that's felt there.

Martin Buber is talking about that too, but he's also talking about a restlessness, an incurable pull towards God, that's inside all of nature, inside the universe itself. It isn't just people who are achingly amorous, it's the whole world, all of nature, the universe itself.

What's being said here? In essence, Buber is saying that what's felt inside the human heart is also present inside every element within nature itself, in atoms, molecules, stones, plants, insects, and animals. There's the same ache for God inside everything that exists, from a dead planet, to a black hole, to a redwood tree, to our pet dogs and cats, to the heart of a saint. And in that there's no distinction between the spiritual and the physical. The one God who made both is drawing them both in the same way.

Pierre Teilhard de Chardin, who was both a scientist and a mystic, believed this interplay between the energy flowing from an erotically charged God and that flowing back from an amorous world, is the energy that undergirds the very structure of the universe, physical and spiritual. For Teilhard, the law of gravity, atomic activity, photosynthesis, ecosystems, electromagnetic fields, animal instinct, sexuality, human friendship, creativity, and altruism, all draw on and manifest one and the same energy, an energy that is forever drawing all things towards each other. If that is true, and it is, then ultimately the law of gravity and the Holy Spirit are part of one and the same energy, one and the same law, one and the same interplay of eros and response.

At first glance it may seem rather unorthodox theologically to put people and physical nature on the same plane. Perhaps too, some might find it offensive to speak of God as "erotically charged." So let me address those concerns.

In terms of God relating to physical nature, orthodox Christian theology and our scriptures affirm that God's coming to us in Christ in the incarnation is an event not just for people, but also for physical creation itself. When Jesus says he has come to save the world he is, in fact, talking about the world and not just the people in the world. Physical creation, no less than humanity, is God's child and God intends to redeem all of his children. Christian theology has never taught that the world will be destroyed at the end of time, but rather (as St. Paul says) physical creation will be transformed and enter into the glorious liberty of the children of God. How will the physical world go to heaven? We don't know; though we can't conceptualize how we will go there either. But we know this: the Christ who took on flesh in the incarnation is also the Cosmic Christ, that is, the Christ through whom all things were made and who binds all creation together. Hence theologians speak of "deep incarnation," namely, of the Christ-event as going deeper than simply saving human beings, as saving physical creation itself.

I can appreciate too that there will be some dis-ease in my speaking of God as "erotic," given that today we generally identify that word with sex. But that's not the meaning of the word. For the Greek philosophers, from whom we took this word, *eros* was identified with love, and with love in all its aspects. Eros did mean sexual attraction and emotional obsession, but it also meant friendship, playfulness, creativity, common sense, and altruism. Eros, properly understood, includes all of those elements, so even if we identify eros with sexuality, there still should be no discomfort in applying this to God. We are made in the image and likeness of God, and thus our sexuality reflects something inside the nature of God. A God who is generative enough to create billions of galaxies and is continually creating billions of people, clearly is sexual and fertile in ways beyond our conception. Moreover, the relentless ache inside of every element and person in the universe for unity with something beyond itself has one and the same thing in mind, consummation in love with God who is Love.

—*In Exile,* November 9, 2020

SOME CHRISTIAN THEOLOGIANS ON LONELINESS

Augustine (354–430)

"You arouse him to take joy in praising you, for you have made us for yourself, and our heart is restless until it rests in you." With these words, Augustine sums up an entire understanding of the human person and provides an explanation for human loneliness, as well.

These words, however, become fully intelligible only when they are placed within Augustine's understanding of the human person as a whole. How did Augustine understand the human person? Why are our hearts restless until they rest in God?

For Augustine, the human person is someone God creates because of God's goodness and love. God's love is so great that it cannot contain itself. It is "effervescent," ever bubbling up and bursting forth to create beings with which to share itself. Hence, the human person is nothing other than something that God's love has created with which to share itself. As humans, then, we are born to participate in the richness of God's very life. Accordingly, since this is our purpose, the only thing that can give us full happiness and completion is, precisely, God's life, full union with God.

However, while we are on earth, separated from full union with God by our creatureliness and by sin, we live a mixed existence, living partly within the city of God and living partly within the city of man. This leaves us incomplete and thirsty, restless and lonely, longing always to bring this pilgrimage to an end, to return to God and our true homeland.

In such a perspective, *our loneliness is really nothing other than our thirst and restlessness to return to God,* to full completion within that richness which is divine life. While we are living on this earth, we are pilgrims, aliens from our true homeland. We live therefore in pain and disquiet, in restlessness and anticipation, as we wait for the journey to end.

We see therefore that, for Augustine, loneliness is both a good and a natural thing. It is God's way of drawing us toward the life for which we were made. God wants us to live inside the divine life, and so God placed within us a strong erotic thirst, a loneliness, that forces us to constantly yearn for God and to be frustrated and not content when we are outside of God's life.

Understanding this properly can be a very liberating insight because, since the dawn of human consciousness, people have ever been at a loss to explain themselves. We never seem to be able to figure out why so frequently when we want to relax, we cannot; why so frequently when we want to work, we do not; and why so frequently when we want to be disciplined, we are not. We are without explanation as to why we are always so restless and unable to sit still. We are constantly surprised (not to mention disappointed) with ourselves. The philosopher Blaise Pascal once remarked, "The sole cause of man's unhappiness is that he does not know how to stay quietly in his room." How true! Yet how natural! For Augustine, this is not a great mystery or an astounding anomaly. We cannot stay quietly in our rooms precisely because God did not build us to stay quietly in a room. We are built to wander, to be restless and lonely. Accordingly, we should not be surprised if we find ourselves incurably in that condition.

Augustine based this understanding of the human person and understanding of loneliness not just on his Christian faith and his Neoplatonic background, but especially on his own life's experience. Most of us are familiar with his life and his search for meaning, a search that led him through philosophy, hedonism, and at times even through rather perverse things. Reading through his Confessions, we can see the tremendous struggle—intellectual, emotional, and moral—that he underwent before he finally came to this understanding of the human person and human loneliness. When he makes his famous statement (perhaps the most quoted line in all of his writings)—"You have made us for yourself, and our heart is restless until it rests in you"—he is not just stating a theological conclusion that he has come to as a result of exegetical and systematic research; he is telling the story of his life, the story of our lives, and the story of every person who has ever searched and cried in loneliness, wandered and wondered in restlessness, and lived in pain while seeing life as through a glass, darkly.

Thomas Aquinas (1224–1274)

Medieval theologian Thomas Aquinas also offers some valuable perspectives on the question of human loneliness. Like Augustine before him, he bases his explanation of loneliness on an understanding of human nature and how he sees it as relating to God. For him, we are lonely because God built us that way. However, while being similar to Augustine on this point, he develops Augustine's understanding of loneliness on three significant points.

(1) *Loneliness is not just a thirst for God, but a thirst for other persons and the world, as well.* For Augustine, we are lonely because our hearts are restless until they attain God. Thomas goes further and adds an important nuance to this explanation. Complete rest for our lonely hearts will, according to him, come only when we are in full union with God and with each other and with all of reality Thus, Thomas would recast slightly the Augustinian dictum, making it read: "You have made us for yourself, and our heart is restless until it rests in you . . . *and others, and the whole and world.*"

(2) *Loneliness is what makes us dynamic beings.* According to Thomas, the human person is a creature whom God has created for a very definite purpose and end. What is that purpose? From explicit Christian revelation, we see that we are made for beatific vision, heaven, union with God and others in a kingdom of love. Also, from philosophy, we see that we are made to attain perfect Being, perfect Love, and perfect Truth. As scholastic philosophers classically put it: The adequate object of our intellect and will (that which can give us total meaning and satisfaction) is union in knowledge and love with all of Being.

As persons, we are called to this end, both by God's explicit word (scripture) and by the erotic urgings innate within our own psychological and physical structure. Built for union, called and drawn toward it in mind and body, it follows logically that we must be capable of attaining it. And, given the fact that we are capable of infinite love and knowledge, it follows that we can never be completely fulfilled, completely happy, or completely at rest until we have attained that end. Lesser ends will simply not satisfy us. We are doomed to critique every experience we have in the light of our ultimate potential. That is why we are always lonely.

Put in summary fashion, Thomas is saying this: We are built for the infinite, to be in perfect intercommunity with God and others. we hunger for this, long for it, and constantly and thirstily reach out for it. But, when we do reach out, we can meet and touch only particular persons and objects. These can fulfill us to a point, but never completely. Our nature is built for more and it demands more. Accordingly, we go through life always somewhat lonely and dissatisfied, restless and unfulfilled, as we perpetually reach out and seek that radical unity with God and others for which we were made.

In such a perspective, loneliness becomes a good thing, a valuable and necessary force in our lives. It is the force that drives us outward to keep searching, to keep reaching, to not give up. It is the force that keeps us dissatisfied with pseudo- and partial solutions, with hedonistic and short-term answers. It is the force that keeps us dynamic, making us restless and dissatisfied when we are stagnant, and making us constantly second-guess all of our experience in the light of the very reason for which we were made.

(3) *Loneliness, if listened to, tells us of God's purpose for us.* In Thomas' view, our loneliness is good not only in that it keeps us dynamic, but also because it keeps us conscriptively focused on the end for which God made us. He explains this as follows: We are made to be in ecstatic union with God and others. This is our purpose. How do we know that purpose? We come to know it not just through explicit Christian revelation but simply by listening to and following the inner dictates and urges of our own being. Through loneliness, God has written the divine plan for us right into the very structures of our heart, mind, and body. Loneliness is God's imprint in us, constantly telling us where we should be going.

An analogy can be used to explain Thomas here: After a clockmaker builds a watch, he does not need to tell it explicitly that its task is to keep time. Rather, he builds it in such a way that, following its own natural dictates, rhythms, and structures, it will naturally keep time. Its own internal mechanisms, its wound-up springs, cause a corresponding tension that naturally causes its hands to move—and the watch to keep time. In that sense, too, it will be a "happy watch" since it will be doing what fulfills it.

Our own human structure and its inbuilt loneliness can be understood in a manner analogous to this. God is the good clockmaker, building our purpose right into our very structure. Thus, if we follow authentically our own inner dictates, laws, and rhythms, we will naturally move toward that end for which we were made. Our own internal mechanisms will push us naturally toward meaning and fulfillment. In our case, however, the mainspring within our internal mechanism, that which causes the tension and ultimately causes our hands to move, is loneliness, a burning thirst for union with God, others, and the world. The very reason why God has made us is structurally imprinted into our very being.

For Thomas, loneliness is the mainspring within our internal makeup. *Desiderium Naturale*, he calls it. Just as the wound-up mainspring of a watch creates a tension that makes the watch's hands move, so loneliness creates a tension inside of us which makes us move. It is the raison d'être of every action we do. We experience this tension at every level within our being: *spiritually,* in our thirst for God; *aesthetically,* in our thirst for beauty; *psychologically,* in our desire for love and unity with others; *emotionally,* in our desire to feel a oneness with others and with all things; *intellectually,* in our thirst for experience and truth; and *physically,* in our sexual tensions.

Loneliness, as we can see, is a good and necessary force within our lives. It makes us tick. Much liberating insight can come from a proper understanding and self-appropriation of this. We all go through life being too surprised at ourselves. Far too often we are surprised at the powerful tensions inside us, surprised at the cataclysmic forces that so often stir deep inside our minds and bodies, surprised at our inability to be quiet and satisfied, surprised at the strength and unyieldingness of our sexual urges, and surprised simply at how much complexity and tension there is in being a human person. Thomas Aquinas was not surprised. Unlike Pascal, he did not marvel at the fact that a human person cannot sit quietly in his room. Furniture and ornaments can stay quietly in his room; their mainspring is not so tense and complex. They were built to stay in rooms. But when God made humans, God had a different purpose in mind and so God gave us a different mainspring, loneliness. To be human, then, is not to sit quietly in a room, but to be a searching, lonely being, wandering from room to room, restlessly looking always for an all-consuming and infinite love and unity.

John of the Cross (1542–1591)

Juan de Yepes y Alvarez, a sixteenth-century Spanish theologian and mystic, more commonly known as John of the Cross, also offers some valuable perspectives on loneliness. In his treatise "The Living Flame of Love," he summarizes his theology of loneliness in three paragraphs:

> The deep caverns of feeling: These caverns are the soul's faculties; memory, intellect, and will. They are as deep as are the boundless goods of which they are capable, since anything less than the infinite fails to fill them. From what they suffer when they are empty, we can gain some knowledge of their enjoyment and when they are filled with God, since one contrary delight sheds light on the other.
>
> In the first place, it is noteworthy that when these caverns of the faculties are not emptied, purged, and cleansed of every affection for creature, they do not feel the vast emptiness of their deep capacity. Any little thing that adheres to them in this life is sufficient to so burden and bewitch them that they do not perceive the harm, nor note the lack of their immense goods, nor know their own capacity.
>
> It is an amazing thing that the least of these goods is enough so to encumber these faculties, capable of infinite goods, that they cannot receive these infinite goods until they are completely empty, as we shall see. Yet when

> these caverns are empty and pure, the thirst, hunger, and yearning of the spiritual feeling is intolerable. Since they have deep cavities they suffer profoundly, for the food they lack, which as I say is God, is also profound.

Why are we lonely? What does our loneliness mean? For John, the answers to those questions are quite similar to those of Augustine and Thomas. His way of expression is different, but the analysis is essentially the same, namely, we are lonely because God built us that way.

John explains this by using the metaphor of caverns. According to him, there are three constitutive faculties to each human person: intellect, will, and memory (mind, heart, and personality). Each of these faculties is seen to be a cavern, a capacity of infinite depth, a "grand canyon" without a bottom. As persons, we are so constituted that in our minds, hearts, and personalities, we are insatiable, bottomless wells, capable of receiving the infinite. God made us that way so that ultimately we could be in union with infinite love and life. Because of this, there can be no fully meaningful and final solution to our loneliness outside of union with the infinite. Therefore, in this life we are always lonely.

On these points John is very similar to Augustine and Thomas. His development of these points, however, produces some unique perspectives.

(1) *There is an immense danger in loneliness.* According to John, if our loneliness is not handled meaningfully and channeled creatively, it becomes a highly dangerous force within our lives. It leads to what he terms "inordinate affectivity" and a corresponding selfish and unhealthy pursuit of pleasure. This, as we saw earlier, if not recognized and checked, can ultimately, be destructive of our personality.

(2) *In order to arrive at our real depth, we must enter into our loneliness.* John has a very exalted notion of the human person. He sees each of us as a cavern of infinite depth, in possession

of great sensitivity and of vast riches within mind, heart, and personality. However, for him, the refusal to enter into our loneliness can condemn us to superficiality, to a life outside of our own depth and richness. Again, he employs a metaphor to explain this.

For him, our mind, heart, and personality are like bottomless canyons. But we can choose not to enter deeply into these canyons. We can let ourselves be frightened off and instead either cling to all kinds of things at the surface of our own canyons, or we can let ourselves be drawn away from our own depth by distracting activity. In either case we never enter deeply into ourselves. In either case, too, we end up living superficially and impoverished, drawing on only a very small part of our own depth and richness.

What does that mean concretely? It means that, to the extent that we go through life running away from our own loneliness, we put a cellophane covering over our own depth and riches and live instead at the surface of our minds, hearts, and personalities. For John, this is probably the biggest problem we face in dealing with our loneliness. We are too frightened of it to enter into it. The canyons of our minds and hearts are so deep and so full of mystery that we try at all costs to avoid entering them deeply. We avoid journeying inward because we are too frightened: frightened because we must make that journey alone; frightened because we know it will involve solitude and perseverance; and frightened because we are entering the unknown. Aloneness, suffering, perseverance, the unknown: All these frighten us. Our own depths frighten us! And so we stall, distract ourselves, drug the pain, party and travel, stay busy, try this and that, cling to people and moments, junk up the surface of our lives, and find any and every excuse to avoid being alone and having to face ourselves. We are too frightened to travel inward. But we pay a price for that, a high one: superficiality and shallowness. So long as we avoid the painful journey inward, to the depth of our caverns, we live at the surface.

(3) *When we first do enter into our loneliness, we enter into the pain of "purgatory."* John of the Cross offers us no painless way to enter loneliness and to come to grips with it. He is very realistic here. The inward journey involves pain, intolerable pain. According to him, once we stop trying to run away from our loneliness and stop trying to fill our thirsty caverns with counterfeit and pseudosolutions, we enter, for a time, into a terrible raging pain, the pain of purgatory, the pain that is felt when we cut ourselves off from pseudosupports and take the plunge inward, into the infinite mystery of ourselves, reality, and God. Eventually this journey leads to a deep peace, but in the early stages it causes intolerable pain. Why?

Because we have stopped using anesthetics. We have stopped numbing, drugging, distracting, and deflecting our lonely thirst. Thus, deprived of anesthetic and of the cellophane covering of superficiality, we can enter and feel fully our own depth. We face ourselves for the first time. Initially this is very painful. We begin to see ourselves as we truly are, infinite caverns, satiable only by the absolutely noncounterfeit, infinite love. We see, too, how, up to now, we have not drawn our strength and support from the infinite, but have drawn on finite things. The realization that we must shift our life-support system, and the process of that shift, is very painful. It is nothing other than the pain of purgatory, the pain of withdrawal and the pain of birth. It is the pain of letting go of a life-support system that, however ineffectual, at least we could understand, and instead, in darkness, altruism, and hope, of moving out and trying to find life support in the mystery of the infinite. It is a process of being born again, of having our Present umbilical cord cut. Like all births, it is a journey from the secure into the unknown; like all births, it involves a certain death. and like all births, too, it is very painful because it is with much groaning of the flesh that new life can be brought forth.

—*The Restless Heart,* 111–122

THE PURPOSE OF RESTLESSNESS

There comes a point in our restlessness when its purpose is no longer to direct us outward, but inward. When instead of letting our restlessness drive us outward to try to satisfy our incompleteness by yet more activity, friendship, sex, work, entertainment, or distraction, we must enter it in such a way as to turn it into solitude.

Solitude, as we know, is not the same thing as loneliness. It is being alone, but it is being alone in such a way that our very incompleteness is a source of quiet strength and not of anxious dissipation. Few spiritual writers have written with as much insight on this question as has Henri Nouwen. For him, the movement to turn our restless incompleteness into a restful solitude has *four* steps:

(1) *Own your pain and incompleteness*. Like an alcoholic cannot be helped until he or she admits helplessness, we too cannot move towards solitude until we acknowledge honestly our pathological restlessness and fundamental sexual unwholeness. Hence, the first step towards solitude is precisely to accept that, here in this life, we will find no final symphony and we may not give our congenital hungers for full consummation free reign but must direct them towards something else.

(2) *Give up false messianic expectations*. Once we have accepted that we are fundamentally dis-eased in that nothing in this life will ever fully complete us, we need then give up our messianic expectations and demands. Hence, we must stop expecting that somewhere, sometime, in some place, we will meet just the right person, the right situation, or the right combination of circumstances so that we can be completely happy. We will stop demanding that our spouses, families, friends, and jobs give us what only God can give us, clear-cut pure joy.

(3) *Go inward*. When we are restless, everything in us screams to move outward, to seek some activity that will soothe the ache. However, to find solitude we must move inward, away from all activity. Ultimately, what turns our restless aching into inner

quiet and peace is not more activity, but sitting still long enough for restlessness to turn to restfulness, compulsion to freedom, impatience to patience, self-absorption to altruism, and heartache to empathy.

(4) *It is a movement that is never made once and for all.* Turning restlessness into restfulness, aching inconsummation into peaceful solitude, is not something that is ever accomplished once and for all. The world is not divided up between two kinds of persons, restless ones and ones who have found solitude. Rather our own lives are divided between two different modes of feeling: some days we are more restless and other days we are more restful, sometimes our congenital sexual aching is one huge heartache and at other times it is a deep well of empathy, and some days we find being alone almost too painful to bear and other days we bask in quiet solitude. Coming to grips with unfulfilled sexual hunger is to, more and more, find the latter.

—*The Holy Longing,* 207–209

3

Sexuality as Sacred Fire

What does a healthy sexuality look like? Ron begins this chapter by affirming the innate goodness and beauty of human sexuality. "A healthy sexuality is the single most powerful vehicle there is to lead us to selflessness and joy." But he also cautions that it is not easy to channel our powerful sexual energies in life-giving ways. Christianity, he admits, still struggles to fully celebrate sexual passion.

In a poignant reflection on marriage from Against an Infinite Horizon, *Ron writes about two couples, both close relatives, whose love he witnessed firsthand. He also defines chastity and celibacy, which are often conflated and poorly understood. Finally, Ron offers a dozen snapshots of "sexuality in its full bloom."*

HEALTHY SEXUALITY

The Greek philosophers used to say that we are fired into life with a madness that comes from the gods and that this energy is the root all love, hate, creativity, joy, and sadness. A Christian should agree with that, then add that God put that great power, sexuality, within us so that, ultimately, we might also create life and, like God, look upon what we have helped create, overflow with a joy that breaks the very casings of our selfishness, and say: "It is good; indeed, it is very good!" A mature sexuality, is when a person looks at what he or she has helped create, swells in a delight that breaks the prison of his or her selfishness, and feels as God feels when God looks at creation.

For this reason sexuality lies at the center of the spiritual life. A healthy sexuality is the single most powerful vehicle there is to lead us to selflessness and joy, just as unhealthy sexuality helps constellate selfishness and unhappiness as does nothing else. We will be happy in this life, depending upon whether or not we have a healthy sexuality.

One of the fundamental tasks of spirituality, therefore, is to help us to understand and channel our sexuality correctly. This, however, is no easy task. Sexuality is such a powerful fire that it is not always easy to channel it in life-giving ways. Its very power, and it is the most powerful force on the planet, makes it a force not just for formidable love, life, and blessing but also for the worst hate, death, and destruction imaginable. Sex is responsible for most of the ecstasies that occur on the planet, but it is also responsible for lots of murders and suicides. It is the most powerful of all fires, the best of all fires, the most dangerous of all fires, and the fire which, ultimately, lies at the base of everything, including the spiritual life.

But how should sexuality be understood? What are the central prongs within a Christian spirituality of sexuality?

Sexuality as an Awareness of Having Been Cut Off

To understand the meaning of sexuality, one must begin with its definition. The roots of a word are not always helpful in clarifying its meaning, but they are in the case of the words *sex* and *sexuality*. The word sex has a Latin root, the verb *secare*. In Latin, *secare* means (literally) *"to cut off," "to sever," "to amputate," "to disconnect from the whole."* To be "sexed," therefore, literally means to be cut off, to be severed from, to be amputated from the whole. Thus, to use a simple example, were you to take a chain-saw and go to a tree and cut off one of its branches, you would have "sexed" that branch. This branch, could it feel and think, would wake up on the ground, severed, cut off, disconnected, a lonely little piece of wood which was once part of a great organism. It would know in its every cell that if it wants to continue living and especially if it wants to produce flowers and bear fruit, it must somehow reconnect itself to the tree.

That is precisely how we wake up in the world. We wake up in our cribs, not serene, but crying—lonely, cut off, severed from the great whole. Long before we even come to self-consciousness and long before we reach puberty when our sexuality constellates so strongly around the desire for sex, we feel ourselves painfully sexed in every cell of our body, psyche, and soul. Sex is a dimension of our very awareness. We wake up in the world and in every cell of our being we ache, consciously and unconsciously, sensing that we are incomplete, unwhole, lonely, cut off, a little piece of something that was once part of a whole. Carl Jung once compared the incompleteness we feel in sexuality to the separated white and yoke of an egg. Together they make a one, a whole. Apart they are incomplete. The sexes are like that. Alone we are essentially incomplete and aching at every level for a wholeness that, at some dark level, we know we have been separated from. We experience ourselves as white or yolk, separated from our other half.

And this is experienced as exceedingly painful—an aching loneliness, an irrational longing, a madness from the gods (as the Greeks put it). But this madness is also a great energy; in fact, it is the greatest energy of all inside us. It is the engine that drives everything else, body and spirit. If this is true, and it is, then we see that sexuality is more than simply a question of having sex and it is becomes very important that we make a critical distinction between *sexuality* and *genitality*. Sex and having sex are not simply identifiable.

Sexuality versus Genitality

Sexuality is an all-encompassing energy inside of us. In one sense, it is identifiable with the principle of life itself. It is the drive for love, communion, community, friendship, family, affection, wholeness, consummation, creativity, self-perpetuation, immorality, joy, delight, humor, and self-transcendence. It is not good to be alone. When God said this about Adam at the dawn of creation, God meant it about every man, woman, child, animal, insect, plant, atom, and molecule in the universe. Sex is the energy inside of us that works incessantly against our being alone.

Genitality, having sex, is only one aspect of that larger reality of sexuality, albeit a very important one. Genitality is particularized, physical consummation, a certain privileged constellation of many of the energies that are contained within our wider erotic energies in one bodily encounter with another person which we commonly term making love.

Upon making this critical distinction, a couple of cautions must immediately go out. On the one hand, genitality (having sex) may never be trivialized or denigrated and seen as something that is too earthy and carnal to be spiritual, as countless Manicheans, Gnostics, and other spiritualists have believed and taught through the centuries. Christianity has for the most part been so influenced by negative and unchristian views on sex that it has never really developed a life-giving spirituality of genitality. For this reason, among others, celibacy has been made too much of a spiritual ideal. This is wrong. Having sex is admittedly not the whole reality of sex, but it is perhaps God's greatest gift to the planet and it offers humans the greatest opportunity for genuine intimacy available this side of eternity. Indeed, some theologians see in sexual encounter a foretaste of the eternal life of heaven and many of the classical mystics use the image of sexual encounter to describe our ultimate union with God and creation.

On the other hand, Christians must also avoid the popular contemporary view that genitality somehow can carry all the things that sexuality is supposed to carry. Popular culture today teaches that one cannot be whole without being healthily sexual. That is correct. However, for the most part, it thinks of sex only as having sex. That is a tragic reduction. Sex is a wide energy and we are healthily sexual when we have love, community, communion, family, friendship, affection, creativity, joy, delight, humor, and self-transcendence in our lives. Having these, as we know, depends on many things and not just on whether or not we sleep alone. One can have a lot of sex and still lack real love, community, family, friendship, and creativity, just as one may be celibate and have these in abundance. We all know the popular dictum (and how true it is) that it is often easier to find a lover than a friend. Sexuality is as much about having friends as it is about having lovers. It is painful to sleep alone but it is perhaps even more painful to sleep alone when you are not sleeping alone. Thus, while genitality should never be denigrated and seen as something that is not spiritual or important, it should not be asked, all by itself, to be responsible for community, friendship, family, and delight within our lives.

The ancient Greek philosophers gave us the word *eros*. For them, however, it meant much more than it does for us today. Generally today we understand it to mean mainly sexual attraction. For the ancient Greeks, eros was a reality with six interpenetrating dimensions: It referred, at one and the same time, to *ludens* (love's playfulness, teasing, and humor); *erotic attraction* (sexual attractiveness and the desire to have sex); *mania* (obsessiveness, falling in love, romance); *pragma* (sensible arrangement in view of family life, home, and community); *philia* (friendship); and *agape* (altruism, selflessness, sacrifice). Unlike us, the ancient Greeks did not ask one aspect of love to carry all the others.

—*The Holy Longing*, 192–196

THE GODDESS ARTEMIS

Ancient Greece expressed much of its psychological and spiritual wisdom inside their myths. They didn't intend these to be taken literally or as historical, but as metaphor and as an archetypal illustration of why life is as it is and how people engage life both generatively and destructively.

And many of these myths are centered on gods and goddesses. They had gods and goddesses to mirror virtually every aspect of life, every aspect of human behavior, and every innate human propensity. Moreover, many of these gods and goddesses were far from moral in their behavior, especially in their sexual lives.

They had messy affairs with each other and with human beings. However, despite the messiness and amorality of their sexual behavior, one of the positive features inside these myths was that, for Ancient Greece, sex was always, somehow, connected to the divine. Even temple prostitution was somehow related to accessing the fertility that emanated from the divine realm.

Within this pantheon of gods and goddesses there was a particular goddess name Artemis. Unlike most of their other goddesses, who were sexually promiscuous, she was chaste and celibate. Her sexual abstinence represented the place and the value of chastity and celibacy. She was pictured as a tall, graceful figure, attractive sexually, but with a beauty that, while sexual, was different from the seductive sexuality of goddesses like Aphrodite and Hera. In the figure of Artemis, sex is pictured as an attractive blend of solitude and integrity. She is frequently pictured as surrounded by members of her own sex or by members of the opposite sex who appear as friends and intimates, but never as lovers.

What's implied here is that sexual desire can remain healthy and generative even while abstaining from sex. Artemis represents a chaste way of being sexual. She tells us that, in the midst of a sexually-soaked world, one can be generative and happy inside of chastity and even inside celibacy. Perhaps even more importantly, Artemis shows us that chastity need not render one anti-sexual and sterile. Rather she shows that sexuality is wider than sex and that sex itself will be richer and more meaningful if it is also connected to chastity. Artemis declares that claiming your solitude and experiencing friendship and other forms of intimacy are not a substitute for sex but one of the rich modalities of sex itself.

Spiritual writer and psychotherapist Thomas Moore, in describing Artemis, writes: "Although she is the most virginal of the goddesses, Artemis is not asexual. She embodies a special kind of sexuality where the accent is on individuality, integrity, and solitude." As such, she is a model not just for celibates but also for people who are sexually active. For the sexually active person, Artemis is the cautionary flag that says: I want to be taken seriously, with my integrity and independence assured.

As well, Moore suggests that, irrespective of whether we are celibate or sexually active, we all "have periods in life or just moments in a day when we need to be alone, disconnected from love and sex, devoted to an interest of our own, withdrawn and remote. [Artemis] tells us that this preference may not be an antisocial rejection of people but simply a deep, positive, even sexual focusing of oneself and one's world."

What's taught by this mythical goddess is a much-needed lesson for our world today. Our age has turned sex into a soteriology, namely, for us, sex isn't perceived as a means towards heaven, it is identified with heaven itself. It's what we're supposed to be living for. One of the consequences of this is that we can no longer blend our adult awareness with chastity, nor with the genuine complexity and richness of sex. Rather, for many of us, chastity and celibacy are seen as a fearful self-protection, which leave one dry, sterile, moralistic, anti-erotic, sexually-uptight, and on the periphery of life's joys. Tied to this too is the notion that all those rich realities so positively highlighted by Artemis (as well as by the classical Christian notion of chastity), namely, friendship, non-sexual forms of intimacy, non-sexual pleasures, and the need for integrity and fidelity within sex, are seen as a substitute for sex, and a second-best one at that, rather than as rich modality of sex itself.

We are psychologically and spiritually impoverished by that notion and it puts undue pressure on our sexual lives. When sex is asked to carry the primary load in terms of human generativity and happiness it cannot help but come up short. And we are seeing that in our world today. —*In Exile,* October 20, 2014

THE SACRAMENT OF MARRIAGE

No amount of preaching shapes a soul as much as does the influence of a good Christian life. If that is true, and it is, then no marriage course is ever as powerful to teach about marriage as is the witness of a good marriage.

I understood this, firsthand, a few weeks ago when I attended the fiftieth wedding anniversary of an uncle and an aunt. Theirs has been a good marriage—good harmony, good hospitality, good family, sustained faith. However, and only they know the full price tag, this did not always come easily. They spent enough years without money and without extras, raising a large family. His first job, clerking in a store, paid him fifty cents a day. She couldn't find any work at all—"women weren't needed in the job market in those days!" There were as well, as in all families, countless other struggles and, in their case, countless more hours spent, by both, beyond their own family concerns, working in church and community circles.

Nearly three hundred of us, family and friends, gathered to toast and roast them. At the end of the banquet my uncle stood up to thank everyone. He ended his comments with the words: "When we got married fifty years ago, we didn't have much, but we had an unconscious trust that if we lived by the Ten Commandments and the laws of the church then things would turn out all right . . . and I think they did."

What an understatement! They turned out more than all right. A good marriage can best be described, I believe, by four images and theirs is the prime analogue of each of these:

- A good marriage is a warm *fireplace*. The love that two people have for each other generates a warm place. But the warmth it creates does not warm just the two people in love; it warms everyone else who comes near them—their children, their neighbors, their community, and everyone who meets them.
- A good marriage is a big *table, loaded with lots of food and drink*. When two people love each other sacramentally that love becomes a place of hospitality, a table where people come to be fed—figuratively and really. Again, love, in a true marriage, feeds not just the two

people who are generating it, but, because it is sacramental, it always contains more than enough surplus to feed everyone who is fortunate enough to meet it.

- A good marriage is a *container that holds suffering*. An old axiom says: "Everything can be borne if it can be shared!" That's true. Anyone fortunate enough to have a true moral partner in this life can bear a lot of suffering. That is even more true in a good marriage where the wife and husband, because of their deep moral and emotional affinity, can carry not just their own sufferings but also can help carry the sufferings of many others.
- Finally, to draw upon a deep Christian image, a good marriage is *Christ's body*, flesh that is "food for the life of the world." Christ left his body to feed the world. A good marriage does precisely that, it feeds everything and everybody around it. Many of us have experienced this in some of the married people we have met. Having them in our lives is a constant source of moral, psychological, religious, and humorous nourishment.

The marriage of my aunt and uncle is, exactly, described by these images. Their relationship to each other is a *fireplace* where many people, including myself, have found warmth. It is a *table*—all their houses have always had big tables, big loaded refrigerators, and big doors that have welcomed and given hospitality and food and drink to everyone who crossed their threshold. And their relationship has been a *container for suffering*. Through the years, thanks to their love for each other, they were able to bear with faith, dignity, soft hearts, and ever-deepening charity all the pain, tragedy, and suffering that came their way. But they were also able to help many other people, including my own family when we lost our parents, to carry their sufferings. Finally, their relationship has been, and remains, *Christ's body, food for the life of the world*. Virtually everyone whose path ever crossed theirs has been fed, nourished, given vitamins in their soul by this marriage.

An age that no longer understands sacrament, might, I submit, look at a marriage like this one to better see what shapes a soul and what constitutes a sacrament. Sometimes the answers we seek are not found in books but in the house across the street. Sometimes too the sacrament we need to feed our souls is found, not just at the communion rail, but in a warm living room and at a loaded table.

Two as One Flesh

This summer one of my sisters died. As much as we all miss her, none of us, including her own children, feels her absence as much as her husband. He doesn't just miss her. Half his life is gone. That is where he is different from her kids: they lost their mum, but still have a whole self left. He wakes up mornings, walks through days, and goes about the business of raising family and crops with some of his own body missing. That is no romantic exaggeration, as everyone who knew them knows. They were married, husband and wife for thirty-four years, and everything about them and their relationship suggested that what was between them was rare.

"And the two shall be one flesh!" That they were, just as the second page of the Bible describes it. Both had left their own families, and a lot of other things, to cling to each other, to be one flesh. When a man and a woman love each other in that way, truly in that way, each dies and something new, some third thing, is born. In my sister and brother-in-law's relationship, you saw this third thing, human love consummated, grown sacramental. Small wonder that my brother-in-law now feels only half alive. For a while he had an ally, a co-conspirator, against the most primal of all loneliness, the one that God himself damned at the origins of history: "It is not good for the man to be alone!" For a time, he was not alone. He was married—married in a way that is worth reflecting upon.

What makes a great marriage? What made my sister and her husband "one flesh" in a way that is so often denied the rest of us? What really marries one person to another? There are all kinds of answers to these questions and, given a culture that constellates so many of its feelings about love around sex and romantic obsession, what was true in their case is normally not what comes first to mind. They weren't Romeo and Juliet. Theirs was not the stuff of Hollywood romances and Iris Murdoch novels. What was so special between them could easily be missed. It had such a quietness to it, a gentleness, softness, and chastity, that it contained nothing of those exaggerated forms that make for great art—and often for tumult, heartbreak, and infidelity in real life. Nothing between them garbled life. Their relationship was, for the most part, too ordinary to notice. They didn't often get the chance to look at each other over crystal wine glasses under romantic lighting, though they yearned for that. They had to catch each other's eye more domestically. For whole years at a stretch, over dirty diapers and dirty dishes, in a house packed with kids, they would meet each other's eyes and both would know that they were home: "At last, bone from my bone, flesh from flesh." They knew what consummation meant. For thirty-four years they had only to look at each other to not be alone.

But what makes this? What needs to be there for someone to look at another and feel that other as bone from my bone, flesh from my flesh, kindred spirit? In today's terminology, what makes someone a soul mate? What do you need to experience with another person to overcome that exile of heart?

Someone looking at my sister and brother-in-law might, more superficially, have seen some obvious things: deep mutual respect, a gentleness between them, uncompromising fidelity to each other, harmony of thought and feelings on most things important, regular prayer together, and a complete trust of each other. Those things are the heart of a marriage. But, in the end, these were, in their case, symptoms really. What connected them, made for bone of my bone, for the harmony, respect, fidelity, and gentleness was something deeper. They had moral affinity. Long before, and concomitant with, sleeping with each other physically, they slept with each other morally.

What's meant by this curious phrase? Each of us has a place inside where we feel most deeply about the right and wrong of things and where what is most precious to us is cherished and guarded. It is when this place is attacked that we feel most violated. It is also the place where, in the end, we feel most alone. More deeply than we long for a sexual partner, we long for someone to sleep with us here.

My sister and brother-in-law found this in each other. They were moral lovers. They found, touched, and protected each other's souls. Everything that was deepest and most precious in each of them was understood, cherished, and safe when the other was around. It made for a great marriage—one flesh, true consummation, all predicated on a great trust and a great chastity. This is a secret worth knowing.

Sex as Sacrament

A Catholic journalist recently commented that the world will begin to take the church seriously when it talks about sex if the church, first of all, affirms what it should always be affirming, namely, that for married persons the marriage bed is their daily eucharist.

Sex as a sacrament. Sex as eucharist. Is this high spiritual truth or is it blasphemy? It can be either since, within a Christian understanding, sex is precisely either sacrament or perversity. In a recent article in *Grail* British psychiatrist Jack Dominion discusses the sacramental role of sex within a marriage. Without denying what traditional Christian thought has always affirmed, that is, that procreation is a function of married sexuality, he goes on to suggest five possibilities (ultimately, sacramental possibilities) which can be realized each time a married couple make love.

First, each time they do make love they, potentially, verify their personal significance to each other. More simply put, each act of sexual intercourse is a reminder (and a celebration) of the fact that they are the most important person in each other's lives. Sexual intercourse, within its proper context, love consecrated through marriage, verifies and celebrates (physically, emotionally, and spiritually) what was pronounced in their marriage vows, namely, "My love is now consecrated, displaced, for you!"

Dietrich Bonhoeffer once told a couple he was marrying: "Today you are young and very much in love. You think that your love will sustain your marriage. Well, I give you the opposite advice—let your marriage sustain your love." Sexual orgasm facilitates a personal encounter that speaks of and demands precisely the type of exclusiveness and fidelity that the marriage vows promise.

Second, sexual intercourse is one of the most powerful acts through which a couple reinforce each other's sexual identity, making, as Dominion puts it, the woman feel fully feminine and the man fully masculine.

Third, sexual intercourse can be, potentially, a most powerful act of reconciliation, healing, and forgiveness. In all relationships, perhaps especially in married ones, wounds will appear (arising from, among other things, different temperaments, disappointment with each other, past histories, weaknesses, and inadequacies) which will, at one level, appear to create an unbridgeable chasm. Sexual orgasm can facilitate a peak experience within which harmony is restored beyond the hurt, not because the hurt is taken away, but because in that peak experience something is felt which, for a second at least, lets persons drop the load of hurt, disappointment, and bitterness and meet in a super-reconciliation which is a foretaste of the reconciliation of heaven itself.

Fourth, sexual intercourse is perhaps, singularly, the most powerful way a couple has of telling each other that they wish to continue in this consecrated relationship. Freud once said we understand the structure of a thing by looking at it when it is broken. Thus we see that within a marriage when the sexual bond is broken, when there is an unwillingness or a hesitancy to sleep with each other, there is, at some level, also some unwillingness or hesitancy to continue the relationship at a very deep level.

Finally, sexual intercourse is, as Dominion so aptly puts it, a rich vein of thanksgiving. Orgasm, within a proper relationship, spawns gratitude.

Given these possibilities for sex, it does not strain the imagination to see that the marriage bed is, potentially, a sacrament, a daily eucharist. A sacrament is, as theology has always said in one fashion or another, someone or something that visibly prolongs a saving action of Christ; something visible, fleshy, tangible, incarnate, that somehow makes God present. More specifically still, what takes place in the marriage bed (between a couple who are properly loving each other) parallels what takes place between ourselves and Christ in the eucharist. Each eucharist also has those five possibilities: In that encounter we say to Christ and Christ says to us: "My life is consecrated, displaced, for you." Through that encounter, as well, we reinforce our identity as Christians, are embraced in a super-reconciliation, announce through word and action that we want to continue in a deep relationship with Christ, and are imbued with and express gratitude.

The marriage bed, like the eucharist, is fleshy, tangible, visible, and incarnate. (Not at all a sacrament for angels!) Like the eucharist too it expresses special love, fidelity, reconciliation, and gratitude in an earthy way. That quality, its earthiness, makes it, like the eucharist, a very powerful and privileged sacrament. Through it the word becomes flesh and dwells among us.

—*Against an Infinite Horizon,* 87–95

ACCEPTING DISAPPOINTMENT IN LOVE

In many of her novels, Anita Brookner, almost as a signature to her work, will make this comment: The first task of a couple in marriage is to console each other for the fact that they cannot not disappoint each other. That's an important insight. Why?

When we are young and hear sadness in love songs, we think that the sadness and disappointment are a prelude to the experience of love. Later we come to realize that the sadness and disappointment ultimately originate not from the fact that love has not taken place, but from the finite, limited character of human love itself. Brookner has it right: The first task in any love is for us to console each other for the limits of our love, for the fact that we cannot not disappoint each other.

Why? Why can't two persons ever be enough for each other? Why is disappointment part of the experience of every relationship, friendship, and marriage?

Because the very way that we are made precludes ever having, in this life, a oneness of mind, heart, and body that fulfils us in such a way that there is no disappointment. Our longing is simply too wide. We long for the infinite and are built for it and so we wake to life and consciousness with longings as deep as a Grand Canyon without a bottom.

In this life then, outside of rare and very transitory mystical experiences, there is no consummation (sexual, emotional, psychological, or even spiritual) with another person that is so deep and all-embracing so as exclude all distance, shadow, and emptiness. No matter how deep a friendship or a marriage and no matter how good, rich in personality, and deep the other person may be, we always find ourselves somewhat disappointed. In this life, there is no union that fills every emptiness inside of us. Somewhere, we always sleep alone.

In essence, there is no union which fulfils perfectly the Genesis prescription that "two become one flesh." No matter how close a marriage or a friendship, two can never ultimately become one.

No matter how deep a union, we always remain separate, two persons who cannot really ever, in this life, make just one heart, one mind, and one body. No love or friendship ever fully takes away our separateness. Sometimes sexual electricity or emotional or spiritual affinity can promise such a oneness. But, in the end, it cannot fully deliver it. No matter how deep and powerful a union, ultimately, we remain, and need to remain, captains of our own hearts, minds, and bodies.

This needs to be recognized, not just to help us deal with the disappointment, but especially so that we do not violate each other. What's implied here?

In this life we are always, to some degree, in exile from each other. We stand alone in some way. Where we feel this most deeply is not in our sexual isolation, but in our moral separateness. What we crave even more deeply than sexual unity is moral affinity, to be truly one heart with another. More than we desire a lover, we desire a kindred spirit, a soul mate. If this is true, then the deepest violations of each other are also not sexual but moral. It's when we try to be captain of somebody else's soul (more so even than of his or her body) that we rape someone. And it is our failure to accept that we will always be somehow separate from each other that creates the pressure inside of us to unhealthily try to be captain of someone else's soul. We violate another's separateness precisely because we cannot accept the disappointment of love.

Finally, beyond even this, we cannot not be disappointed in love because, in the end, we are all, in some way, limited, inadequate, blemished, dull, and boring. None of us is God. No matter how rich our personalities or attractive our bodies, none of us can indefinitely excite and generate novelty, sexual electricity, and emotional pleasure, within a relationship. A relationship is like a long trip and, as Dan Berrigan puts it, "there's bound to be some long dull stretches. Don't travel with someone who expects you to be exciting all the time!"

What's the lesson in this? Stoicism and cynicism about love and romance? To the contrary: The recognition that, in love, we cannot not disappoint each other is what makes it possible for us to remain inside of marriage, friendship, celibacy, and respect. It's when we demand not to be disappointed that we grow angry, make unrealistic demands, and put pressure on each other's moral and sexual integrity. Conversely, when we recognize the limits of love, when we accept an inevitable separateness, moral loneliness, and disappointment, we can begin to console each other in our friendships and our marriages. In that consolation, since it touches so deeply the core of our souls, we can, in fact, begin to find the threads that can bind us into a oneness of heart beyond disappointment. —*In Exile,* July 15, 2007

UNDERSTANDING CHASTITY

In the Christian view of things, chastity is one of the keys to a healthy sexuality. This however needs to be correctly understood. First, there is the concept of chastity itself: Chastity is not the same thing as celibacy. To be chaste does not mean that one does not have sex. Nor does it mean that one is a prude. My parents were two of the most chaste persons I ever met, yet they obviously enjoyed sex—as a large family and a warm, vivacious bond between them gave more than ample evidence of. Chastity is, first of all, not even primarily a sexual concept, though, given the power and urgency of sex, faults in chastity are often within the area of sexuality.

Chastity has to do with all experiencing. It is about the appropriateness of any experience. Ultimately, chastity is reverence—and sin, all sin, is irreverence. To be chaste is to experience people, things, places, entertainment, the phases of our lives, and sex in a way that does not violate them or ourselves. To be chaste is to experience things reverently, in such a way that the experience leaves both them and ourselves more, not less, integrated.

Thus, we are chaste when we relate to others in a way that does not transgress their moral, psychological, emotional, aesthetic, and sexual boundaries. That is an abstract way of saying that we are chaste when we do not let impatience, irreverence, or selfishness ruin what is gift by somehow violating it. Conversely, we lack chastity when we cross boundaries prematurely or irreverently, when we violate anything and somehow reduce what it is. Chastity is respect, reverence, and patience. Its fruits are integration, gratitude, and joy. Lack of chastity is impatience, irreverence, and violation. Its fruits are disintegration of soul, bitterness, and cynicism.

Whenever there is violence, disrespect, emotional chaos, lack of community, bitterness, cynicism, and sexual irresponsibility, there is a lack of chastity. Those are its infallible indicators.

Sex, precisely because it is such a powerful fire, always needs the protection of chastity. As Carl Jung suggests, we should never be naïve about the imperialistic power of energy. All energy, especially sexual energy, is not always friendly and it often seeks to take us across borders prematurely or irreverently. There is more than a little wisdom in some of the classical sexual taboos. Fire that is so powerful and sacred, sexual fire, needs to be disciplined and contained by more things than just our emotional state on a given day. The wisdom of the ages, some codified in the commandments and some buried archetypally in our instincts, tells us that, before the fire of sex, we should stand in a certain reverence and holy awe, knowing that divine fire demands that we have our shoes off. Before anything as powerful as sex there need to be some taboos.

Again, of course, our culture objects. Few things are as subject to cynicism today as is the concept of sexual chastity. Contemporary culture considers the overcoming of chastity a moral victory, one that has finally helped set us free sexually. Christians could perhaps take that claim more seriously if this supposed sexual liberation had in fact translated into more respect between the sexes and into sex that actually relieves loneliness, builds lasting community, builds more stable souls, results in less sexual exploitation of others, and helps create a society of less lonely, more loving, more gracious, and happier adults. Sadly, that is not the case and one is reminded of Albert Camus' lament that there is a time when moving beyond chastity is considered a victory, but this soon turns into a defeat.

A final comment regarding chastity: Someone once said that Christianity does not understand sexual passion while the world does not understand chastity. That is an over-simplification, given that there are important individual voices on both sides that do not fit the description, but the statement is true as a generalization and says something very important. Christianity has struggled, and still does, to healthily and fully celebrate sexual passion. The world, for its part, has struggled, and still does, to honestly and courageously look at what happens to our innocence and our happiness when we denigrate chastity. Both need to learn from each other. Passion and chastity, sex and purity, must be brought together.

Christianity must have the courage to let go of some of its fears and timidities and learn to celebrate the goodness of sexual passion, of sex. Indeed it must be the moral force that challenges the culture to celebrate the goodness of sex. As long as it hesitates to do this, it will, at this level at least, remain the enemy of legitimate delight and creativity. Chastity outside of the goodness of sex is frigidity. On the other hand, our culture must relearn the value of chastity and purity. It must admit how much of its emotional pain and chaos is the result of trivializing sex and ignoring the value of chastity and purity. As long as the world continues to see chastity as naïveté, fear, and Victorian morality, it will remain its own enemy. Sexual passion is only something of depth when it is related to chastity and purity. It is archetypal, not incidental, that we want to get married in white.

—*The Holy Longing*, 201–204

CELIBACY AS SOLIDARITY WITH THE POOR

Few persons today believe that there is much sense in the vow of celibacy. In spite of this, celibacy remains common, far more common, in fact, than is generally admitted. Millions of people are celibate. For most of these, being alone in this way has nothing to do with wanting celibacy and even less with making religious vows. Most celibates are that way by conscription, not choice.

This is an important piece of information that should be brought out front and center as we struggle with the question of consecrated celibacy within Catholicism. Today consecrated celibacy is under siege. Gone are the days, and this is a healthy sign, when celibacy was seen as a higher state, with marriage and sex considered as somehow second-rate, not noble but better than "burning in the flesh." Today, the starting point for any theology of sexuality is that "it is not good to be alone," that marriage and sexual union are what God intended as the norm.

Celibacy, therefore, is not normal. To be celibate, as Merton once put it, is to live in a loneliness that God himself condemned. Given that truth, more and more people are saying that the church should never ask celibacy of anyone and that a commitment to vowed celibacy is not a sign of healthy life, but bespeaks rather a fear of sex.

That celibacy indicates an unhealthy theology of sex is far from true in every case. What is universally true is that celibacy is not, and can never be, the norm sexually. The universe works in pairs, from birds through humanity. And if this is so, what possible justification can there be for vowed celibacy? On what possible basis can the church ask celibacy from so many of its ministers? Why live celibacy, if one is not forced into it by unwanted circumstance?

Because Christ lived it. At the end of the day, that single line is the sole basis for any valid justification. But that line, itself, must be properly understood. Christ's celibacy in no way suggests that celibacy is a higher state, nor that married people cannot, in their own way, imitate the manner in which Jesus incarnated himself as a sexual being. In fact, the proper way to ask the question is not: "Why did Christ remain celibate?" Asked this way, the answer too easily suggests precisely that celibacy is a higher state. The question is more accurately put this way: "What did Christ try to say to us through the way he incarnated himself as a sexual being?" If asked this way, the answer to the question will have meaning for both married people and celibates.

So why did Christ incarnate his sexuality in this manner? What was he trying to teach us? Among many other things, through his celibacy, Christ was trying to tell us that love and sex are not always the same thing, that chastity, waiting, and inconsummation have an important role to play within the interim eschatological age we live in, and that, ultimately, in our sexuality we are meant to embrace everyone. But his celibacy had another purpose too. It was part of his solidarity with the poor.

How so? Simply put, when Christ went to bed alone at night he was in real solidarity with the many persons who, not by choice but by circumstance, sleep alone. And there is a real poverty, a painful searing one, in this kind of aloneness. The poor are not just those who are more manifestly victimized by poverty, violence, war, and unjust economic systems. There are other less obvious manifestations of poverty, violence, and injustice. Enforced celibacy is one of them.

Anyone who is because of unwanted circumstance (physical unattractiveness, emotional instability, advanced age, geographical separation, frigidity or uptightness, bad history, or simple bad luck) effectively blocked from enjoying sexual consummation is a victim of a most painful poverty. This is particularly true today in a culture that so idealizes sexual intimacy and the right sexual relationship. To sleep alone is to be poor. To sleep alone is to be stigmatized. To sleep alone is to be outside the norm for human intimacy and to feel acutely the sting of that.

When Jesus went to bed alone he was in solidarity with that pain, in solidarity with the poor. A vow of celibacy, whatever its negatives, also does that for a person, it puts him or her into a privileged solidarity with a special kind of poverty, the loneliness of those who sleep alone, not because they want to, but because circumstance denies them from enjoying one of the deepest human experience that there is, sexual consummation.

—*In Exile,* June 14, 1995

A MATURE SEXUALITY

Sexuality is a beautiful, good, extremely powerful, sacred energy, given us by God and experienced in every cell of our being as an irrepressible urge to overcome our incompleteness, to move towards unity and consummation with that which is beyond us. It is also the pulse to celebrate, to give and to receive delight, to find our way back to the Garden of Eden where we can be naked, shameless, and without worry and work as we make love in the moonlight.

Ultimately, though, all these hungers, in their full maturity, culminate on one thing: They want to make us co-creators with God . . . mothers and fathers, artisans and creators, big brothers and big sisters, nurses and healers, teachers and consolers, farmers and producers, administrators and community builders . . . co-responsible with God for the planet, standing with God and smiling at and blessing the world.

Given that definition, we see that sexuality in its mature bloom does not necessarily look like the love scenes (perfect bodies, perfect emotion, perfect light) in a Hollywood movie. What does sexuality in its full bloom look like?

- When you see a young mother, so beaming with delight at her own child that, for that moment, all selfishness within her has given way to the sheer joy of seeing her child happy you are seeing sexuality in its mature bloom.
- When you see a grandfather so proud of his grandson who has just received his diploma, that, for that moment, his spirit is only compassion, altruism, and joy you are seeing sexuality in its mature bloom.
- When you see an artist, after long frustration, look with such satisfaction on a work she has just completed that everything else for the moment is blotted out, you are seeing sexuality in its mature bloom.
- When you see a young man, cold and wet, but happy to have been of service, standing on a dock where he has carried the unconscious body of a child he has just saved from drowning, you are seeing sexuality in it mature bloom.
- When you see someone throw back his or her head in genuine laughter, caught off guard by the surprise of joy itself, you are seeing sexuality in its mature bloom.
- When you see an elderly nun who, never having slept with a man, been married, or given birth to a child, has through years of selfless service become a person whose very compassion gives her a mischievous smile, you are seeing sexuality in its mature bloom.
- When you see a community gathered round a grave, making peace with tragedy and consoling each other so

that life can go on, you are seeing sexuality in its mature bloom.

- When you see an elderly husband and wife who after nearly half a century of marriage have made such peace with each other's humanity that now they can quietly share a bowl of soup, content just to know that the other is there, you are seeing sexuality in its mature bloom.
- When you see a table, surrounded by a family, laughing, arguing, and sharing life with each other, you are seeing sexuality in its mature bloom.
- When you see a Mother Teresa dress the wounds of a street-person in Calcutta or an Oscar Romero give his life in defense of the poor, you are seeing sexuality in its mature bloom.
- When you see any person—man, woman, or child—who in a moment of service, affection, love, friendship, creativity, joy, or compassion, is, for that moment, so caught up in what is beyond him or her that for that instant his or her separateness from others is overcome, you are seeing sexuality in its mature bloom.
- When you see God, having just created the earth or just seen Jesus baptized in the Jordan river, look down on what has just happened and say, "It is good; in this I take delight!"; you are seeing sexuality in its mature bloom.

Sexuality is not simply about finding a lover or even finding a friend. It is about overcoming separateness by giving life and blessing it.

Thus, in its maturity, sexuality is about giving oneself over to community, friendship, family, service, creativity, humor, delight, and martyrdom so that, with God, we can help bring life into the world.

—*In Exile,* May 28, 1998

MOURNING OUR VIRGINITY

In the Jewish scriptures there's a story that's unique both in its capacity to shock and to fascinate. A king, Jepthah, is at war and things are going badly. Praying in desperation, he makes a promise to God that, should he win this battle, he would, upon returning home, sacrifice on the altar the first person he meets.

Some days God has nothing better to do than to hear such prayers. Jepthah's prayer is granted and he wins the battle, but, upon returning home, he is deeply distressed because the first person he meets is his own daughter, in the full bloom of youth. He loves her deeply, grieves his foolish vow, and is ready to break it for her sake.

But she asks him to go ahead with it. She accepts to die on the altar of sacrifice, except for one thing (in stories that bare the soul there is always "one thing"). In her case, the one thing is this: She will now die a virgin, unconsummated, unfulfilled, not having achieved full intimacy, and not having given birth to children. And so she asks her father for time in the desert (forty days, the time it takes the desert to do its work) before she dies, to grieve her virginity, the incompleteness of her life.

Her father grants her wish and she goes out into the desert with her companions (themselves virgins) for forty days to bewail that she will die a virgin. After this, she returns and is ready to die on the altar of sacrifice.

There's a rather nasty patriarchal character to this story (such were the times) and, of course, we are right to abhor the very idea of human sacrifice, but this particular story is not historical and is not meant literally. It's archetype, metaphor, a poetry of the soul within which death and virginity are not meant in their literal sense. What do death and virginity mean in this story?

They're metaphors inside a parable meant to teach a profound truth, namely, all of us, no matter age or state in life, must, at some point, mourn what's incomplete and not consummated in our lives.

We are all Jepthah's daughters. In the end, like her, we all die virgins, having lived incomplete lives, not having achieved the intimacy we craved, and having yearned to create a lot more things than we were able to birth. In this life, nobody gets the full symphony. There's a place inside us where we all "bewail our virginity," and this is true too of married people, just as it is of celibates. At some deep level, this side of eternity, we all sleep alone.

We need to mourn this, whatever form that might take. When we fail to do this, we go through life disappointed, dissatisfied with our lives, restless inside our own skins, prone to anger, and forever expecting, unrealistically, that someone or something—a marriage partner, a family, a child, a church, a sexual partner, a friend, a career, or an achievement—can take all of our loneliness away, give us the complete symphony, and (metaphorically) consummate our lives so that we aren't virgins any more.

Of course that's impossible, only God can do that. Our yearnings and our needs are infinite because we are Grand Canyons without a bottom.

Recognizing and accepting this isn't one of our strengths. Most everything inside of our culture today conspires to keep us from admitting this. No more for us the old prayer, "To thee we send up our sighs, mourning and weeping in this valley of tears." Good for past generations, but not for us. The last thing we like to admit is tears, the helpless frustration of our lives at times, and the incontrovertible fact of our own virginity.

We suffer a lot of restlessness, disappointment, and bitterness because of this. Until, like Jepthah's daughter, we can recognize and admit and honor how we really feel, we will forever be fighting something or somebody—usually those persons and things closest to us.

The daydreams of our youth eventually die, though perhaps as we get older we replay them just to feel old sentiments (our own version of "The Way We Were") rather than with any kind of practical hope. Time and disappointment have done their work, we no longer look for the daydreams to come true and the dreams themselves look pretty flat in the context of our actual lives. But what created those dreams all those years back hasn't changed; indeed there's a part of us now that's more idealistic than before and we ache just as much as we ever did, even now when we accept that daydreams don't come true.

—*In Exile,* August 22, 2004

PART TWO

Guidelines for a Generative Spirituality

4

The Incarnation at the Root of All Christian Spirituality

Why would God take on human flesh? In this chapter, Ron retraces his own path toward a better understanding of the incarnation. "The incarnation teaches unequivocally that we find salvation not by escaping the body and the things of this earth, but by entering them more deeply and correctly."

He also revisits the Christmas story and its symbols. Jesus was not born in a cathedral with the sweet smell of incense perfuming the air and soft organ music playing in the background. He was born in a stable with its animal smells and with all the attendant mess of an ordinary human birth. God entered our world not as a superhuman, invincible being, but as a helpless infant. What the incarnation tells us is that God is to be found in the ordinary: in our workplaces, in our family lives, in our wounds, and in each other's faces.

OUR MISCONCEPTION OF THE INCARNATION

The central mystery within all of Christianity, undergirding everything else, is the mystery of the incarnation. Unfortunately, it is also the mystery that is the most misunderstood or, more accurately, to coin a phrase, under-understood. It is not so much that we misunderstand what the incarnation means, it is more that we grasp only the smallest tip of a great iceberg. We miss its meaning by not seeing its immensity.

Generally, we think of the incarnation this way: In the beginning, God created the world and everything in it, concluding with the creation of humanity. But humanity soon sinned (original sin) and became helpless to save itself. God, in his goodness and mercy, however, decided to save humanity, despite its sin. So God prepared a people by calling the patriarchs and then the prophets. Through them, God slowly readied the people (the Jewish scriptures). Finally, when the time was right, God sent his own son, Jesus, who was born in Palestine nearly 2000 years ago. Jesus was God, but also fully a man. He had two natures: one human, the other divine. Jesus walked this earth for thirty-three years. He revealed God's nature, taught great truths, healed people, worked miracles, but eventually was falsely accused, arrested, crucified, and died. He rose three days later and, for the next 40 days, made various appearances to his followers. At the end of this time, with his followers now more adjusted to the new reality of the resurrection, he took them to a hill-side outside of Jerusalem, blessed them, and ascended, physically, to heaven.

In this concept, God walked this earth, physically, for thirty-three years, and then returned to heaven, leaving us the Holy Spirit, a real but less physical presence of God. The physical body of Jesus, the word made flesh, was with us for thirty-three years and is now in heaven.

What is wrong with this? It is right—in its own symbolic, beautiful language—about many things: our sin, God's mercy, God coming physically to earth. Where it is wrong is that it gives the impression that the incarnation was a thirty-year experiment, a one-shot incursion by God into human history. In this version, God came to earth physically and then, after thirty-three years, went back home. It uses the past tense for the incarnation and that is a dangerous under-understanding. The incarnation is still going on and it is just as real and as radically physical as when Jesus of Nazareth, in the flesh, walked the dirt roads of Palestine. How can this be so? . . .

Why would God want to take on human flesh? Why would an infinite power want to limit itself within the confines of history and a human body? Why incarnation?

There is a marvelous story told about a four-year-old child who awoke one night frightened, convinced that in the darkness around her there were all kinds of spooks and monsters. Alone, frightened, she ran to her parents' bedroom. Her mother calmed her down and, taking her by the hand, led her back to her own room where she put on a light and reassured the child with these words: "You needn't be afraid, you are not alone here. God is in the room with you." The child, replied: "I know that God is here, but I need someone in this room who has some skin!"

In essence, that story gives us the reason for the incarnation, as well as an excellent definition of it. God takes on flesh because, like this young girl, we all need someone with us who has some skin. A God who is everywhere is just as easily nowhere. We believe in what we can touch, see, hear, smell, and taste. We are not angels, without bodies, but sensual creatures in the true sense of the word, sensuality. We have five senses and we are present in the world through those senses. We know through them, communicate through them, and are open to each other and the world only through them. And God, having created our nature, respects how it operates. Thus, God deals with us through our senses. The Jesus who walked the roads of Palestine could be seen, touched, and heard. In the incarnation, God became physical because we are creatures of the senses who, at a point, need a God with some skin. —*The Holy Longing,* 75–77

ORDINARY GOODNESS AND OUR SPIRITUAL JOURNEY

The spirituality writer, Tom Stella, tells a story about three monks at prayer in their monastery chapel. The first monk imagines himself being carried up to heaven by the angels. The second monk imagines himself already in heaven, chanting God's praises with the angels and saints. The third monk cannot focus on any holy thoughts but can only think about the great hamburger he had eaten just before coming to chapel. That night, when the devil was filing his report for the day, he wrote: "Today

I tried to tempt three monks, but I only succeeded with two of them."

There's more depth to this story that initially meets the eye. I wish that, years ago, I had grasped how both angels and great hamburgers play a role in our spiritual journey. You see, for too many years, I identified the spiritual quest with only explicit religious thoughts, prayers, and actions. If I was in church, I was spiritual, whereas if I was enjoying a good meal with friends, I was merely human. If I was praying and could concentrate my thoughts and feelings on some holy or inspiring thing, I felt I was praying and was, for that time, spiritual and religious; whereas if I was distracted, fatigued, or too sleepy to concentrate, I felt I had prayed poorly. When I was doing explicitly religious things or making more-obvious moral decisions, I felt religious, everything else was, to my mind, mere humanism.

While I was not particularly Manichaean or negative on the things of this world, nonetheless the good things of creation (of life, of family and friendship, of the human body, of sexuality, of food and drink) were never understood as spiritual, as religious. In my mind, there was a pretty sharp distinction between heaven and earth, the holy and the profane, the divine and the human, between the spiritual and the earthly. This was especially true for the more earthy aspects of life, namely, food, drink, sex, and bodily pleasures of any kind. At best, these were distractions from the spiritual; at worst, they were negative temptations tripping me up, obstacles to spirituality.

But, by stumbling often enough, we eventually learn: I tried to live like the first two monks, with my mind on spiritual things, but the third monk kept tripping me up, ironically not least when I was in church or at prayer. While in church or at prayer and trying to force mind and heart onto the things of the spirit, I would forever find myself assailed by things that, supposedly, had no place in church: memories and anticipations of gatherings with friends, anxieties about relationships, anxieties about unfinished tasks, thoughts about my favorite sports teams, thoughts of wonderful meals with pasta and wine, of grilled steaks and bacon-burgers, and, most pagan of all, sexual fantasies that seemed the very antithesis of all that's spiritual.

It took some years and better spiritual guidance to learn that many of these tensions were predicated on a poor and faulty understanding of Christian spirituality and of God's intent and design in creating us. God did not design our nature in one way, that is, to be sensual and to be so rooted deeply in the things of this earth, and then demand that we live as if we were not corporeal and as if the good things of this earth were only sham and obstacles to salvation, as opposed to being an integral part of salvation. Moreover, the incarnation, the mystery of God becoming corporeal, sensual, taking on human flesh, teaches unequivocally that we find salvation not by escaping the body and the things of this earth but by entering them more deeply and correctly. Jesus affirmed the resurrection of the bodily, not the flight of the soul.

—*In Exile,* May 30, 2016

IN PRAISE OF SKIN

In her book, *Nature and Other Mothers,* Brenda Peterson has a marvelous little essay entitled "In Praise of Skin." Her reflections begin on a personal level. When she was thirty-five years old, for reasons that doctors were unable to properly diagnose, she broke out in a rash that left her skin dotted with red marks, like an adult with chicken-pox. For months she saw doctors and tried various remedies, including an unlimited prescription for cortisone cream. Nothing worked. Eventually she went to see her step-grandmother who made a more primal, and accurate, diagnosis: skin needs to be touched.

Her step grandmother told her: "Your body's skin is harder-working and more wide-open than the human heart; it's a sad thing to see how skin gets passed over, barely touched except in sex, or sickness, or deep trouble. Why, we pay so little mind to our skin, we might as well be living inside a foreign country." Then she proceeded to cure her. How? By touching, massaging, and caressing her skin. Eventually the spots all disappeared and her skin became healthy again.

Our skin, as Peterson goes on to point out, is our body's biggest organ. It breathes, filters, protects, and is more important than the heart in that it is possible to live with one-third of your heart blocked, but you will die if you lose one-third of your skin. It is not incidental, she submits, that the deadliest killer of our time, AIDS, begins not with some plague-like virus invading the body, but with the breaking of skin. Skin, she insists, needs to be taken more seriously, caressed more often. It also needs to be better theologized-about.

Somehow our spiritualities have been slow off the mark and rather timid in doing this. We still want for a fertile theology of the body, of skin, of the Eucharist, of the incarnation (and all of these are tied together). So much within spirituality, even when it tries hard to be holistic, is still dis-embodied, platonic, reluctant to take seriously the very foundation of Christianity, namely, that in the incarnation God takes on real flesh, skin. We are better, it seems, at honoring skin in theory than in taking it seriously in real life. How we honor the body in actual life never quite approximates our theologizing. We still struggle mightily when it gets to actually touching, caressing, and honoring our skin and we all live long seasons when our skin is too lonely for touch. Untouched skin is rife with fever spots, like the ones Peterson speaks of, save in our case these are visible mostly in our attitudes. Part of the problem is simple: we don't get touched enough.

For Christians, among all the religions of the world, this shouldn't be the case since we believe in that, in becoming flesh, God legitimizes skin, praises skin, enters it, honors it, caresses it, and kisses it. Among all the religions of the world, we stand out because, for us, salvation is never a question of stepping outside of skin, but of having skin itself glorified. That is why Jesus never preached simple immortality of the soul, but insisted on the resurrection of the body. Christian heaven is not a state beyond skin. This teaching, that salvation includes the body, was and remains scandalous, something difficult to accept. At any given time in history the vast majority of persons, if they believe in salvation at all, believe that it exists somehow in an escape from the physical body, a stepping outside of skin.

For Christians, however, the body is not something from which one is ever meant to escape. Rather the body is to be understood as a temple of the holy spirit, a church, a sacred place where God can come and make a home. Skin then is sacred, deserving of praise. This is true, especially true, when skin meets skin, in sacramental sex, and temple commingles with temple. Not an easy thing for us to accept. It seems too earthy to be spiritual. Consequently we generally lack the courage to accept a theology of sexuality that is earthy enough to do justice to how shockingly physical the incarnation really is. In sacramental sex there is Eucharist, just as in Eucharist, God enters, caresses, and kisses human skin. Andre Dubos, the Cajun essayist and novelist, used to say: "Without the Eucharist, God is a monologue." Well put, especially in what is implicitly affirmed. With the Eucharist, God becomes more than words, more than a belief, more than a teaching. In the Eucharist, God, like Brenda Peterson's step-grandmother, becomes the great healer who touches, caresses, massages, and kisses our skin.

In praise of skin. A wonderfully-coined phrase that could serve as a subtitle for the incarnation! Karl Rahner once said that Christmas, God becoming flesh, gives us permission to be happy. He might well have added that it also gives us permission to praise and cherish the sacramentality of human skin.

—*In Exile,* June 4, 2000

THE EARTHINESS OF CHRISTMAS

Christmas means many things, but, at its heart, lies the concept of the incarnation, namely, the idea that God takes on human flesh, a human body, becomes physical. At Christmas, "the word was made flesh."

That's significant for many reasons. Among other things, the fact that God is born into our material world and takes on a human body blesses and sanctifies the physical world and our own bodies. It also assures us that we can find meaning and salvation without having to denigrate either our bodies or the physical world.

This is clear in the Christmas message and is taught explicitly in the way in which Jesus is born. His birth was real, physical, earthy, and, like all human births, messy.

We don't often allow ourselves to think like that. Mostly we idealize and spiritualize the birth of Jesus so as to imagine it as privileged, somehow miraculous, and thus removed from the mess, blood, smells, and brute physicality of normal human birth. But, as scripture assures us, Jesus was fully human in every way and that means too that he was born through the pain, mess, and earthiness of normal childbirth, complete with all that attends that—blood, messy afterbirth, the need for washing.

Moreover, scripture tells us that Jesus was not born in a cathedral, with the sweet smell of incense perfuming the air, stained-glass windows providing a special light, or soft organ music intimating the presence of the sacred. Indeed he wasn't even born in a hospital, where modern medicine and sanitation help cover the mess and the smells of childbirth. The Gospels tell us instead that he was born in a barn and then laid into an animals' feeding trough.

Contemporary biblical scholarship nuances this somewhat by telling us that we don't really know exactly where Jesus was born and that the Gospel writers don't necessarily want us to believe that he was born in a barn and physically placed in a manger. But the Gospels do want us to take those symbols seriously, and that still makes the point: Jesus' birth is placed inside a stable because, among other things, barns don't look like cathedrals and animals don't smell like incense. There's a brute earthiness to a barn, smells you don't get in church. As for the manger, the feeding trough, well, that makes sense too, given that Jesus will tell us that his "flesh is food for the life of the world." If one of the main purposes of Jesus' life is to end up as food, as Eucharist, on a table (we call an altar), shouldn't he be born in a feeding trough? The wood of the manger and the wood of the altar are one and the same, feeding tables, both of them.

But it's difficult for us both to imagine and to accept how truly physical, earthy, and messy all of this really is. Everyone struggles with this, conservatives and liberals alike: Conservatives are forever wanting to make Jesus' actual physical birth a miraculous event, with Mary delivering Jesus in some privileged way so that there isn't at his birth the normal groaning, blood, and mess of childbirth. Liberals don't fare much better. They're forever trying to turn the event of Jesus' birth into something more symbolic than physical (which then, like the conservatives' miracle, doesn't have any real blood).

The same is true for most World Religions. Invariably salvation is seen as an escape from the flesh, an escape from the physical, an escape from dirt, an escape from mess, all done in the name of the spiritual. The way to God, in most religious traditions and in most ordinary imaginations, involves escaping the physical and frowning upon mess.

But that's not the way of Christianity, as the birth of Jesus makes plain. In the incarnation, Christmas, God enters the world, becomes physical, and, by doing that, assures us that the spiritual does not set itself against the physical, that the sacred is not antithetical to the smells of the human body, and that God is not just found in churches and in places that are clean and reverent. The old moral dualisms—the spiritual against the physical, the clean against the messy—break down in the incarnation.

What Christmas teaches us is that God is as much domestic as monastic, a God of the body as well as of the soul, a God who is found in barns as well as in churches, in kitchens as well as in cathedrals.

Among the many things we celebrate at Christmas therefore is the sacredness of our own lives, in all their physicality. What's made holy by Jesus' birth? Most everything that's physical: nature, our homes, our kitchens, our workplaces, our barns, our restaurants, our bars, our sports facilities, and, not least, our own bodies, including sex and the way babies are born.

Spirit too, of course, is blessed and made holy by the incarnation, but the Word was already spiritual. At Christmas, it "was made flesh."

—*In Exile,* December 26, 2004

BORN INTO THE ORDINARY

Christmas is about God in the ordinary. After the birth of Christ, we need not look to the extraordinary, the spectacular, the miraculous to find God. God is now found where we live, in our kitchens, at our tables, in our wounds and in each other's faces. That is hard to believe and always has been. When Jesus was on earth, virtually no one believed he was the Messiah precisely because he was so ordinary, so unlike what they'd imagined God to be. People were looking for a Messiah. When finally Christ did appear, they were disappointed. They'd expected a superstar, a king, a miracle worker, someone who would, by miracle and hammer, vindicate good, destroy evil and turn the world rightfully upside down. Jesus didn't live up to those expectations. Born in a barn, preaching meekness and gentleness, unwilling to use power in a forceful way, there was little hammer and few miracles. Mainly, there was ordinariness.

It is curious that scripture refuses to describe what Jesus looked like. It never tells us whether he was short or tall, with beard or without, had light or dark hair, or blue or brown eyes. Neither does it ever assign to him anything extraordinary in terms of psychological countenance: for example, it never tells us that when Jesus entered a room, his eyes were so penetrating and his gaze so awesome that people knew they were in the presence of something extraordinary. No, scripture doesn't describe him because, in terms of physical appearance, Jesus wasn't worth describing, he looked like everyone else. Even after the resurrection, he is mistaken for a gardener, a cook, a traveler. People had trouble recognizing Jesus as God incarnate because he was so ordinary, so immersed in the things they took for granted. He was just a carpenter's son and he looked like everyone else.

Things haven't changed much in 2,000 years. Seldom does Christ meet expectations. We, like his contemporaries, are constantly looking beyond the ordinary, beyond the gardener, the cook, and the traveler, to try to find a miraculous Christ. It is for this reason that we fly to Fatima or Lourdes to see a spot where the Blessed Virgin might have cried and left us a message, but fail to see the significance of tears shed at our own breakfast table. We are intrigued by Padre Pio who had the wounds of Christ in his hands, but fail to see the wounds of Christ in those suffering around us, or in our own emotional and moral wounds. We pray for visions but seldom watch a sunset. We marvel at the gift of tongues, but are bored listening to babies. We desire proofs for the existence of God even as life in all its marvels continues all around us. We tend to look for God everywhere, except in the place where the incarnation took place—our flesh.

Nikos Kazantzakis once wrote: "God is not found in monasteries, but in our homes! Wherever you find husband and wife, that's where you find God: wherever children and petty cares and cooking and arguments and reconciliation are, that's where God is, too. The God I'm telling about, the domestic one, not the monastic one, that's the real God." Christmas celebrates the domestic God, the God born into ordinary life.

Several years ago, at a prayer seminar I was attending, a lady was giving a talk on Zen. She was describing how she spent more than two hours a day in meditation and how she would, through this practice, have very deep and lucid connections with the transcendent. During the question period, I asked her how she would compare the feelings of God that she experienced during meditation with the feelings she had when she ate dinner with her family. "No comparison," she replied. "Eating dinner with my family can be a good experience, holy even in its own way. But the experience of God in meditation is much more real. The way God is experienced in meditation dwarfs everything else."

I do not want to question the importance of meditation, nor indeed the value of Lourdes, Fatima and Padre Pio, but I am

Christian enough to be pagan enough to demand some qualifications here. We should pray meditatively, and perhaps we can benefit from Fatima, Lourdes and Padre Pio. But, in the end, we must realize that God is domestic more than monastic.

1 John 4:7–16, says: "God is love and whoever abides in love abides in God and God abides in him/her." Love is a thing that happens in ordinary life, in kitchens, at tables, in workplaces, in families, in the flesh. God abides in us when we abide there. The Christ-child is also to be found in church, in the sacraments and in private meditations (for these, too, are ordinary). All of these are ordinary and the incarnation crawls into them and helps us, there, to abide in God. —*In Exile,* December 2, 1986

CHRISTMAS AS SHATTERING THE CONTAINERS OF OUR EXPECTATIONS

Funny how God invariably shatters the containers of our expectations. We have a notion of how God should act and God ends up acting in a way that shatters all of those expectations and yet fulfills our expectations in a deeper way. That's certainly true of what happened in Bethlehem at the first Christmas.

For centuries, men and women of faith, aware of their helplessness to rectify everything that's wrong in life, had been praying for God to come to earth as a Messiah, a Savior, to clean up the earth and right all that's wrong with it. Exactly how this was to happen was perhaps more of an inchoate longing for justice, a hungry hope, than any kind of clear vision, at least until the great Jewish prophets came along. Eventually prophets like Isaiah began to articulate a vision of what would happen when the Messiah came. In these visions, the Messiah would usher in a "Messianic Age," a new time, when everything would be made right. There would be prosperity for the poor, healing for the sick, freedom from every type of enslavement, and justice for all (including punishment for the wicked). The poor and the meek would inherit the earth because the long-sought Messiah would simply overpower all evil, drive the wicked off the face of the earth, and make all things right.

And after all those centuries of waiting, of longing, what did we get? What did we get? A helpless, naked baby, unable to feed himself. That wasn't the way anyone expected this to happen. They had expected a Superhuman, a Superstar, someone whose muscle, intellect, physical stature, invulnerability, and invincibility would simply dwarf all the powers on the planet in a way that there could be no argument, no resistance, no standing against its presence.

That's still the way, mostly, we fantasize how God's power should work in our world. But, as we know from the first Christmas, that's not normally the way God works. What was revealed in Bethlehem is that normally we meet the presence and power of God in our world as a helpless infant lying in the straw, vulnerable, seemingly powerless, touching us subliminally.

Why? Why doesn't the all-powerful Creator of the universe flex more muscle? Why is God normally revealed more in the body of an infant than in that of Superstar? Why? Because the power of God works to melt hearts rather than break them, and that's what vulnerability and helplessness can do. That's what infants can do. God's power, at least God's power to draw us into intimacy with each other, doesn't normally work through might, muscles, and cool (invulnerability). It works through a lot of things, but it works with a special power through vulnerability and helplessness. Intimacy is predicated on vulnerability. You cannot overpower another person so as to make him or her love you, unless you overpower his or her heart the way an infant does. We can seduce each other through attractiveness, draw admiration through our talents, and intimidate each other through superior strength, but none of these will ultimately provide the basis for a shared community of life for long . . . but the powerlessness and innocence of a baby can provide that.

God's power, like a baby sleeping in its crib, lies in our world as a quiet invitation, not as a threat or coercion. When Christ took on flesh in our world in Bethlehem two thousand years ago and then died seemingly helpless on a cross in Jerusalem some thirty years later, this is what was revealed: the God who is incarnated in Jesus Christ enters into human suffering rather than stands clear of it, is in solidarity with us rather than standing apart from us, manifests that the route to glory is downward rather than upward, stands with the poor and powerless rather than with the rich and powerful, invites rather than coerces, and is more manifest in a baby than in a superstar.

But that isn't always easy to grasp, nor accept. We are often frustrated and impatient with God who, as scripture tells, can seem slow to act. Jesus promised that the poor and the meek would inherit the earth and this seems forever belied by what's actually happening in the world. The rich are getting richer and the poor don't seem to be inheriting much. What good does a helpless infant do apropos to this? Where do we see messianic power acting?

Well, again the containers of our expectations need to be shattered. What does it mean "to inherit the earth"? To be a superstar? To be rich and famous? To have power over others? To walk into a room and be instantly recognized and admired as being significant and important? Is that the way we "inherit the earth"? Or, do we "inherit the earth" when a coldness is melted in our hearts and we are brought back to our primal goodness by the smile of a baby? —*In Exile,* December 21, 2020

TOUCHING OUR LOVED ONES INSIDE THE BODY OF CHRIST

Part of the wonder of the incarnation is the astonishing fact that we can do for each other what Jesus did for us. Jesus gives us that power: Whatever you bind on earth will be bound in heaven; whatever you loose on earth will be loosed in heaven. . . . Whose sins you forgive they are forgiven.

If you are part of the Body of Christ, when you forgive someone, he or she is forgiven. If you love someone, he or she is being loved by Christ because the Body of Christ is not just the body of Jesus but is also the body of believers. To be touched, loved, and forgiven by a member of the body of believers is to be touched, loved, and forgiven by Christ. Hell is possible only when someone has put himself completely out of the range of love and forgiveness so as to render himself incapable of being loved and forgiven. And this is not so much a question of rejecting explicit religious or moral teaching as it is of rejecting love as it is offered among the community of the sincere. Put more simply:

If someone whom you love strays from the church in terms of faith practice and morality, as long as you continue to love that person and hold him or her in love and forgiveness, he or she is touching the "hem of Christ's garment," is being held to the Body of Christ, and is being forgiven by God, irrespective of his or her official external relationship to the church. How?

They are touching the Body of Christ because your touch is Christ's touch. When you touch someone, unless that person actively rejects your love and forgiveness, he or she is relating to the Body of Christ. And this is true even beyond death: If someone close to you dies in a state which, externally at least, has him or her at odds with the visible church, your love and forgiveness will continue to bind that person to the Body of Christ and will continue to offer forgiveness to that individual, even after death.

G.K. Chesterton once expressed this in a parable: "*A man who was entirely careless of spiritual affairs died and went to hell. And he was much missed on earth by his old friends. His business agent went down to the gates of hell to see if there was any chance of bringing him back. But though he pleaded for the gates to be opened, the iron bars never yielded. His priest also went and argued: 'He was not really a bad fellow; given time he would have matured. Let him out, please!' The gate remained stubbornly shut against all their voices. Finally his mother came; she did not beg for his release. Quietly, and with a strange catch in her voice, she said to Satan: 'Let me in.' Immediately the great doors swung open upon their hinges. For love goes down through the gates of hell and there redeems the dead."*

In the incarnation, God takes on human flesh: in Jesus, in the Eucharist, and in all who are sincere in faith. The incredible power and mercy that came into our world in Jesus is still with us, at least if we choose to activate it. We are the Body of Christ. What Jesus did for us, we can do for each other. Our love and forgiveness are the cords that connect our loved ones to God, to salvation, and to the community of saints, even when they are no longer walking the path of explicit faith.

Too good to be true? Yes, surely. But how else to describe the mystery of the incarnation! —*In Exile,* June 6, 2010

HOLY THURSDAY AND THE EUCHARIST

One of the things we celebrate during Holy Week is the institution of the Eucharist. This mystery, as we know, makes God present, real and physical, in the world in a multiplicity of ways. What happens at a Eucharist? Among other things, what happens at every Eucharist is that, as a community, our reality as the Body of Christ is intensified. What is meant by that?

In scripture, the phrase *"the body of Christ"* is used to connote *three* realities simultaneously: *Jesus*, the God-man who walked the roads of Palestine for thirty-three years; *the Eucharist,* which continues to give concrete physical flesh to God, as Jesus did; and *the community of believers* who also, like the Eucharist, continues to make the physical reality of God present in the world. All three of these are the body of Christ. Moreover when scripture speaks of the latter two realities, the Eucharist and the Community of believers, as the Body of Christ it is not using the term metaphorically. It *never says* that we are *like* the Body of Christ, or that we *represent* the Body of Christ or *replace* it, nor even that we are the *mystical* body of Christ. It simply says that we *are* the Body of Christ.

This has implications beyond what we normally realize. It doesn't just mean that in the Eucharistic species, the bread and wine, we have the real physical presence of Christ, but it means as well, and this is where we often water it down, that, in the community of believers too we have God on earth as really as that God was once physically present in Jesus. The community gathered for worship, and even when it is not at worship, is really the anointed, physical, real presence of God on earth. That sounds strong, and it is. Like the incarnation itself, this conception both stretches and scandalizes the imagination. It stretches it because we cannot conceive of what is so infinite and perfect in something so finite and flawed. It scandalizes because the imagination balks at the concept of a God that is so accessible, so tied to the ordinary, and so bound to human flesh with all its flaws.

Yet that is our belief and that is the mystery of the Eucharist. To try to explain it more simply: At the Eucharistic prayer at the liturgy, the priest says the words: "This is my body. This is my blood." When he says those words, and in the invocation to the Holy Spirit that usually just precedes those words, he is not only asking that the bread and wine be changed into the reality of Christ, he is also, and just as much, asking that the people present, the congregation, be changed into the body and blood of Christ.

St. Augustine, in a homily he gave to Christians who were receiving the Eucharist for the first time, once said it this way: *"You ought to know that what you will receive, what you ought to receive daily, the bread that you see upon the altar which has been sanctified by the word of God, is the body of Christ. The cup, or more accurately what the cup contains, sanctified by the word of God, is the blood of Christ. By these, the bread and wine, Christ wanted to entrust us with his body and blood which he shed for the forgiveness of our sins. If you receive this well, you are what you receive."*

Augustine goes on in the same homily to point out the meaning of the symbolism of the loaf of bread and the cup of wine that serve as Eucharistic species. A piece of bread is made up because individual kernels of wheat have been crushed and brought together and then, under heat and fire, baked into one loaf. Likewise for the wine: It is made up of individual grapes that have been crushed and thus brought together into one cup. The unity that results is, in each case, contingent upon a certain giving up of individualism. This is part of the transformation that the Eucharistic prayer asks of us, namely, the breaking down of our own egos, agendas, and bitter lack of forgiveness, so that we can be one with others in a community. Later on, in that same homily, Augustine tells those receiving communion that they should receive it in this way, "*so that you have yourselves in mind.*"

In another homily he uses even stronger words. He tells the neophytes who are about to receive communion: "*Be what you see, and receive what you are.*" *(Estote quod videtis, et accipite quod estis.)*

Receive what you are! That is the real imperative within the Eucharist. What Jesus wanted to give us at the last supper was not just his presence and God's forgiveness under the species of bread and wine, but that same reality in the faces, hands, and bodies of those who partake of that bread and wine. At a Eucharist, we, not just the bread and wine, are meant to change.

—*In Exile*, March 25, 1999

INCARNATION—ANOTHER MEANING OF CHRISTMAS

Some years ago at a religious conference a man approached the microphone and after apologizing for what he felt would be an inappropriate question, asked this: "I love my dog. When he dies will he go to heaven? Do animals have eternal life?"

The answer to that might come as a surprise to many of us, but, looked at through the eyes of Christian faith, yes, his dog can go to heaven. It's one of the meanings of Christmas. God came into the world to save the world, not just the people living in it. The incarnation has meaning for humanity, but also for the cosmos itself. We don't know exactly what that means and our imaginations aren't up to the task of picturing it, but, because of the incarnation, dogs too can go to heaven. Is this fanciful? No, it's scriptural teaching.

At Christmas was celebrate the birth of Jesus and see in his birth the beginning of the mystery of the incarnation unfolding in history, the mystery of God becoming human in physical flesh in order to save the world. What we tend to struggle with though is how we understand what's meant by Christ saving the world. Most of us take that to mean that Christ came into the world to save the people, those of us with self-awareness and eternal souls.

That's true, but our faith also asks us to believe that God's saving activity in the Christ extends to more than only human beings and more than even animals and other living things. God's saving activity in Christ reaches so deep that it saves creation itself—the oceans, the mountains, the soil that grows our food, the desert sands, and the earth itself. Christ came to save all of those things too, not just us, the people.

Where, you might ask, does scripture teach this? It teaches it most everywhere in implicit ways though it teaches it quite explicitly in a number of different places. For example, in the Epistle to the Romans (8, 19–22) St. Paul writes: I consider that our present sufferings are not worth comparing with the glory that will be revealed in us. For the creation waits in eager expectation for the children of God to be revealed. For the creation was subjected to frustration, not by its own choice, but by the will of the one who subjected it, in hope that creation itself will be liberated from its bondage to decay and brought into the freedom and glory of the children of God. We know that the whole creation has been groaning as in the pains of childbirth right up to the present time.

This may come as a surprise to us since, until quite recently, our preaching and catechesis has not often made this explicit. However what St. Paul is saying here is that physical creation itself, the cosmic world, will, at the end of time, be transformed in some glorious way and enter into heaven, just as human beings do. He's also saying that, like us, it too somehow senses its mortality and groans to be set free from its present limits.

We need to ask ourselves this question? What do we believe will happen to physical creation at the end of time? Will it be destroyed, burnt-up, annihilated? Or, will it simply be abandoned and left empty and deserted like a stage after a play has ended, while we go on to life elsewhere? Scripture informs us otherwise, that is, it tells us that physical creation itself, our planet earth, will also be transformed ("liberated from its bondage to decay") and enter into heaven with us. How will this happen? We can't imagine it, just as we can't imagine our own transformed state. But scripture assures us that it will happen because, like ourselves, our world, physical creation, is also destined to die, and, like us, it intuits its mortality and groans under that sentence, aching to be set free from its limitations and become immortal.

Science agrees. It tells us that physical creation is mortal, that the sun is burning out, that energy is ever-so-slowly decreasing and that the earth as we know it will someday die. The earth is as mortal as we are and so if it's to have a future it needs to be saved by Something or Someone from outside itself. That Something and Someone are revealed in the mystery of the incarnation within which God takes on physical flesh in Christ in order to save the world—and what he came to save was not just us, the people living on this earth, but rather, "the world," the planet itself, and everything on it.

Jesus assured us that nothing is ever ultimately lost. No hair falls from someone's head and no sparrow falls from the sky and simply disappears forever, as if it had never been.

God created, loves, cares for, and ultimately resurrects every bit of creation for all eternity—including a beloved dog.

—*In Exile*, December 16, 2019

5

Prayer and the Perennial Invitation to Always Go Deeper

In selections from his columns and his book The Shattered Lantern, *Ron stresses the importance of daily prayer while recognizing that it can be boring and hard to sustain. He encourages readers to pray in whatever way works best for them, in whatever way is freeing for the soul: "read scripture, read a passage from a serious book, journal, paint a picture, garden, write poetry, write a letter to a friend you haven't seen in a long time."*

There is no bad way to pray, he assures us, and there is no single starting point. The important thing is that we show up regularly and open ourselves to God and to deeper intimacy. To put "skin" on that principle, he offers a brilliant parable about the dutiful adult child who shows up, day after day, to visit a widowed parent in an assisted living facility.

Ron's practical definitions of the various forms of Christian prayer are particularly eye-opening. Priestly Prayer, for example, is not only for ordained ministers; all Christians are called to pray in such a way that we "give voice to the earth itself." In this chapter, he also shares with readers two breathtaking original prayers.

WE ARE MADE FOR LOVE

Spirituality is as real as science. But that is not easy to understand or believe. We live in a world where what is real has been reduced to what is physical, to what can be empirically measured, seen, touched, tasted, smelled. We live in a world that is for the most part spiritually tone-deaf, where all the goods are in the store window, digitized, reduced to a flat-screen. And so, prayer is a struggle. So are a lot of other things. When the surface is all there is, it is hard to be enchanted by anything, to see depth, to be deeply touched by poetry, faith, and love. But these are what we long for: depth, poetry, faith, love.

Indeed we are made for love. We are made for intimacy with each other and with God. As Saint Augustine so classically put it, "You have made us for yourself, Lord, and our hearts are restless until they rest in you." But the deep meaning of our longing is not always so obvious. Today most of us do not see our restless longing as pushing us towards the infinite. We have trivialized and tamed our longing. Instead of longing for the transcendent, we anesthetize and distract ourselves by focusing our desires on the good life, on sex, on money, on success, and on whatever else everybody has. There is nothing bad about these things, but if we define our deepest longings as directed towards these things in themselves, we end up mostly disappointed and empty. Our disquiet persists and we remain restless and tired in a way that drains us of energy rather than in a place of solitude where our very striving gives us energy.

Ultimately, our restless aching is a yearning for God. We need to connect with God. We need prayer. We know this, both in our more reflective moments and in our more desperate moments. It is then that we feel our need for prayer and try to go to that deep place. But, given our lack of trust and our lack of practice, we struggle to get there. We do not know how to pray or how to sustain ourselves in prayer.

There is no bad way to pray and there is no one starting point for prayer. All the great spiritual masters offer only one non-negotiable rule: You have to show up for prayer and you have to show up regularly. Everything else is negotiable and respects your unique struggles.

There is a beautiful text in the Gospels that captures, in a stark metaphor, our need for prayer. One morning, after Simon Peter, James and John had "toiled all night" and caught nothing, no fish, only their own emptiness, Jesus comes to them and invites them to go out to the deeper waters, to "put out into the deep." They do, and they catch so many fish their boat begins to sink. (Luke 5:1–7)

These reflections on prayer are an invitation that echoes that invitation from Jesus: When we are catching nothing but our own emptiness, it is time to "put out into the deep."

—*Prayer: Our Deepest Longing,* vii–ix

PRAYER AS LIFTING MIND AND HEART TO GOD

One classical definition of prayer defines it this way: "Prayer is lifting mind and heart to God."

That's a wonderful and accurate description of prayer, the problem is that we rarely do that. It's rare that we actually open mind and heart to God in order to show God what's really there. Instead we treat God as a parental-figure or as a visiting dignitary and tell God what we think God wants to hear rather than what's really on our minds and hearts.

As a result we have a pretty narrow range of thoughts and feelings that we consider suitable for prayer. Most of what we actually think and feel is considered too base for prayer. We feel we are praying only when we have attentive thoughts and warm feelings, when we feel like praising God, when we feel altruistic, pure, centered, when we have good feelings towards God, others, and nature, when we feel the desire to pray more, or when we yearn for moral improvement.

Such thoughts and feelings do make for prayer, but we can't turn them on like a water tap. Many times, perhaps most times, we experience other thoughts and feelings: boredom, tiredness, dissipation, bitterness, sexual fantasy, and sometimes even a positive distaste for church, prayer, and moral improvement. We don't feel that it is valid to lift these bitter thoughts and impure feelings to God. Instead we try to crank up the thoughts and feelings that we think we should be having when we pray.

There is some legitimacy in this. Classically, spiritual masters have distinguished between prayer and distraction. Prayer, they point out, requires an effort of concentration, of attentiveness, an act of will. It isn't simply daydreaming or letting a stream of consciousness occur.

But prayer is "lifting mind and heart to God" and that means lifting up, at any given moment, exactly what's there and not what, ideally, might be there. It would be nice if we always felt warm, reverent, altruistic, full of faith, chaste, hopeful, connected with others and nature, happy about who we are and what life has dealt us. But that isn't the case. We all have moments and even seasons of doubt, anger, alienation, pettiness, boredom, obsession, and tiredness. Our thoughts are not always holy and our hearts are not always warm or pure. It's at times like this we need prayer and what we need to take to prayer is, precisely, those bitter thoughts and unholy feelings.

All thoughts and feelings are valid material for prayer. Simply put: When you go to pray, lift up what's inside of you at that moment. If you are bored, lift up that boredom; if you are angry, lift up your anger; if you are sexually obsessed, lift up your sexual fantasies; if you are tired, lift up that tiredness; if you feel selfish, don't be afraid to let God see that. Jesus said that we must become like little children to enter the kingdom of heaven. One of the qualities in children to which this refers is precisely their honesty in showing their feelings. Children don't hide their sulks, pouts, and tantrums. A good mother handles these rather easily, often with a smile. God is up to the task. In prayer, we can be transparent, no matter how murderous, adulterous, or irreverent our thoughts and feelings might seem.

If we do that, it makes it easier for us to "pray always," as scripture asks. What does this mean? Obviously it doesn't mean that we should always be at formal prayer, that we should strive to be full-time contemplatives, or even that we should seize every possible occasion we can to pray formally.

To "pray always" invites us rather to live our lives against a certain horizon. It doesn't necessarily mean to stop work and go to formal prayer, important though that is at times. The point is rather that we need to do everything within the context of a certain awareness, like a married man who goes on a business trip and who, in the midst of a demanding schedule of meetings and social engagements, is somehow always anchored in a certain consciousness that he has a spouse and children at home. Despite distance and various preoccupations, he knows that he is "married always." That awareness, more than the occasional explicit phone call home, is what keeps him anchored in his most important relationship.

Our relationship with God is the same. We need to "pray always" by doing everything out of that kind of awareness. Moreover, when we do spend time in formal prayer, we need, like children do, to tell God exactly how we feel and invite God to deal with that. Rabbi Abraham Heschel points out how, in prayer, the great figures of scripture did not always easily acquiesce to God and say: "Thy will be done!" They sometimes fought bitterly and said: "Thy will be changed!" That can be good prayer. It lifts mind and heart to God.

—*In Exile,* March 2, 2003

AFFECTIVE PRAYER

A couple of years ago, I attended a six-day retreat given by Robert Michel, an Oblate colleague and a highly sought-after spiritual mentor. His approach was disarming. Most of us are forever looking for something novel, at the cutting-edge, outside the box, something complex, but what he offered was stunningly simple and down-to-earth. He spent the whole time trying to teach us how to pray in an affective way.

What exactly does that mean, to pray affectively? In essence, what he told us might be summarized this way: *"You must try to pray so that, in your prayer, you open yourself in such a way that sometime—perhaps not today, but sometime—you are able to hear God say to you: 'I love you!' These words, addressed to you by God, are the most important words you will ever hear because, before you hear them, nothing is ever completely right with you, but, after you hear them, something will be right in your life at a very deep level."*

These are simple words, but they capture what we ultimately try to do when we "lift mind and heart to God" in prayer.

In the end, prayer's essence, its mission-statement, its deep raison d'être, is simply this: We need to open ourselves to God in such a way that we are capable of hearing God say to us, individually, "I love you!"

This might sound pious and sentimental. It's anything but that. Don't be put off by simplicity. The deeper something is the simpler it will be. That's why we have trouble understanding the deep things, be they of science or the heart. What separates the great minds (Augustine, Aquinas, Descartes, Whitehead, Einstein, Lonergan) from the rest of us is their capacity to grasp the simple. Anyone can understand what's complex, but we have trouble grasping the principle of relativity, the concept of being, the concept of love, and things about the nature of the God, for exactly the opposite reason. They're too simple. The simpler something is, the harder it is to wrap our minds around it and the more we need to make it complex in order to understand it. That's true too of prayer. It's so simple that we rarely lay bare its essence. It has ever been thus, it would seem.

John's Gospel already makes that point. The Gospel of John, as we know, structures itself very differently from the other Gospels. John has no infancy narratives or early life of Jesus. In his Gospel, we meet Jesus as an adult right on the first page and the first words out of Jesus' mouth are a question: "What are you looking for?" That question remains throughout the rest of the Gospel as an hermeneutical coloring suggesting that beneath everything else a certain search is going on. A lot of things are happening on the surface, but underneath, there remains always the nagging, restless question: "What are you looking for?"

Jesus answers that question explicitly only at the end of the Gospel, on the morning of the resurrection. Mary Magdala goes looking for him, carrying spices with which to embalm his dead body. Jesus meets her, alive and in no need of embalming, but she doesn't recognize him. Bewildered, but sincere, she asks Jesus where she might find Jesus (something, I suspect, we do often enough in prayer). Jesus, for his part, repeats for her the question he opened the Gospel with: "What are you looking for?" Then he answers it:

With deep affection, he pronounces her name: "Mary." In doing that, he tells her what she and everyone else are forever looking for, God's voice, one-to-one, speaking unconditional love, gently saying your name. In the end, that's what we are all looking for and most need. It's what gives us substance, identity, and justification beyond our own efforts to make ourselves lovable, worthwhile, and immortal. We are forever in fear of our own seeming insubstantiality. How to give ourselves significance? We need to hear God, affectionately, one-to-one, pronounce our names: "Carolyn!" "Julia!" "Kern!" "Gisele!" "Steve!" "Sophia!" Nothing will heal us more of restlessness, bitterness, and insecurity than to hear God say: "I love you!"

Moreover since prayer is meant to be a mutual thing, it's important too that we respond in kind: Part of affective prayer is also that we, one- to-one, with affection, occasionally at least, say the same thing to God: "I love you!" In all long-term, affectionate relationships the partners have to occasionally prompt each other to hear expressions of affection and reassurance. It's not good enough to tell a marriage partner or a friend just once "I love you!" It needs to be said regularly. The relationship of prayer is no different. —*In Exile,* March 23, 2003

PRIESTLY PRAYER—PRAYER FOR THE WORLD

One of the responsibilities of being an adult is that of praying for the world. Like the high priests of old, we need to offer up prayers daily for others. Indeed we are all priests, ordained by the oils of baptism and consecrated by the burdens of life that have given us wrinkles and grey hair. As adults, elders, priests, we need, as scripture puts it, "to make prayer and entreaty, aloud and in silent tears, for ourselves and for the people." All of us, lay and cleric alike, need to offer up priestly prayer each day.

But how do we do that? How do we pray priestly prayer? We pray as priests, as Jesus prayed in the 17th chapter of John's Gospel, every time we sacrifice self-interest for the good of others. That's priestly prayer in its widest sense. However, we pray that prayer, formally and sacramentally, whenever we pray the prayer of the church, namely, the Eucharist or the Divine Office. This kind of prayer, called liturgy, is what keeps incarnate the priestly prayer of Christ.

In priestly prayer we pray not just for ourselves, nor ideally by ourselves, but we pray as a microcosm of the whole world, even as we pray for the whole world. In this kind of prayer we lift up our voices to God, not as a private offering, but in such a way as to give a voice to the earth itself. In essence, when we pray at the Eucharist or at the Divine Office, we are saying this:

> *Lord, God, I stand before you as a microcosm of the earth itself, to give it voice: See in my openness, the world's openness, in my infidelity, the world's infidelity; in my sincerity, the world's sincerity, in my hypocrisy, the world's hypocrisy; in my generosity, the world's generosity, in my selfishness, the world's selfishness; in my attentiveness, the world's attentiveness, in my distraction, the world's distraction; in my desire to praise you, the world's desire to praise you, and in my self-preoccupation, the world's forgetfulness of you. For I am of the earth, a piece of earth, and the earth opens or closes to you through my body, my soul, and my voice. I am your priest on earth.*
>
> *And what I hold up for you today is all that is in this world, both of joy and of suffering. I offer you the bread of the world's achievements, even as I offer you the wine of its failure, the blood of all that's crushed as those achievements take place. I offer you the powerful of our world, our rich, our famous, our athletes, our*

> *artists, our movie stars, our entrepreneurs, our young, our healthy, and everything that's creative and bursting with life, even as I offer you those who are weak, feeble, aged, crushed, sick, dying, and victimized. I offer to you all the pagan beauties, pleasures, and joys of this life, even as I stand with you under the cross, affirming that the one who is excluded from earthily pleasure is the cornerstone of the community. I offer you the strong and arrogant, along with the weak and gentle of heart, asking you to bless both and to stretch my heart so that it can, like you, hold and bless everything that is. I offer you both the wonders and the pains of this world, your world.*

To pray like this is to pray liturgically, as priest. And we pray like this each time we go to the Eucharist or when we, with others or alone, pray the Divine Office of the church. It is particularly this latter prayer, the Divine Office (also called "Breviary" or "Liturgy of the hours"), that is available daily as the priestly prayer for those of us who are not ordained ministers in the church. And this is especially true for two of those liturgical hours, Lauds (Morning Prayer) and Vespers (Evening Prayer). They, unlike the other hours which are more the particular domain of monks and professional contemplatives, are the ordinary priestly prayer of the laity.

And what is important in praying them is to remember that these are not prayers that we say for ourselves, nor indeed prayers whose formulae we need personally to find meaningful or relevant. Unlike private prayer and contemplation, where we should change methods whenever praying becomes dry or sterile, Lauds and Vespers are prayers of the universal church that are in essence intended to be communal and priestly. They don't have to be relevant for our private lives. We pray them as elders, as baptized adults, as priests, to invoke God's blessing upon the world.

And whenever we do pray them we take on a universal voice. We are no longer just a private individual praying, but are, in microcosm, the voice, body, and soul of the earth itself, continuing the high priesthood of Christ, offering prayers and entreaties, aloud and in silent tears, to God for the sake of the world.

—*In Exile,* March 16, 2003

CONTEMPLATION AND MEDITATION

In classical Christian spirituality, there are two essential ways of praying: mediation and contemplation. This distinction itself is based upon a prior one: very early on in Christian spiritual writings, authors distinguished between something they called *praxis* and something they called *theoria. Praxis* referred to everything we can do in our attempt to reach God and others, namely, works of charity and justice, discursive prayer, and ascetical practices. *Theoria* referred to what happens within us when God and others were actually met and undergone. Hence, praxis refers to what is active and *theoria* to what is receptive and passive. On the basis of this, classical Christian spirituality has made a distinction between meditation and contemplation.

Thus, prayer is called meditation when we are active within it. This, for example, would be a meditation: you decide to spend a half hour in prayer. You sit down in some quiet place and pick up the Bible. You then find a text you want to meditate on and begin your prayer. You read the text slowly and try to let it speak to you. It does. You begin to feel consolation from God, challenge from God, sorrow for your sins, joy in being blessed by God. You feel yourself becoming more insightful. You pray for others. But you also experience distractions. Every so often, perhaps frequently, your mind wanders and you catch yourself thinking about other things—your heartaches and headaches. When these distractions occur, you catch yourself and bring yourself back to what you are praying about. As you are doing all of this, all this activity, all this *praxis,* you are meditating.

Contemplation, centering prayer, is quite different. Unlike meditation, which is an exercise in concentration, it is an exercise in refusing to concentrate on anything, including holy thoughts and divine inspirations. This, for example, would be contemplation: you decide to spend a half hour in prayer. You sit down in some quiet place. However, for contemplation you do not bring the Bible, nor do you bring anything to pray on or about. You begin contemplating by making a brief act of meditation. You actively focus yourself on what you are about to do, prayer, and tell God that you are here to pray, that this next half hour will be prayer. Then you calm and center yourself, perhaps using a breathing technique and a prayer word (though these are optional). Then you begin to contemplate. What do you do? Nothing. You let your heart and mind go and you interfere in the stream of feelings and consciousness only when you catch yourself concentrating very long on anything, including holy thoughts and divine inspirations. In contemplation there is no distinction between bad distractions and holy thoughts. Everything is relative. You try to hang onto God by refusing to hang onto anything else, including thoughts and feelings about God. The whole time of prayer, save for a very brief explicit act of meditation at the beginning and again at the end, consists in this stream of consciousness and feeling. The discipline is more of not concentrating than of concentrating.

But how is this prayer? If contemplation consists simply in stream of consciousness, with a brief act of intention for prayer thrown in at the beginning and the end, by what right do we speak of this as prayer and how will that make us more aware of God? The answer to that is best understood within the analogy, the parable, of the fish and the ocean.

Imagine you are the mother fish and your child comes to you and says: "Mummy, where is this water we hear so much about?" Suppose, since this is a parable and anything is possible, you could do this. To give your child some sense of water, even though it is totally immersed within it, you could set up at the bottom of the ocean a slide projector and a television set and show your child pictures, slides, and videos of water. As ironic as it would be, these pictures, which are not water, would in fact give your child, who is living in water, some idea of what water is. Eventually, after having shown your child hours of pictures of water, you might then want to turn off all the videos and the slide projector and simply tell the child: "Now you have some idea of what water is, you've seen pictures of it. Now I want you to simply sit in it and let it flow through you." That image, in essence, shows what meditation and contemplation of God are.

When we pray by meditation, we are watching the slides and the videos, so to speak. All thoughts and feelings about God, even scripture itself, is not God. Good as they are, they are not the reality. At a point, they must give way to the reality—meditation must give way to contemplation—and instead of sitting and thinking and feeling *about* God we must sit *in* God. Meditation is watching the slides and the videos. It brings concepts, thoughts, and feelings about the reality. Contemplation is sitting in the reality. Normally it does not feel like prayer.

For this reason, contemplation should not be evaluated like meditation. How do you know whether or not you are praying, or have prayed? In meditation this is done during and immediately after the prayer. We are praying when we are not entertaining distractions, when our thoughts and feelings are focused on God, though even in meditation, ultimately, the effects within one's life are the real criteria which tell whether or not someone is praying. Contemplation, however, must be evaluated in a quite different manner than meditation.

Suppose you are sitting in contemplative prayer regularly. How do you know whether or not you are actually praying or wasting your time? Unlike meditation, you do not make any assessment whatever during or immediately after prayer. Instead you do contemplative prayer for a substantial period of time, several months perhaps, and then check yourself: Am I now more restful than restless; more free than compulsive; more calm than hyper; more patient than impatient; more humble than competitive; more self-forgetful than self-preoccupied; and more grateful than bitter? If there is progress in these things, then I am praying and God is more vitally within my life.

Blessed are the pure of heart, for they shall see God. If a sense of God's presence is absent within our lives, more than likely restlessness, obsessions, impatience, competitiveness, self-preoccupation, and bitterness are not. Small wonder God cannot break in! Contemplative prayer, practiced regularly as a discipline, is an invaluable exercise for purifying awareness, restoring wonder, and helping us to regain the ancient instinct for astonishment. —*The Shattered Lantern, 196–200*

THE VALUE OF RITUAL IN SUSTAINING PRAYER

Love and prayer work the same: The neophyte's mistake is to think that they can be sustained simply through good feelings and good intention, without the help of a ritual-container and a sustaining rhythm. That's naïve, however sincere. Love and prayer can only be sustained through ritual, routine, and rhythm. Why?

What eventually makes us stop praying, John of the Cross says, is simple boredom, tiredness, lack of energy. It's hard, very hard, existentially impossible, to crank-up the energy, day in and day out, to pray with real affectivity, real feeling, and real heart. We simply cannot sustain that kind of energy and enthusiasm. We're human beings, limited in our energies, and chronically too-tired, dissipated, and torn in various directions to sustain prayer on the basis of feelings. We need something else to help us. What?

Ritual—a rhythm, a routine. Monks have secrets worth knowing and anyone who has ever been to a monastery knows that monks (who pray often and a lot) sustain themselves in prayer not through feeling, variety, or creativity, but through ritual, rhythm, and routine. Monastic prayer is simple, often rote, has a clear durational-expectancy, and is structured so as to allow each monk the freedom to invest himself or hold back, in terms of energy and heart, depending upon his disposition on a given day. That's wise anthropology.

Prayer is like eating. There needs to be a good rhythm between big banquets (high celebration, high aesthetics, lots of time, proper formality) and the everyday family supper (simple, no-frills, short, predictable). A family that tries to eat every meal as if it were a banquet soon finds that most of its members are looking for an excuse to be absent. With good reason. Everyone needs to eat every day, but nobody has energy for a banquet every day. The same holds true for prayer. One wonders whether the huge drop-off of people who used to attend church services daily isn't connected to this. People attended daily services more when those services were short, routine, predictable, and gave them the freedom to be as present or absent (in terms of emotional investment) as their energy and heart allowed on that given day.

Today, unfortunately, we are misled by a number of misconceptions about prayer and liturgy. Too commonly, we accept the following set of axioms as wise: Creativity and variety are always good. Every prayer-celebration should be one of high energy. Longer is better than shorter. Either you should pray with feeling or you shouldn't pray at all. Ritual is meaningless unless we are emotionally invested in it.

Each of these axioms is over-romantic, ill thought-out, anthropologically naïve, and not helpful in sustaining a life a prayer. Prayer is a relationship, a long-term one, and lives by those rules. Relating to anyone long-term has its ups and downs. Nobody can be interesting all the time, sustain high energy all the time, or fully invest himself or herself all the time. Never travel with anyone who expects you to be interesting, lively, and emotionally-invested all the time. Real life doesn't work that way. Neither does prayer. What sustains a relationship long-term is ritual, routine, a regular rhythm that incarnates the commitment.

That's why the saints and the great spiritual writers have always said that there is only one, non-negotiable, rule for prayer: "Show up! Show up regularly!" The ups and downs of our minds and hearts are of secondary importance.

—*In Exile,* April 6, 2003

DEEPER THINGS UNDER THE SURFACE

Imagine this. You are the dutiful daughter or son and your mother is widowed and living in an assisted living facility. You happen to be living close by while your sister is living across the country, thousands of miles away. So the weight falls on you to be the one to help take care of your mother. You dutifully visit her each day. Every afternoon, on route home from work, you stop and spend an hour with her as she has her early dinner. And you do this faithfully, five times a week, year after year.

As you spend this hour each day with your mother, year after year, how many times during the course of a year will you have a truly stimulating and deep conversation with your mother? Once? Twice? Never? What are you talking about each day? Trivial things: the weather, your favorite sports team, what your kids are doing, the latest show on television, her aches and pains, and the mundane details of your own life. Occasionally you might even doze off for a while as she eats her early dinner. In a good year, perhaps once or twice, the conversation will take on some depth and the two of you will share more deeply about something of importance; but, save for that rare occasion, you will simply be filling in the time each day with superficial conversation.

But, and this is the question, are those daily visits with your mother in fact superficial, merely functionary because your conversations aren't deep? Are you simply going through the motions of intimate relationship because of duty? Is anything deep happening?

Well, compare this with your sister who is (conveniently) living across the country and comes home once a year to visit your mother. When she visits, both she and your mother are wonderfully animated, they embrace enthusiastically, shed some tears upon seeing each other, and seemingly talk about things beyond the weather, their favorite sports teams, and their own tiredness. And you could kill them both! It seems that in this once-a-year meeting they have something that you, who visit daily, do not have. But is this true? Is what is happening between your sister and your mother in fact deeper than what is occurring each day when you visit your mother?

Absolutely not. What they have is, no doubt, more emotional and more affective, but it is, at the end of day, not particularly deep. When your mother dies, you will know your mother better than anyone else knows her and you will be much closer to her than your sister. Why? Because through all those days when you visited her and seemed to talk about nothing beyond the weather, some deeper things were happening under the surface. When your sister visited your mother things were happening on the surface (though emotionally and affectively the surface can look wonderfully more intriguing than what lies beneath it). That is why honeymoons look better than marriage.

What your sister had with your mother is what novices experience in prayer and what couples experience on a honeymoon. What you had with your mother is what people experience in prayer and relationships when they are faithful over a long period of time. At a certain level of intimacy in all our relationships, including our relationship with God in prayer, the emotions and the affectivity (wonderful as they are) will become less and less important and simple presence, just being together, will become paramount. Previous to that, the important things were happening on the surface and emotions and affectivity were important; now deep bonding is happening beneath the surface and emotions and affectivity recede in importance. At a certain depth of relationship just being present to each other is what is important.

Too often, both popular psychology and popular spirituality do not really grasp this and consequently confuse the novice for the proficient, the honeymoon for the wedding, and the surface for the depth. In all of our relationships, we cannot make promises as to how we will always feel, but we can make promises to always be faithful, to show up, to be there, even if we are only talking about the weather, our favorite sports team, the latest television program, or our own tiredness. And it is okay occasionally to fall asleep while there because as Thérèse of Lisieux once said: a little child is equally pleasing to its parents, awake or asleep, probably more asleep! That also holds true for prayer. God does not mind us occasionally napping while at prayer because we are there and that is enough. The great Spanish doctor of the soul John of the Cross tells us that as we travel deeper into any relationship, be it with God in prayer, with each other in intimacy, or with the community at large in service, eventually the surface will be less emotive and less affective and *the deeper things will begin to happen under the surface.*

—*In Exile*, July 6, 2020

PRAYER AS SEEKING DEPTH

In our more reflective moments we sense the importance of prayer; yet, we struggle to pray. Sustained, deep prayer doesn't come easy for us. Why?

First of all, we struggle to make time for prayer. Prayer doesn't accomplish anything practical for us, it's a waste of time in terms of tending to the pressures and tasks of daily life, and so we hesitate to go there. Coupled with this, we find it hard to trust that prayer actually works and brings about something real in our lives. Beyond that, we struggle to concentrate when we try to pray. Once we do settle in to pray, we soon feel ourselves overwhelmed by daydreams, unfinished conversations, half-forgotten melodies, heartaches, agendas, and the impending tasks that face us as soon as we get up from our place of prayer. Finally, we struggle to pray because we really don't know how to pray. We might be familiar with various forms of prayer, from devotional prayers to different kinds of meditation, but we generally lack the confidence to believe that our own particular way of praying, with all its distractions and missteps, is prayer in the deep sense.

One of the places we can turn for help is the Gospel of Luke. More so than any of the other Gospels, his is the Gospel of prayer. In Luke's Gospel there are more descriptions of Jesus in prayer than in all the other Gospels combined. Luke gives us glimpses of Jesus praying in virtually every kind of situation: He prays when he is joy-filled, he prays when he is in agony, he prays with others around him, and he prays when he is alone at night, withdrawn from all human contact. He prays high on a mountain, on a sacred place, and he prays on the level plane, where ordinary life happens. In Luke's Gospel, Jesus prays a lot.

And the lesson isn't lost on his disciples. They sense that Jesus' real depth and power are drawn from his prayer. They know that what makes him so special, so unlike any other religious figure, is that he is linked at some deep place to a power outside of this world. And they want this for themselves. That's why they approach Jesus and ask him: "Lord, teach us to pray!"

But we must be careful not to misunderstand what constituted their attraction and what they were asking for when they asked Jesus to teach them how to pray. They sensed that what Jesus drew from the depth of his prayer was not, first of all, his power to do miracles or to silence his enemies with some kind of superior intelligence. What impressed them and what they wanted too for their own lives was the depth and graciousness of his soul.

The power they admired and wanted was Jesus' power to love and forgive his enemies rather than embarrass and crush them. What they wanted was Jesus' power to transform a room, not by some miraculous deed, but by a disarming innocence and vulnerability that, like a baby's presence, has everyone solicitously guarding his or her behavior and language. What they wanted was his power to renounce life in self-sacrifice, even while retaining the enviable capacity to enjoy the pleasures of life without guilt. What they wanted was Jesus' power to be big-hearted, to love beyond his own tribe, and to love poor and rich alike, to live inside of charity, joy, peace, patience, goodness, longsuffering, fidelity, mildness, and chastity, despite everything within life that militates against these virtues. What they wanted was Jesus' depth and graciousness of soul.

And they recognized that this power did not come from within himself, but from a source outside him. They saw that he connected to a deep source through prayer, through constantly lifting to God what was on his mind and in his heart. They saw it and they wanted that depth-connection too, for themselves. So they asked Jesus to teach them how to pray.

Ultimately, we too want Jesus' depth and graciousness in our own lives. Like Jesus' disciples, we also know that we can only attain this through prayer, through accessing a power that lies inside the deepest deep of our souls and beyond our souls. We know too that the route to that depth lies in journeying inward, in silence, through both the pain and the quiet, the chaos and the peace, that come to us when we still ourselves to pray.

In our more reflective moments, and in our more desperate moments, we feel our need for prayer and try to go to that deep place. But, given our lack of trust and our lack of practice, we struggle to get there. We don't know how to pray or how to sustain ourselves in prayer.

But in this we are in good company, with Jesus' disciples. And so a good beginning is to recognize what we need and where it is found. We need to begin with a plea: Lord teach us to pray!

—*In Exile,* November 28, 2011

TURNING OUR EYES TOWARD HEAVEN

It's not easy to be centered, rooted, secure in who we are, able to give the world our best. More commonly, we find ourselves adrift, unsure of ourselves, with most of what's best in us still frustrated, buried, waiting for a better day. Too many things, it seems, conspire against us living out what's truest and best inside us.

We'd like to be grounded, be ourselves, have a clear direction in life, be free of compulsions, and live out more our dignity, goodness, and creativity; but too many things push us the opposite way. Ideology, anger, bitterness, envy, restlessness, confusion, moral compromise, and the simple need to get by, all pull us down and we end up giving into various compensations (as substitutes for what we really want) and thus quietly despair of ever carrying our dignity, talents, and solitude at any high level.

Why does it happen? The fault is with prayer, or lack of it. We cannot stay steady in a churning sea without a good anchor, cannot avoid giving into compensation unless what's highest in us is given enough expression, and cannot deal with the issues of finitude unless we have some transcendent focus. Unless we are anchored in something beyond the here and now there is a good chance that we will drown in the present moment.

Jesus models the kind of prayer we need to cope with a world that goes mad at times and with a heart prone to drink in that madness. The Gospels describe Jesus praying in different ways, but sometimes they simply say: "He turned his eyes towards heaven!" The same expression is used of other great faith-figures— Stephen, Paul, the early martyrs—and it's used of them at those times when the forces of madness are precisely threatening to kill them. When the world around them is going mad, they "turn their eyes towards heaven." The phrase hasn't been lost on artists.

Virtually every painting of someone being martyred has this motif, the martyr has his or her eyes lifted up towards heaven, in contrast to the eyes of the executioners and onlookers which are cast downwards in hatred, envy, and group-think or in the blank stare of mindlessness.

Jesus lifted his eyes towards heaven and that freed him of hatred, envy, group-think, and mindlessness. What does this mean? How did he turn his eyes towards heaven?

What made Jesus different (and what makes any prayerful person different) is not intellectual insight, superior willpower, less fiery emotions, or monastic withdrawal from the temptations of the world. Prayer is not a question of insight, of being smarter than anyone else; nor of will, of being stronger than anyone else; nor of emotional restraint or sexual aloofness, of being less passionate than anyone else; nor of withdrawal, of being less exposed to temptation than anyone else. Prayer is a question of unity and surrender, of uniting one's will with someone else and surrendering one's will to that other. Prayer is the desire to be in union with someone, especially in union with that other's will.

Perhaps the people that have understood this best are Alcoholics Anonymous groups. They long ago realized that it's not by strength of will or by intellectual insight that we keep from drowning. Nobody with an addiction of any kind has ever studied or willed their way out of that. Through pain and humiliation, he or she has eventually come to realize there is only one way out of helplessness, surrender of one's will to a higher power, God. In essence, people get together at Alcoholics Anonymous meetings to (as scripture would put it) "turn their eyes towards heaven."

Each of us needs to find our own way of doing this if we are to cope with the forces that threaten to drown us. It's not through study or willpower that we will rise above ideology, anger, bitterness, discouragement, jealousy, restlessness, confusion, dissatisfaction, moral ineptitude, the endless practical demands of life, and the compensations we give into in order to cope with all of this. We will always be adrift, until we, like Jesus, regularly "turn our eyes towards heaven." In my experience, the extraordinary people that I have known and admired all have had the same secret, they prayed privately. —*In Exile,* November 10, 2002

PARALYSIS, EXASPERATION, AND HELPLESSNESS AS PRAYER

Several years ago I received an email that literally stopped my breath. A man who had been for many years an intellectual and faith mentor to me, a man whom I thoroughly trusted, and a man with whom I had developed a life-giving friendship, had killed both his wife and himself in a murder-suicide. The news left me gasping for air, paralyzed in terms of how to understand and accept this as well as how to pray in the face of this.

I had neither words of explanation nor words for prayer. My heart and my head were like two water pumps working a dry well, useless and frustrated. Whatever consolation I had was drawn from an assurance from persons who knew him more intimately that there had been major signs of mental deterioration in the time leading up to this horrible event and they were morally certain that this was the result of an organic dysfunction in his brain, not an indication of his person. Yet . . . how does one pray in a situation like this? There aren't any words.

And we have all experienced situations like this: the tragic death of someone we love by murder, suicide, overdose, or accident. Or, the exasperation and helplessness we feel in the face of the many seemingly senseless events we see daily in our world: Terrorists killing thousands of innocent people; natural disasters leaving countless persons dead or homeless; mass killings by deranged individuals in New York, Paris, Las Vegas, Florida, San Bernardino, Sandy Hook, among other places; and millions of refugees having to flee their homelands because of war or poverty. And we all know people who have received terminal sentences in medical clinics and had to face what seems an unfair death: young children whose lives are just starting and who shouldn't be asked at so tender an age to have to process mortality and young mothers dying whose children still desperately need them.

In the face of these things, we aren't just exasperated by the senselessness of the situation we struggle too to find both heart and words with which to pray. How do we pray when we are paralyzed by senselessness and tragedy? How do we pray when we no longer have the heart for it?

St. Paul tells us that when we don't know how to pray, the Spirit in groans too deep for words prays through us. What an extraordinary text! Paul tells us that when we can still find the words with which to pray this is not our deepest prayer. Likewise when we still have the heart to pray, this too is not our deepest prayer. Our deepest prayer is when we are rendered mute and groaning in exasperation, in frustration, in helplessness. Wordless exasperation is often our deepest prayer. We pray most deeply when we are so driven to our knees so as to be unable to do anything except surrender to helplessness. Our groaning, wordless, seemingly the antithesis of prayer, is indeed our prayer. It is the Spirit praying through us. How so?

The Spirit of God, the Holy Spirit, is, as scripture assures us, the spirit of love, joy, peace, patience, goodness, longsuffering, fidelity, mildness, faith, and chastity. And that Spirit lives deep within us, placed there by God in our very make-up and put into us even more deeply by our baptism. When we are exasperated and driven to our knees by a tragedy which is too painful and senseless to accept and absorb our groans of helplessness are in fact the Spirit of God groaning in us, suffering all that it isn't, yearning for goodness, beseeching God in a language beyond words.

Sometimes we can find the heart and the words with which to pray, but there are other times when, in the words of the Book of Lamentation, all we can do is put our mouths to the dust and wait. The poet, Rainer Maria Rilke, once gave this advice to a person who had written him, lamenting that in the face of a devastating loss he was so paralyzed that he did not know what he could possibly do with the pain he was experiencing. Rilke's advice: Give that heaviness back to the earth itself, the earth is heavy, mountains are heavy, the seas are heavy. In effect: Let your groaning be your prayer!

When we don't know how to pray, the Spirit in groans too deep for words prays through us. So every time we are face-to-face with a tragic situation that leaves us stuttering, mute, and so without heart that all we can do is say, I can't explain this! I can't accept this! I can't deal with this! This is senseless! I am paralyzed in my emotions! I am paralyzed in my faith! I no longer have the heart to pray, it can be consoling to know that this paralyzing exasperation is our prayer—and perhaps the deepest and most sincere prayer we have ever offered.

—*In Exile,* November 6, 2017

LONGING FOR SOLITUDE

Eight hundred years ago, the poet, Rumi wrote: *What I want is to leap out of this personality and then sit apart from that leaping. I've lived too long where I can be reached.*

Isn't that true for all of us, especially today! Our lives are often like over-packed suitcases. It seems like we are always busy, always over-pressured, always one phone call, one text message, one email, one visit, and one task behind. We are forever anxious about what we have still left undone, about whom we have disappointed, about unmet expectations.

Moreover, inside of all of that, we can forever be reached. We have no quiet island to escape to, no haven of solitude. We can always be reached. Half the world has our contact numbers and we feel pressure to be available all the time. So we often feel as if we are on a treadmill from which we would want to step off. And within all that busyness, pressure, noise, and tiredness we long for solitude, long for some quiet, peaceful island where all the pressure and noise will stop and we can sit in simple rest.

That's a healthy yearning. It's our soul speaking. Like our bodies, our souls too keep trying to tell us what they need. They need solitude. But solitude isn't easy to find. Why?

Solitude is an elusive thing that needs to find us rather than us finding it. We tend to picture solitude in a naïve way as something that we can "soak ourselves in" as we would soak ourselves in a warm bath. We tend to picture solitude this way: We are busy, pressured, and tired. We finally have a chance to slip away for a weekend. We rent a cabin, complete with a fireplace, in a secluded woods. We pack some food, some wine, and some soft music and we resist packing any phones, iPads, or laptops. This is to be a quiet weekend, a time to drink wine by the fireplace and listen to the birds sing, a time of solitude.

But solitude cannot be so easily programmed. We can set up all the optimum conditions for it, but that is no guarantee we will find it. It has to find us, or, more accurately, a certain something inside of us has to be awake to its presence. Let me share a personal experience:

Several years ago, when I was still teaching theology at a college, I made arrangements to spend two months in summer living at a Trappist monastery. I was seeking solitude, seeking to slow down my life. I had just finished a very-pressured semester, teaching, doing formation work, giving talks and workshops, and trying to do some writing. I had a near-delicious fantasy of what was to meet me at the monastery. I would have two wonderful months of solitude: I would light the fireplace in the guesthouse and sit quietly by it. I would take a quiet walk in the woods behind the monastery. I would sit on an outdoor rocking chair by a little lake on the property and smoke my pipe. I would enjoy wholesome food, eating in silence as I listened to a monk reading aloud from a spiritual book, and, best of all, I would join the monks for their prayers—singing the office in choir, celebrating the Eucharist, and sitting in quiet meditation with them in their stillness chapel.

I arrived at the monastery at mid-afternoon, hastily unpacked, and set about immediately to do these things. By late evening I had mowed them all down, like a lawn that had been waiting to be cut: I had lit the fire and sat by it. I had taken a walk in the woods, smoked my pipe on the rocking chair by lake, joined the monks in choir for vespers, sat in meditation with them afterwards for a half an hour, ate a wholesome supper in silence, and then joined them again for sung compline. By bedtime the first evening I had already done all the things I had fantasized would bring me solitude and I went to bed restless, anxious about how I would survive the next two months without television, newspapers, phone calls, socializing with friends, and my regular work to distract me. I had done all the right solitude activities and had not found solitude, but had found restlessness instead. It took several weeks before my body and mind slowed down enough for me to find a basic restfulness, before I could even begin to nibble at the edges of solitude.

Solitude is not something we turn on like a water faucet. It needs a body and mind slowed down enough to be attentive to the present moment. We are in solitude when, as Merton says, we fully taste the water we are drinking, feel the warmth of our blankets, and are restful enough to be content inside our own skin. We don't often accomplish this, despite sincere effort, but we need to keep making new beginnings. —*In Exile,* July 1, 2012

A PRAYER FOR STILLNESS

Be still and know that I am God. Scripture assures us that if we are still we will come to know God, but arriving at stillness is easier said than done. As Blaise Pascal once stated, "All the miseries of the human person come from the fact that no one can sit still for one hour." Achieving stillness seems beyond us and this leaves us with a certain dilemma, we need stillness to find God, but we need God's help to find stillness. With this in mind, I offer a prayer for stillness.

God of stillness and of quiet . . .

- *Still the restlessness of my youth: still that hunger that would have me be everywhere, that hunger to be connected to everyone, that wants to see and taste all that is, that robs me of peace on a Friday night. Quiet those grandiose dreams that want me to stand out, to be special. Give me the grace to live more contentedly inside my own skin.*
- *Still the fever I inhale from all the energy that surrounds me, that makes my life feel small. Let me know that my own life is enough, that I need not make an assertion of myself, even as the whole world beckons this of me from a million electronic screens. Give me the grace to sit at peace inside my own life.*
- *Still my sexuality, order my promiscuous desires, my lusts, my polymorphous aching, my relentless need for more*

intimacy. Quiet and order my earthy desires without taking them away. Give me the grace to see others without a selfish sexual color.

- *Still my anxiety, my heartaches, my worries, and stop me from always being outside the present moment. Let each day's worries be sufficient onto themselves. Give me the grace to know that you have pronounced my name in love, that my name written in heaven, that I am free to live without anxiety.*
- *Still my unrelenting need to be busy all the time, to occupy myself, to be always planning for tomorrow, to fill every minute with some activity, to seek distraction rather than quiet. Give me themes with age. Soothe the unacknowledged anger I feel from not achieving much of what I've wanted in life, the failure that I feel in the face of all that I've left untried and unfinished. Still in me the bitterness that comes from failure. Save me from the jealousy that comes unbidden as I begrudgingly accept the limits of my life. Give me the grace to accept what circumstance and failure have dealt me.*
- *Still in me the fear of my own shadow, the fear I feel in the face of the powerful, dark forces that unconsciously threaten me. Give me the courage to face my darkness as well as my luminosity. Give me the grace to not be fearful before my own complexity.*
- *Still in me the congenital fear that I'm unloved, that I'm unlovable, that love has to be earned, that I need to be more worthy. Silence in me the nagging suspicion that I'm forever missing out, that I'm odd, an outsider, that things are unfair, and that I'm not being respected and recognized for who I am. Give me the grace to know that I'm a beloved child of a God whose love need not be earned.*
- *Still in me my false fear of you, my propensity for a misguided piety, my need to treat you like a distant and feared dignitary rather than as a warm friend. Give me the grace*

to relate to you in a robust way, as a trusted friend with whom I can jest, wrestle, and relate to in humor and intimacy.

- *Still my unforgiving thoughts, the grudges I nurse from my past, from the betrayals I've suffered, from the negativity and abuses I've been subject to. Quiet in me the guilt I carry from my own betrayals. Still in me all that's wounded, unresolved, bitter, and unforgiving. Give the quiet that comes from forgiveness.*
- *Still in me my doubts, my anxieties about your existence, about your concern, and about your fidelity. Calm inside me the compulsion to leave a mark, to plant a tree, to have a child, to write a book, to create some form of immortality for myself. Give me the grace to trust, even in darkness and doubt, that you will give me immortality.*

Still my heart so that I may know that you are God, that I may know that you create and sustain my every breath, that you breathe the whole universe into existence every second, that everyone, myself no less than everyone else, is your beloved, that you want our lives to flourish, that you desire our happiness, that nothing falls outside your love and care, and that everything and everybody is safe in your gentle, caring hands, in this world and the next.

—*In Exile,* September 25, 2017

6

Entering the Mystery of Passivity—On Aging and Dying

No one looks forward to growing old and frail, least of all in a culture that idealizes youth. Ron admits it was a jolt the day he looked in a mirror and realized he no longer was a young man. Over time, though, he has discovered the hidden "intelligence" of the aging process.

Our souls, Ron explains in this chapter, do not age the way our bodies do. They mature and become richer and more textured, like the best wines. The paradox is that courage and grace can be more evident in a person who is weak and helpless than in one who has unlimited power and strength. The example of Jesus, especially in the Passion narratives, has profound lessons to offer us.

Finally, Ron reflects on his experience of death at family members' bedsides and at funeral services he's attended. Why is it that some deaths leave mourners uneasy and burdened, while others, even heart-breaking deaths, elicit feelings of gratitude, warmth, and joy? Ultimately, we all hope that our deaths, like our lives, will be a source of blessing and a gift to others. Ron shines a beam of light on the path ahead.

THE INTELLIGENCE INSIDE OF THE AGING PROCESS

What can God and nature have had in mind when they designed the aging process? Why is it that just when our mental prowess, our human maturity, and our emotional freedom are at their peak, the body begins to fall apart?

Our faith, of course, because it opens us to a perspective beyond our biological lives, sheds some light on these questions, though it doesn't always give us a language within which to grasp more reflectively what is happening to us in the aging process. Sometimes a secular perspective can be helpful and that is the case here.

The psychologist James Hillman, in a brilliant book on aging entitled, *The Force of Character and Lasting Life,* takes up these questions. What did God and nature have in mind when designing the aging process? He answers with a metaphor: The best wines have to be aged in cracked old barrels. The last years of our lives are meant to mellow the soul and most everything inside our biology conspires together to ensure that this happens. The soul must be properly aged before it leaves. There's intelligence inside of life, he asserts, that intends aging just as it intends growth in youth. It's a huge mistake to read the signs of aging as indications of dying rather than as initiations into another way of life. Each physical diminishment (from why we have to get up at night to go to the bathroom to why our skin sags and goes dry) is designed to mature the soul. And they do their work without our consent, relentlessly and ruthlessly.

The aging process, he asserts, eventually turns us all into monks and that, indeed, is its plan, just as it once pumped all those excessive hormones into our bodies to drive us out of our homes at puberty. And God again is in on this conspiracy. Aging isn't always pleasant or easy; but there's a rhyme and reason to the process. Aging deliteralizes biology. The soul finally gets to trump the body and it rises to the fore: "We can imagine aging as a transformation in beauty as much as in biology," writes Hillman.

Increasingly, as we age, our task is not productivity, but reflection, not utility, but character. In Hillman's words: "Earlier years must focus on getting things done, while later years consider what was done and how." The former is a function of generativity, we are meant to give our lives away; the latter is a function of dying, we are also meant to give our deaths away.

—*In Exile,* January 20, 2013

A LESSON IN AGING

We live in a culture that idealizes youth and marginalizes the old. And, as James Hillman says, the old don't let go easily either of the throne or the drive that took them there. I know; I'm aging.

For most of my life, I've been able to think of myself as young. Because I was born late in the year, October, I was always younger than most of my classmates, graduated from high school at age seventeen, entered the seminary at that tender age, was ordained to the priesthood at age twenty-five, did an advanced degree within the next year, and was teaching graduate theology at age twenty-six, the youngest member on the faculty. I was proud of that, achieving those things so early. And so I always thought of myself as young, even as the years piled up and my body began to betray my conception of myself as young.

Moreover, for most of those years, I tried to stay young too in soul, staying on top of what was shaping youth culture, its movies, its popular songs, its lingo. During my years in seminary and for a good number of years after ordination, I was involved in youth ministry, helping give youth retreats in various high schools and colleges. At that time, I could name all the popular songs, movies, and trends, speak youth's language, and I prided myself in being young.

But nature offers no exemptions. Nobody stays young forever. Moreover, aging doesn't normally announce its arrival. You're mostly blind to it until one day you see yourself in a mirror, see a recent photo of yourself, or get a diagnosis from your doctor and suddenly you're hit on the head with the unwelcome realization that you're no longer a young person. That usually comes as a surprise. Aging generally makes itself known in ways that have you denying it, fighting it, and accepting it only piecemeal, and with some bitterness.

But that day comes round for everyone when you're surprised, stunned, that what you are seeing in the mirror is so different from how you have been imagining yourself and you ask yourself: "Is this really me? Am I this old person? Is this what I look like?" Moreover you begin to notice that young people are forming their circles away from you, that they're more interested in their own kind, which doesn't include you, and you look silly and out of place when you try to dress, act, and speak like they do. There comes a day when you have to accept that you're no longer young in in the world's eyes—nor in your own.

Moreover gravity doesn't just affect your body, pulling things downward, so too for the soul. It's pulled downward along with the body, though aging means something very different here. The soul doesn't age, it matures. You can stay young in soul long after the body betrays you. Indeed we're meant to be always young in spirit.

Souls carry life differently than do bodies because bodies are built to eventually die. Inside of every living body the life-principle has an exit strategy. It has no such strategy inside a soul, only a strategy to deepen, grow richer, and more textured. Aging forces us, mostly against our will, to listen to our soul more deeply and more honestly so as to draw from its deeper wells and begin to make peace with its complexity, its shadow, and its deepest proclivities.

So, in the end, aging is a gift, even if unwanted. Aging takes us to a deeper place, whether we want to go or not.

—*In Exile,* August 26, 2019

THE ROUTE TO DEPTH AND WISDOM

John Updike, after recovering from a serious illness, wrote a poem he called, "Fever."It ends this way: *But it is a truth long known that some secrets are hidden from health.*

Deep down we already know this, but as a personal truth this is not something we appropriate in a classroom, from parents or mentors, or even from religious teaching. These just tell us that this is true, but knowing it does not itself impart wisdom. Wisdom is acquired, as Updike says, through a personal experience of serious illness, serious loss, or serious humiliation.

The late James Hillman, writing as an agnostic, came to the same conclusion. I remember hearing him at a large conference where, at a point in his talk, he challenged his audience with words to this effect: Think back, honestly and with courage, and ask yourself: What are the experiences in your life that have made you deep, that have given you character? In almost every case, you will have to admit that it was some humiliation or abuse you had to endure, some experience of powerlessness, helplessness, frustration, illness, or exclusion. It is not the things that brought glory or adulation into your life that gave you depth and character, the time you were the valedictorian for your class or the time you were the star athlete. These did not bring you depth. Rather the experience of powerlessness, inferiority, is what made you wise.

I recall too as a graduate student sitting in on a series of lectures by the renowned Polish psychiatrist, Kasmir Dabrowski who had written a number of books around a concept he termed, "positive disintegration." His essential thesis was that it is only by falling apart that we ever grow to higher levels of maturity and wisdom. Once, during a lecture, he was asked: "Why do we grow through the disintegrating experiences such as falling ill, falling apart, or being humiliated? Would it not be more logical to grow through the positive experiences of being loved, being affirmed, being successful, being healthy, and being admired? Shouldn't that fire gratitude inside us and, acting out of that gratitude, we should become more generous and wise?"

He gave this response: *Ideally, maturity and wisdom should grow out of experiences of strength and success; and maybe in some instances they do. However, as a psychiatrist, all I can say is that in forty years of clinical practice I have never seen it. I have only seen people transformed to higher levels of maturity through the experience of breaking down.*

Jesus, it would seem, agrees. Take, for example, the incident in the Gospels where James and John come and ask whether they might be given the seats at his right hand and left hand when he comes into his glory. It is significant that he takes their question seriously. He does not (in this instance) chide them for seeking their own glory; what he does instead is redefine glory and the route to it. He asks them: "Can you drink the cup?" They, naïve as to what is being asked of them, responded: "Yes, we can!" Jesus then tells them something to which they are even more naïve. He assures them that they will drink the cup, since eventually everyone will, but tells them that they still might not receive the glory because being seated in glory is still contingent upon something else.

What? What is "the cup"? How is drinking it the route to glory? And why might we not receive the glory even if we do drink the cup?

The cup, as is revealed later, is the cup of suffering and humiliation, the one Jesus has to drink during his passion and dying, the cup he asks his Father to spare him from when in Gethsemane he prays in agony: "Let this cup pass from me!"

In essence, what Jesus is telling James and John is this: *There is no route to Easter Sunday except through Good Friday.* There is no route to depth and wisdom except through suffering and humiliation. The connection is intrinsic, like the pain and groans of a woman are necessary to her when giving birth to a child. Further still, Jesus is also saying that deep suffering will not automatically bring wisdom. Why not? Because, while there is an intrinsic connection between deep suffering and greater depth in our lives, the catch is that bitter suffering can make us deep in bitterness, anger, envy, and hatred just as easily as it can make us deep in compassion, forgiveness, empathy, and wisdom. We can have the pain, and not get the wisdom.

Fever! The primary symptom of being infected with the coronavirus, *Covid-19*, is a high fever. Fever has now beset our world. The hope is that, after it so dangerously raises both our bodily and psychic temperatures, it will also reveal to us some of the secrets that are hidden from health. What are they? We don't know yet. They will only be revealed inside the fever.

—*In Exile,* May 4, 2020

FLOWERS AND THE RICH YOUNG MAN

To be mature is to be able to give off life and to be a principle of blessing.

But what does this mean? How does one give off life and be a principle of blessing and how is this the essence of maturity and generativity?

An image can be useful here. Imagine a flower: As a seedling and budding young flower it is, in a manner of speaking, essentially selfish. At this stage, it is primarily consumed with taking things into itself, with its own growth. That remains true until it reaches the stage just past its bloom. At that point, it begins to die and in that movement it gives off its seed and is then consumed with giving itself away. It becomes generative at the precise moment when it begins to die and its capacity to give its seed is directly contingent upon its own death.

There are myriad lessons in that about maturity, mature love, mature sexuality, and mature growth. In that movement from seedling to young plant to bloom to giving off seed in death we see nature's paradigm for maturity and generativity. In a flower, when full maturity is reached, life becomes consumed in giving itself away, at the cost of its own death.

In a flower, though, all of this is conscriptive, blind raw forces in the hardwiring of things relentlessly spinning themselves out. There are no choices made. As human beings we have another option, to give off our seed without dying, to let go of our seed with our bloom still intact. But this makes for some things that nature never intended: adults still consumed with taking things in, adults still obsessed with their own growth; boy fathers, girl mothers, child adults, puerile teachers, self-seeking authorities, abusive clergy, and parents who are still so caught up in the search for their own bloom so as to be unable to give off their lives for their children.

No one can truly bless another without dying. That's what makes a blessing so powerful. Nature prescribes that. The flowers know it. Generativity depends upon a willingness to die, to let go of both the search for one's bloom and of that bloom itself.

You see that in blessing adults: good mothers, fathers, teachers, clergy, mentors, uncles, aunts, and friends of all kinds. These, the generative adults, do not look like Peter Pan or Tinkerbell (who look like children), nor do they look like movie stars or athletes or those superb physically conditioned specimens that have just showered and walked out of the exercise club (who symbolize the bloom). No. Blessing adults, of both genders, are recognized by their stretch marks, their scars, their physical waning, and by the very fact that they are dying and their lives are no longer consumed with, precisely, trying to create and hang on to their own bloom.

In the Gospels, when Jesus challenges the rich young man to sell all that he has and give the money to the poor and come and follow him, the young man does not respond because what Jesus was asking of him, to let go of his riches, meant exactly that he would have to let go of his bloom. He was most sincere, but he could not do what Jesus asked. He wanted still to give his seed without dying, to become generative with his bloom still intact. He went away sad.

Flowers go away, but they don't go away sad. They bless the earth, first with their bloom and then with their seed. Unlike the rich young man, in their maturity they sacrifice their bloom to give out all they have.

Innate in nature lies a lesson: Don't give off your seed if your primary concern is still your own bloom. —*In Exile,* May 8, 1996

GROWING TO OUR DEEPEST CENTER

It's interesting to note that the word "Gospel" means "good news," not "good advice." The Gospels are not so much a spiritual and moral theology book that tell us what we should be doing, but are more an account of what God has already done for us, is still doing for us, and the wonderful dignity that this bestows on us. Of course the idea is that since we are gifted in this way our actions should reflect that dignity rather than what's less lofty and more petty inside us. Morality is not a command, it's an invitation; not a threat, but a reminder of who we truly are. We become taller and less petty when we remember what kind of family we ultimately come from.

In essence, we all have two souls, two hearts, and two minds. Inside of each of us there's a soul, heart, and mind that's petty, that's been hurt, that wants vengeance, that wants to protect itself, that's frightened of what's different, that's prone to gossip, that's racist, that perennially feels cheated. Seen in a certain light, all of us are as small in stature as the pre-converted Zacchaeus. But there's also a tall, big-hearted person inside each of us, someone who wants to warmly embrace the whole world, beyond personal hurt, selfishness, race, creed, and politics.

We are always both, grand and petty. The world isn't divided up between big-hearted and small-minded people. Rather our days are divided up between those moments when we are big-hearted, generous, warm, hospitable, unafraid, wanting to embrace everyone and those moments when we are petty, selfish, over-aware of the unfairness of life, frightened, and seeking only to protect ourselves and our own safety and interests. We are both tall and short at the same time and either of these can manifest itself from minute to minute.

But, as we all know, we are most truly ourselves when what's tall in us takes over and gives back to the world what the short, petty person wrongly takes. John of the Cross, the great mystic, made this insight the center-piece of his theology of healing. For him, this is the way we heal:

We heal not by confronting all of our wounds and selfishness head-on, which would overwhelm us and drown us in discouragement, but by growing to what he calls "our deepest center." For him, this center is not first of all some deep place of solitude inside the soul, but rather the furthest place of growth that we can attain, the optimum of our potential. To grow to what our deepest DNA has destined us for is what makes us whole, makes us tall—humanly, spiritually, and morally.

Thus, if John of the Cross were your spiritual director and you went to him with some moral flaw or character deficiency, his first counsel would be: What are you good at? What have you been blessed with? Where, in your life and work, does God's goodness and beauty most shine through? If you can grow more and more towards that goodness, it will fan into an ever larger flame which eventually will become a fire that cauterizes your faults. When you walk tall there will be less and less room for what's small and petty to manifest itself.

But to walk tall means to walk within our God-given dignity. Nothing else, ultimately, gives us as large an identity. That's useful too to remember when we challenge each other: Gospel-challenge doesn't shame us with our pettiness, it invites us to what's already best inside us. —*In Exile,* August 10, 2003

THE LAST TEMPTATION

The last temptation is the greatest treason:
To do the right deed for the wrong reason.

T.S. Eliot wrote those words to describe how difficult it is to purge our motivation of selfish concerns, to do things for reasons that are not ultimately about ourselves. In Eliot's *Murder in the Cathedral*, his main character is Thomas Becket, the Archbishop of Canterbury, who is martyred for his faith. From every outward appearance, Becket is a saint, unselfish, motivated by faith and love. But as Eliot teases out in *Murder in the Cathedral*, the outward narrative doesn't tell the deeper story, doesn't show what's more radically at issue. It's not that Thomas Becket wasn't a saint or wasn't honest in his motivation for doing good works; rather there's still a "last temptation" that he needed to overcome on the road to becoming a full saint. Beneath the surface narrative there's always a deeper, more-subtle, invisible, moral battle going on, a "last temptation" that must be overcome. What's that temptation?

It's a temptation that comes disguised as a grace and tempts us in this way: be unselfish, be faithful, do good things, never compromise the truth, be about others, carry your solitude at a high level, be above the mediocrity of the crowd, be that exceptional moral person, accept martyrdom if it is asked of you. But why? For what reason?

There are many motives for why we want to be good, but the one that disguises itself as a grace and is really a negative temptation is this one: be good because of the respect, admiration, and permanent good name it will win you, for the genuine glory that this brings. This is the temptation faced by a good person. Wanting a good name is not a bad thing, but in the end it's still about ourselves.

In my more reflective moments, I'm haunted by this and left with self-doubts. Am I really doing what I am doing for Jesus, for others, for the world, or am I doing it for my own good name and how I can then feel good about that? Am I doing it so that others might lead fuller, less fearful, lives or am I doing it for the respect it garners for me? When I'm teaching is my real motivation to make others fall in love with Jesus or to have them admire me for my insights? When I write books and articles, am I really trying to dispense wisdom or am I trying to show how wise I am? It this about God or about me?

Perhaps we can never really answer these questions since our motivation is always mixed and it's impossible to sort this out exactly. But still, we owe it to others and to ourselves to scrutinize ourselves over this in prayer, in conscience, in spiritual direction, and in discussion with others. How do we overcome that "last temptation," to do the right things and not make it about ourselves?

The struggle to overcome selfishness and motivate ourselves by a clear, honest altruism can be an impossible battle to win. Classically, the churches have told us there are seven deadly sins (pride, greed, wrath, envy, lust, gluttony, sloth) that are tied to our very nature and with which we will struggle our whole lives. And the problem is that the more we seem to overcome them, the more they manage to simply disguise themselves in more subtle forms in our lives. For example, take Jesus' counsel to not be proud and take the most prestigious place at table and then be embarrassed by being asked to move to a lower place, but rather humbly taking the lowest seat so as to be invited to move higher. That's sound practical advice, no doubt, but it can also be a recipe for a pride we can really be proud of. Once we have displayed our humility and been publicly recognized for it, then we can feel a truly superior pride in how humble we've been! It's the same for all of the deadly sins. As we succeed in not giving in to crasser temptations, they re-root themselves in subtler forms within us.

Our faults display themselves publicly and crassly when we're immature, but the hard fact is that they generally don't disappear when we are mature. They simply take on more subtle forms.

—*In Exile,* August 31, 2020

THE LESSONS OF THE PASSION

What exactly was the Passion of Jesus?

As Christians, we believe that Jesus gave us both his life and his death. Too often, however, we do not distinguish between the two, though we should: Jesus gave his life for us in one way, through his activity; he gave his death for us in another way, through his passivity, his passion.

It is easy to misunderstand what the Gospels mean by the Passion of Jesus. When we use the word passion in relationship to Jesus' suffering we spontaneously connect it to the idea of passion as pain, the pain of the crucifixion, of scourging, of whips, of nails in his hands, of humiliation before the crowd. The Passion of Jesus does refer to these, but the word asks for a different focus here. The English word passion takes it root in the Latin, *passio,* meaning passivity, and that's its real connotation here. The word "patient" also derives from this. Hence what the Passion narratives describe is Jesus' passivity, his becoming a "patient." He gives his death to us through his passivity, just as he had previously given his life to us through his activity.

Indeed the Gospels of Matthew, Mark, and Luke can each be neatly divided into two distinct parts: In each Gospel we can split off everything that is narrated until Jesus' arrest in the Garden of Gethsemane and call this part of the Gospel: The Activity of Jesus Christ. Then we could take the section of the Gospels that we call "the Passion" and call that section: The Passivity of Jesus Christ. This would in fact help clarify an important distinction: Jesus gave his life for us through his activity whereas he gave his death for us through his passivity. Hence: Up until his arrest, the Gospels describe Jesus as active, as doing in things, as being in charge, preaching, teaching, performing miracles, consoling people. After his arrest, all the verbs become passive: he is led away, manhandled by the authorities, whipped, helped in carrying his cross, and ultimately nailed to the cross. After his arrest, like a patient in palliative care or hospice, he no longer does anything; rather others do it for him and to him. He is passive, a patient, and in that passivity he gave his death for us.

There are many lessons in this, not least the fact that life and love are given not just in what we do for others but also, and perhaps even more deeply, in what we absorb at those times when we are helplessness, when we have no choice except to be a "patient."

—*In Exile,* March 30, 2015

THE SUMMER OF MY DISCONTENT

Nothing in my youth remains as clear in my mind and as formative of my soul as is the summer when I was fourteen years old. For any boy, that's an awkward age, even at the best of times. For me, that summer was not the best of times.

It began ordinarily enough. The most important things in my young life then were sports and looking good. I was obsessed with trying to make the high school softball team and the parish junior baseball team. To make those teams would be to look good, to be able to strut a bit, to have some confidence with the opposite sex, and to have a better place among my friends, to have, as it were, a bit of immortality, as fourteen-year-olds define it. But that summer dealt me a different kind of immortality, not the kind a fourteen-year-old wants to deal with.

I came to breakfast one morning at the beginning of May and was told that one of our neighbor's sons, a young man in his twenties, had, the previous night, committed suicide by hanging himself in a barn. No event, no death, no tragedy, no loss of love, not anything, has ever rocked the foundations of my soul as did that suicide. It's not that I fell to pieces and was unable to control my tears. The opposite, I went numb and never cried for years. But that was not the story, dealing with death was.

At fourteen, you have no understanding of death, especially of that kind, suicide. Years later, I would begin to understand that sometimes a man or woman can have so sensitive a soul that, at a point, something snaps and, not unlike a heart attack or stroke, it takes that person unwillingly out of this life. But on that day in May all those years ago, and through all that summer, I didn't have that understanding, nor the peace that comes of it, and so my young thoughts and feelings churned in every direction but found no restful place to stop: When all you've experienced is life and all you can dream of is life, what sense can be made of death, especially the suicide of a young, healthy person whose athletically-endowed body I envied?

It was the fact of suicide (that black hole inside of human understanding and formerly even inside of our Christian faith) that so jolted, but it was more. It was the brute inevitability of death itself, especially of my own some day, that ate away inside of me. I had seen dead people before, though not many, but they were all already old, had lived long enough, to my young reasoning. This person hadn't lived long at all and the seeming unnecessary character of his death was like an atom bomb to my young soul. What is the purpose of making a baseball team, of popularity, of all of my young dreams and plans, if this, after all, can happen?

I agonized and fretted, silently though. Curiously too my reaction was not, it seemed, a religious one. On the contrary, I wanted to think of nothing religious at all. Distraction, reading magazines about Hollywood stars and athlete's exploits, seemed the route to go; after all, to a fourteen-year-old, they, the rich, the glamorous, with their beautiful bodies and exciting, graced lives, offer an exemption from death and all its terrors.

And so went my summer—compounded further by two other young deaths in our district and school; first, the death of another young man in his twenties, killed in an industrial mishap and then the death, in a horseback riding accident, of one of my classmates. I remember spending more than one evening staring at a dark sky and wondering: "Where are they? Are they still alive somewhere? What really is behind those clouds? God? Another life? Terror and hell? Love and an ecstasy that I can't imagine?" Such are the metaphysics of a fourteen-year-old.

Slowly, as happens with these things, a calm returned. Life, with all its promises, demands, and numbing distractions, eventually brings you back to the ordinary with its health, aches, and pleasures. I stopped staring at the dark sky and asking those metaphysical questions. But, underneath, something had shifted. I had been through my first dark night of the soul and I'd learned something.

I knew now, in a way I never imagined before, that life is fragile, that everyone dies, that I too will die someday. I knew too that life is not just about life here, but about something bigger, infinitely bigger. I am a priest because of that—because of that summer of discontent, when my fourteen-year-old soul was forced to do some metaphysics and my internal furniture was forever re-arranged. —*In Exile,* April 25, 1999

UNDERGOING OUR OWN PASSION

Ten years ago, my sister, Helen, an Ursuline nun, died of cancer. A nun for more than thirty years, she much loved her vocation and was much loved within it. For most of those thirty years, she served as a den-mother to hundreds of young women who attended an academy run by her order. She loved those young women and was for them a mother, an older sister, and a mentor. For the last twenty years of her life, after our own mother died, she also served in that same capacity for our family, organizing us and keeping us together. Through all those years she was the active-one, the consummate-doer, the one that others expected to take charge. She relished the role. She loved doing things for others.

Nine months before she died, cancer struck her brutally and she spent the last months of her life bed-ridden. Now things needed to be done for her and to her. Doctors, nurses, her sisters in community, and others, took turns taking care of her. And, like Jesus from the time of his arrest until the moment of his death, her body too was humiliated, led around by others, stripped, prodded, and stared at by curious passers-by. Indeed, like Jesus, she died thirsty, with a sponge held to her lips by someone else.

This was her passion. She, the one who had spent so many years doing things for others, now had to submit to having things done to her. But, and this is the point, like Jesus, she was able in that period of her life, when she was helpless and no longer in charge, to give life and meaning to others in a deeper way than she could when she was active and doing so many things for others.

There's a great lesson in this, not the least of which is how we view the terminally ill, the severely handicapped, and the sick. There's a lesson too on how we might understand ourselves when we are ill, helpless, and in need of care from others.

The lesson is that we, like Jesus, give as much to others in our passivities as in our activities. When we are no longer in charge, beaten down by whatever, humiliated, suffering, and unable even to make ourselves understood by our loved ones, we are undergoing our passion and, like Jesus in his passion, have in that the opportunity to give our love and ourselves to others in a very deep way.

—*In Exile*, February 24, 2002

THE GRACE WITHIN PASSIVITY

A friend of mine shares this story. She grew up with five siblings and an alcoholic father. The effect of her father's alcoholism was devastating on her family. Here's how she tells the story:

> *By the time my father died his alcoholism had destroyed our family. None of us kids could talk to each other anymore. We'd drifted apart to different parts of the country and had nothing to do with each other. My mother was a saint and kept trying through the years to have us reconcile with each other, inviting us to gather for Thanksgiving and Christmas and the like, but it never worked. All her efforts were for nothing. We hated each other. Then as my mother lay dying of cancer, in hospice, bedridden, and eventually in a coma, we, her kids, gathered by her bedside, watching her die, and she, helpless and unable to speak, was able to accomplish what she couldn't achieve through all those years when she could speak. Watching her die, we reconciled.*

We all know similar stories of someone in their dying, when they were too helpless to speak or act, powerfully impacting, more powerfully than they ever did in word or action, those around them, pouring out a grace that blessed their loved ones. Sometimes, of course, this isn't a question of reconciling a family but of powerfully strengthening their existing unity.

The lesson is that we don't just do important things for each other and impact each other's lives by what we actively do for each other; we also do life-changing things for each other in what we passively absorb in helplessness.

Unfortunately, this is not something our present culture, with its emphasis on health, productivity, achievement, and power very much understands. We no longer much understand or value the powerful grace that is given off by someone dying of a terminal illness; nor the powerful grace present in a person with a disability, or indeed the grace that's present in our own physical and personal disabilities. Nor do we much understand what we are giving to our families, friends, and colleagues when we, in powerlessness, have to absorb neglect, slights, and misunderstanding. When a culture begins to talk about euthanasia it is an infallible indication that we no longer understand the grace within passivity.

In his writings, Henri Nouwen makes a distinction between what he terms our "achievements" and our "fruitfulness." *Achievements* stem more directly from our activities: What have we positively accomplished? What have we actively done for others? And our achievements stop when we are no longer active. *Fruitfulness*, on the other hand, goes far beyond what we have actively accomplished and is sourced as much by what we have passively absorbed as by what we actively produced. The family described above reconciled not because of their mother's achievements, but because of her fruitfulness. Such is the mystery of passivity.

—*In Exile,* October 21, 2019

"BLOOD AND WATER POURED OUT"

Paradox is everywhere: Sometimes the things you think will make you happy end up saddening you and sometimes the very thing that breaks your heart is also the thing that opens it to warmth and gratitude. Sometimes it's death itself that pours out life.

We see this in the language that surrounds the death of Jesus in the Gospels. In some of the Gospels, the moment of Jesus' death brings with it a series of apocalyptic-type cataclysms—the temple veil is ripped, top to bottom, and a series of earthquakes shake the earth, opens graves, and the saints begin to walk around. Among other things, what this says is that Jesus' death strips away the veil that blocks us from seeing what's inside of God and, after Jesus' death, we are to believe that the graves are empty, our loved ones aren't there, but with Jesus, alive, elsewhere.

John's Gospel though has a different image: He tells us that after Jesus died, the soldiers came and pierced his side with a sword and "immediately blood and water poured out." Classically theologians have been quick to read the origin of the sacraments into that, namely, the blood and water refer to Eucharist and Baptism. No doubt that's true, but there's something more immediate there.

What are "blood" and "water"? Blood carries life through our bodies. It's the flow of life. In a manner of speaking, blood is life itself. Water keeps us alive, quenches thirst, and, importantly too, washes us clean. What John is saying when he says that "blood and water" flowed out of the dead body of Jesus is that Jesus died in such a way that his death became for those who loved him and for those of us who continue to love him a source of life, health, and cleansing. After he died, those who loved him, paradoxically, experienced his death not as something that drained life from them and made them feel guilty, but the opposite: As sad and heart-breaking as was his death, those who loved him experienced it as something which gave them deeper life, let them breathe more freely, and freed them from feelings of guilt. That's an incredible paradox but we are not without parallels within our own experience to help us understand this. We all too have experienced blood and water flowing out at the funeral of someone we've loved.

During the past several years, the most genuinely joy-filled occasions I've gone to were three particular funerals, each a farewell to a man who died relatively young, the victim of cancer. Two of the men were in the mid-fifties and the other was a young seventy. But in each case, the man had lived, and then died, in a way so as to make his death his final gift to his family and his loved ones.

In each case, all of us who were at the funeral walked out of church deeply sad but, at the same time, strangely more free, more open to life and love, more grateful at some deep level, and more free from that free-floating guilt that can so easily rob our lives of delight. In every case, almost tangibly, blood and water flowed from their casket. That's not just a metaphor.

We experience this negatively as well: Sometimes someone we know dies and his or her death has the opposite effect. No blood or water flows. Rather that person's death somehow asphyxiates us, stops our blood, gives us trouble breathing, and we feel guilty about having known this person and about all the things we did, didn't do, or should have done. A sword has pieced someone's side, but no blood and water are flowing out.

I remember a conversation with one of those men whose funerals were so joy-filled. Visiting him in palliative care, I asked him if he was afraid of anything. He answered: "No, I'm not afraid of dying, though I'm finding this hard. It's hard to describe the loneliness of it. I have a very loving family and so many friends and someone is holding my hand almost constantly, but I am deeply alone inside of this. People can love you, but they can't go into this with you. But I'm only really afraid of one thing, of not doing this with dignity. I want to make this, the way I die, my final act of love for my family. I want to do this right!" He did. We cried at his funeral but we all walked out of the church afterwards more free, more loving, less wrapped in guilt.

Sometimes the very thing that breaks your heart is the thing that most warms it and the very life that is taken from you is what opens up the flow of blood inside of you. Our task, in the end, is to do what this man did, die in such a way that our going away is our final gift to those whom we love.

—*In Exile,* January 20, 2008

LEAVING PEACE BEHIND AS OUR FAREWELL GIFT

There is such a thing as a good death, a clean one, a death that, however sad, leaves behind a sense of peace. I have been witness to it many times. Sometimes this is recognized explicitly when someone dies, sometimes unconsciously. It is known by its fruit.

I remember sitting with a man dying of cancer in his mid-fifties, leaving behind a young family, who said to me: "I don't believe I have an enemy in the world, at least I don't know if I do. I've no unfinished business." I heard something similar from a young woman also dying of cancer and also leaving behind a young family. Her words: "I thought that I'd cried all the tears I had, but then yesterday when I saw my youngest daughter I found out that I had a lot more tears still to cry. But I'm at peace. It's hard, but I've nothing left that I haven't given." And I've been at deathbeds other times when none of this was articulated in words, but all of it was clearly spoken in that loving awkwardness and silence you often witness around deathbeds. There is a way of dying that leaves peace behind.

In the Gospel of John, Jesus gives a long farewell speech at the Last Supper on the night before he dies. His disciples, understandably, are shaken, afraid, and not prepared to accept the brute reality of his impending death. He tries to calm them, reassure them, give them things to cling to, and he ends with these words: *I am going away, but I will leave you a final gift, the gift of my peace.*

I suspect that almost everyone reading this will have had an experience of grieving the death of a loved one, a parent, spouse, child, or friend, and finding, at least after a time, beneath the grief a warm sense of peace whenever the memory of the loved one surfaces or is evoked. I lost both of my parents when I was in my early twenties and, sad as were their farewells, every memory of them now evokes a warmth. Their farewell gift was the gift of peace.

In trying to understanding this, it is important to distinguish between *being wanted* and *being needed.* When I lost my parents at a young age, I still desperately wanted them (and believed that I still needed them), but I came to realize in the peace that eventually settled upon our family after their deaths that our pain was in still wanting them and not in any longer needing them. In their living and their dying they had already given us what we needed. There was nothing else we needed from them. Now we just missed them and, irrespective of the sadness of their departure, our relationship was complete. We were at peace.

The challenge for all of us now, of course, is on the other side of this equation, namely, the challenge to live in such a way that peace will be our final farewell gift to our families, our loved ones, our faith community, and our world. How do we do that? How do we leave the gift of peace to those we leave behind?

Peace, as we know, is a whole lot more than the simple absence of war and strife. Peace is constituted by two things: harmony and completeness. To be at peace something has to have an inner consistency so that all of its movements are in harmony with each other and it must also have a completeness so that it is not still aching for something it is missing. Peace is the opposite of internal discord or of longing for something we lack. When we are not at peace it is because we are experiencing chaos or sensing some unfinished business inside us.

Positively then, what constitutes peace? When Jesus promises peace as his farewell gift, he identifies it with the Holy Spirit; and, as we know, that is the spirit of *charity, joy, peace, patience, goodness, longsuffering, fidelity, mildness,* and *chastity.*

How do we leave these behind when we leave? Well, death is no different than life. When some people leave anything, a job, a marriage, a family, or a community, they leave chaos behind, a legacy of disharmony, unfinished business, anger, bitterness, jealousy, and division. Their memory is felt always as a cold pain. They are not missed, even as their memory haunts. Some people on the other hand leave behind a legacy of harmony and completeness, a spirit of understanding, compassion, affirmation, and unity. These people are missed but the ache is a warm one, a nurturing one, one of happy memory.

Going away in death has exactly the same dynamic. By the way we live and die we will leave behind either a spirit that perennially haunts the peace of our loved ones, or we will leave behind a spirit that brings a warmth every time our memory is evoked.

—*In Exile,* May 11, 2020

FAITH, DOUBT, AND DYING

We tend to nurse a certain naïveté about what faith means in the face of death. The common notion among us as Christians is that if someone has a genuine faith she should be able to face death without fear or doubt. The implication then of course is that having fear and doubt when one is dying is an indication of a weak faith. While it's true that many people with a strong faith do face death calmly and without fear, that's not always the case, nor necessarily the norm.

We can begin with Jesus. Surely he had real faith and yet, in the moments just before his death, he called out in both fear and doubt. His cry of anguish, "My God, my God, why have you forsaken me," came from a genuine anguish that was not, as we sometimes piously postulate, uttered for divine effect, not really meant, but something for us to hear. Moments before he died, Jesus suffered real fear and real doubt. Where was his faith? Well, that depends upon how we understand faith and the specific modality it can take on in our dying.

In her famous study of the stages of dying, Elisabeth Kübler-Ross, suggests there are five stages we undergo in the dying process: Denial, Anger, Bargaining, Depression, Acceptance. Our first response to receiving a terminal diagnosis is denial—*This is not happening!* Then when we have to accept that it is happening our reaction is anger—*Why me!* Eventually anger gives way to bargaining—*How much time can I still draw out of this?* This is followed by depression and finally, when nothing serves us any longer, there's acceptance—*I'm going to die.* This is all very true.

But in a deeply insightful book, *The Grace in Dying,* Kathleen Dowling Singh, basing her insights upon the experience of sitting at the bedside of many dying people, suggests there are additional stages: Doubt, Resignation, and Ecstasy. Those stages help shed light on how Jesus faced his death.

The night before he died, in Gethsemane, Jesus accepted his death, clearly. But that acceptance was not yet full resignation.

That only took place the next day on the cross in a final surrender when, as the Gospels put it, he bowed his head and gave over his spirit. And, just before that, he experienced an awful fear that what he had always believed in and taught about God was perhaps not so. Maybe the heavens were empty and maybe what we deem as God's promises amount only to wishful thinking.

But, as we know, he didn't give into that doubt, but rather, inside of its darkness, gave himself over in trust. Jesus died in faith—though not in what we often naïvely believe faith to be. To die in faith does not always mean that we die calmly, without fear and doubt.

For instance, the renowned biblical scholar, Raymond E. Brown, commenting on the fear of death inside the community of the Beloved Disciple, writes:

> The finality of death and the uncertainties it creates causes trembling among those who have spent their lives professing Christ. Indeed, among the small community of Johannine disciples, it was not unusual for people to confess that doubts had come into their minds as they encountered death. . . . .The Lazarus story is placed at the end of Jesus' public ministry in John to teach us that when confronted with the visible reality of the grave, all need to hear and embrace the bold message that Jesus proclaimed: "I am the life." . . . For John, no matter how often we renew our faith, there is the supreme testing by death. Whether the death of a loved one or one's own death, it is the moment when one realizes that it all depends on God. During our lives we have been able to shield ourselves from having to face this in a raw way. Confronted by death, mortality, all defenses fall away.

Sometimes people with a deep faith face death in calm and peace. But sometimes they don't and the fear and doubt that threatens them then is not necessarily a sign of a weak or faltering faith. It can be the opposite, as we see in Jesus. Inside a person of faith, fear and doubt in the face of death is what the mystics call "the dark night of the spirit" . . . and this is what's going on inside that experience: The raw fear and doubt we are experiencing at that time make it impossible for us to mistake our own selves and our own life-force for God. When we have to accept to die in trust inside of what seems like absolute negation and can only cry out in anguish to an apparent emptiness then it is no longer possible to confuse God with our own feelings and ego. In that, we experience the ultimate purification of soul. We can have a deep faith and still find ourselves with doubt and fear in the face of death. Just look at Jesus.

—*In Exile,* November 4, 2019

REDEMPTION FOR ALL

The Belgian spirituality writer, Benoît Standaert, suggests that the greatest miracle is "that the freely given exists, that there is love that makes whole and that embraces what has been lost, that chooses what had been rejected, that forgives what has been found guilty beyond appeal, that unites what had seemingly been torn apart forever."

In other words, the greatest miracle is that there's redemption for all that's wrong with us.

- There's redemption from all we've failed to live up to because of our inadequacies.
- There's redemption from our wounds, from all that's left us physically, emotionally, and spiritually limping and cold.
- There's redemption from injustice, from the unfairness we suffer ourselves and from the hurt which we inflict knowingly or unknowingly on others.
- There's redemption from our mistakes, our moral failures, our infidelities, our sins.
- There's redemption from relationships gone sour, from marriages, families, and friendships that have been torn apart by misunderstanding, hatred, selfishness, and violence.
- There's redemption from suicide and murder.

Nothing falls outside the scope of God's power to forgive, to resurrect and make new, fresh, innocent, and joyful again.

—*In Exile,* July 2, 2018

GIVING OUR DEATHS TO OUR LOVED ONES

Just as elders are meant to teach the young how to live they are also meant to teach them how to die. That's the final lesson we are meant to give the young, to die in such a way that our deaths are our final blessing to them.

Henri Nouwen writes:

> Yes, there is such a thing as a good death. We ourselves are responsible for the way we die. We have to choose between clinging to life in such a way that death becomes nothing but a failure, or letting go of life in freedom so that we can be given to others as a source of hope. This is a crucial choice and we have to "work" on that choice every day of our lives. Death does not have to be our final failure, our final defeat in the struggle of life, our unavoidable fate. If our deepest human desire is, indeed, to give ourselves to others, than we can make our death our final gift.

What does this really mean? At every funeral we have some sense of it. We feel what we don't understand. When someone we know dies, we are left with a feeling, a tone, a color, something in the air, of either guilt or blessing. The feeling isn't based so much upon whether the person died accidently or naturally, was young or old, or whether or not we were present to him or her at the time of death. It takes root rather in how that person lived and how he or she related to life in general, more so than how he or she related specifically to us. That's part of the mystery of death. It releases a spirit.

Before he died, Jesus told his disciples that it was only after he was gone that they would be able to grasp what he really meant for them. That is true for everyone. Only after we have died will our spirits fully reveal themselves. And this works in two ways: If our spirits have been loving, death will reveal our real beauty (which, in this life, is always limited by wounds and shortcomings). Conversely, if our spirits, at the core, have been petty and bitter, our deaths will also reveal that. The death of a generous, gracious soul releases blessing and makes others feel free, just as the death of a bitter, clinging soul pours out accusation and makes others feel guilty.

How can I make my death a gift for others? By the way I live. If I live in bitterness and non-forgiveness, always full of accusation, then my death will pour those things out among my family and loved ones. That's what people will feel at my funeral because that's the air and color that emanates from my soul, now made transparent. Conversely, if I live in graciousness, in admiration, in forgiveness, and am willing when it's time to decrease so that others can increase then what will be poured out at my death is blessing. My death will mean new freedom and courage for those who knew me. They will be able to go on with their lives with less fear, less guilt, knowing that it is best for them that I go away and that, like Jesus, I am helping to prepare a place for them.

But this isn't automatic, nor easy. It's something we have to "work at," painfully, every day of our lives. And what do we have to work at? At blessing others, especially the young, at admiring their energy, beauty, and achievement without envy, bitterness, or cynicism. This involves, especially as we grow older, saying what John the Baptist said when Jesus appeared: "He must increase and I must decrease!" As we age, the real task of life and love is to continually hand over, without bitterness, regret, or envy, all the things that were once so much our own (power, attention, popularity, usefulness, turf of every sort). Part of this, the hardest part of all, is forgiveness. To exit gracefully, we have to first forgive others, God, and ourselves for the fact that our lives didn't turn out the way they might have. That's easier said than done.

Our deaths, like our lives, are either a source of blessing or frustration to those around us. Ultimately the choice is ours. The final task of life is to live in such a way that, when we die, our deaths, like our lives, sweeten rather than embitter the air.

—*In Exile,* November 11, 2001

7

Faith, Doubt, and Dark Nights within the Spiritual Journey

What do we do when doubts about God make us waver in our faith? Many Christians have faced what St. John of the Cross calls "a dark night of the soul." Mother Teresa described her religious experience as empty, lonely, and dark. Jesus cried out on the cross, "My God, my God, why have you forsaken me?"

Ron explains that even ordinary Christians are likely to face periods of doubt and unbelief. We needn't be alarmed by God's seeming absence. While not minimizing the pain and confusion such an experience may bring, our inability to sense God's presence does not mean that God has abandoned us. It means God can now enter our lives in a deeper way—a way not easily grasped by our imagination or by our physical senses. The Gospels tell us that God's presence in the world is quiet and hidden, like the yeast that leavens dough. So it is in our souls, especially as our spiritual life matures. In that darkness, Ron writes, "real faith begins."

DARK NIGHTS AND MATURITY

In one of his books on contemplative prayer, Thomas Keating shares with us a line that he occasionally uses in spiritual direction. People come to him, sharing how they used to have a warm and solid sense of God in their lives but now complain that all that warmth and confidence have disappeared and they're left struggling with belief and struggling to pray as they used to. They feel a deep sense of loss and invariably this is their question: "What's wrong with me?" Keating's answer: *God is wrong with you!*

His answer, in essence, says this: Despite your pain, there is something very right with you. You have moved past being a religious neophyte, past an initiatory stage of religious growth, which was right for you for its time, and are now being led into a deeper, not lesser, faith. Moreover, that loss of fervor has brought you to a deeper maturity. So, in effect, what you're asking is this: I used to be quite sure of myself religiously and, no doubt, probably somewhat arrogant and judgmental. I felt I understood God and religion and I looked with some disdain at the world. Then the bottom fell out of my faith and my certainty and I'm now finding myself a lot less sure of myself, considerably more humble, more empathetic, and less judgmental. What's wrong with me?

Asked in this way, the question answers itself. Clearly that person is growing, not regressing.

Lost is a place too! Christina Crawford wrote those words, describing her own painful journey through darkness into a deeper maturity. To be saved, we have to first realize that we're lost, and usually some kind of bottom has to fall out of our lives for us to come to that realization. Sometimes there's no other cure for arrogance and presumption than a painful loss of certitude about our own ideas about God, faith, and religion. John of the Cross suggests that a deeper religious faith begins when, as he puts it, we are forced to understand more by not understanding than by understanding. But that can be a very confusing and painful experience that precisely prompts the feeling: What's wrong with me?

A curious, paradoxical dynamic lies behind this: We tend to confuse faith with our capacity on any given day to conjure up a concept of God and imagine God's existence. Moreover we think our faith is strongest at those times when we have affective and emotive feelings attached to our imaginations about God. Our faith feels strongest when bolstered by and inflamed by feelings of fervor. Great spiritual writers will tell us that this stage of fervor is a good stage in our faith, but an initiatory one, one more commonly experienced when we are neophytes. Experience tends to support this. In the earlier stages of a religious journey it is common to possess strong, affective images and feelings about God. At this stage, our relationship with God parallels the relationship between a couple on their honeymoon. On your honeymoon you have strong emotions and possess a certain certainty about your love, but it's a place you come home from. A honeymoon is an initiatory stage in love, a valuable gift, but something that disappears after it has done its work. A honeymoon is not a marriage, though often confused with one. It's the same with faith; strong imaginative images of God are not faith, though they're often confused with it.

Strong imaginative images and strong feelings about God are, in the end, just that, images. Wonderful, but images nonetheless, icons. An image is not the reality. An icon can be beautiful and helpful and point us in the right direction, but when mistaken for the reality it becomes an idol. For this reason, the great spiritual writers tell us that God at certain moments of our spiritual journey "takes away" our certainty and deprives us of all warm, felt feelings in faith. God does this precisely so that we cannot turn our icons into idols, so that we cannot let the experience of faith get in the way of the end of faith itself, namely, an encounter with the reality and person of God.

Mystics such as John of the Cross call this experience of seemingly losing our faith, "a dark night of the soul." This describes the experience where we used to feel God's presence with a certain warmth and solidity, but now we feel like God is non-existent and we are left in doubt. This is what Jesus experienced on the cross and this is what Mother Teresa wrote about in her journals.

And while that darkness can be confusing, it can also be maturing: It can help move us from being arrogant, judgmental, religious neophytes to being humble, empathic men and women, living inside a cloud of unknowing, understanding more by not understanding than by understanding, helpfully lost in a darkness we cannot manipulate or control, so as to finally be pushed into genuine faith, hope, and charity. —*In Exile,* November 9, 2015

MOTHER TERESA'S FAITH

A recent book on Mother Teresa, *Mother Teresa: Come Be My Light,* makes public a huge volume of her intimate correspondence and in it we see what looks like a very intense, fifty-year, struggle with faith and belief.

Again and again, she describes her religious experience as "dry," "empty," "lonely," "torturous," "dark," "devoid of all feeling." During the last half-century of her life, it seems, she was unable to feel or imagine God's existence.

Many people have been confused and upset by this. How can this be? How can this woman, a paradigm of faith, have experienced such doubts?

And so some are making that judgment that her faith wasn't real. Their view is that she lived the life of a saint, but died the death of an atheist. For doctrinaire atheists, her confession of doubt is manna from the abyss. Christopher Hitchens, for example, writes: *"She was no more exempt from the realization that religion is a human fabrication than any other person, and that her attempted cure was more and more professions of faith could only have deepened the pit that she dug for herself."*

What's to be said about all of this? Was Mother Teresa an atheist?

Hardly! In a deeper understanding of faith, her doubts and feelings of abandonment are not only explicable, they're predictable:

What Mother Teresa underwent is called *"a dark night of the soul."* This is what Jesus suffered on the cross when he cried out: *"My God, my God, why have you forsaken me?"* When he uttered those words, he meant them. At that moment, he felt exactly what Mother Teresa felt so acutely for more than fifty years, namely, the sense that God is absent, that God is dead, that there isn't any God. But this isn't the absence of faith or the absence of God, it is rather a deeper presence of God, a presence which, precisely because it goes beyond feeling and imagination, can only be felt as an emptiness, nothingness, absence, non-existence.

But how can this make sense? How can faith feel like doubt? How can God's deeper presence feel like God's non-existence? And, perhaps more importantly, why? Why would faith work like this?

The literature around the *"dark night of the soul"* makes this point: Sometimes when we are unable to induce any kind of feeling that God exists, when we are unable to imagine God's existence, the reason is because God is now coming into our lives in such a way that we cannot manipulate the experience through ego, narcissism, self-advantage, self-glorification, and self-mirroring. This purifies our experience of God because only when all of our own lights are off can we grasp divine light in its purity. Only when we are completely empty of ourselves inside an experience, when our heads and hearts are pumping dry, can God touch us in a way that makes it impossible for us to inject ourselves into the experience, so that we are worshiping God, not ourselves.

And this is painful. It is experienced precisely as darkness, emptiness, doubt, abandonment. But this is, in fact, *"the test"* that we pray God to spare us from whenever we pray Matthew's version of the Lord's Prayer—*"Do not put us to the test."*

Moreover this experience is usually given to those who have the maturity to handle it, spiritual athletes, those who pray for and truly want a searing "purity of heart," people like Mother Teresa. They ask Jesus to experience and feel everything as he did. He just answers their prayers!

Henri Nouwen, in a book entitled, *In Memorium*, shares a similar thing about his mother: She was, he states, the most faith-filled and generous woman he had ever met. So when he stood at her bedside as she was dying he had every right to expect that her death would be a serene witness to a life of deep faith. But what happened, on the surface at least, seemed the exact reverse. She struggled, was seized by doubts, cried out, and died inside a certain darkness. Only later, after prayer and reflection, did this make sense. His mother had prayed her whole life to die like Jesus—and so she did! A common soldier dies without fear, Jesus died afraid.

In a remarkable book, *The Crucified God*, Jürgen Moltmann writes: *"Our faith begins at the point where atheists suppose that it must end. Our faith begins with the bleakness and power which is the night of the cross, abandonment, temptation, and doubt about everything that exists! Our faith must be born where it is abandoned by all tangible reality; it must be born of nothingness, it must taste this nothingness and be given it to taste in a way no philosophy of nihilism can imagine."*

Mother Teresa understood all of this. That is why her seeming doubt did not lead her away from God and her vocation but instead riveted her to it with a depth and purity that, more than anything else, tell us precisely what faith really is.

—*In Exile,* September 9, 2007

GOD'S QUIET PRESENCE IN OUR LIVES

The poet, Rumi, submits that we live with a deep secret that sometimes we know, and then not.

That can be very helpful in understanding our faith. One of the reasons why we struggle with faith is that God's presence inside us and in our world is rarely dramatic, overwhelming, sensational, something impossible to ignore. God doesn't work like that. Rather God's presence, much to our frustration and loss of patience sometimes, is something that lies quiet and seemingly helpless inside us. It rarely makes a huge splash.

Because we are not sufficiently aware of this, we tend to misunderstand the dynamics of faith and find ourselves habitually trying to ground our faith on precisely something that is loud and dramatic. We are forever looking for something beyond what God gives us. But we should know from the very way God was born into our world, that faith needs to ground itself on something that is quiet and undramatic. Jesus, as we know, was born into our world with no fanfare and no power, a baby lying helpless in the straw, another child among millions. Nothing spectacular to human eyes surrounded his birth. Then, during his ministry, he never performed miracles to prove his divinity; but only as acts of compassion or to reveal something about God. Jesus never used divine power in an attempt to prove that God exists, beyond doubt. His ministry, like his birth, wasn't an attempt to prove God's existence. It was intended rather to teach us what God is like and that God loves us unconditionally.

Moreover, Jesus' teaching about God's presence in our lives also makes clear that this presence is mostly quiet and hidden, a plant growing silently as we sleep, yeast leavening dough in a manner hidden from our eyes, summer slowly turning a barren tree green, an insignificant mustard plant eventually surprising us with its growth, a man or woman forgiving an enemy. God, it seems, works in ways that are quiet and hidden from our eyes. The God that Jesus incarnates is neither dramatic nor splashy.

And there's an important faith-lesson in this. Simply put, God lies inside us, deep inside, but in a way that's almost non-existent, almost unfelt, largely unnoticed, and easily ignored. However, while that presence is never overpowering, it has within it a gentle, unremitting imperative, a compulsion towards something higher, which invites us to draw upon it. And, if we do draw upon it, it gushes up in us in an infinite stream that instructs us, nurtures us, and fills us with endless energy.

This is important for understanding faith. God lies inside us as an invitation that fully respects our freedom, never overpowers us; but also never goes away. It lies there precisely like a baby lying helpless in the straw, gently beckoning us, but helpless in itself to make us pick it up.

For example, C.S. Lewis, in explaining why he finally became, in his words, "the most reluctant convert in the history of Christendom," writes that, for years, he was able to effectively ignore a voice inside him, precisely, because it was almost non-existent, almost unfelt, and largely unnoticed. On the other hand, in retrospect, he realized it had always been there, a gentle, incessant nudge, beckoning him to draw from it, something he eventually recognized as a gentle, but unyielding, imperative, a "compulsion" which, if obeyed, leads to liberation.

Ruth Burrows, the British Carmelite and mystic, describes a similar experience in her autobiography, *Before the Living God*. Chronicling her late adolescent years, Burrows describes both her religious flightiness and her lack of attraction to the religious life at that time in her life. Yet she eventually ends up not only being serious about religion but becoming a Carmelite nun. What happened? One day, in a chapel, almost against her will, triggered by a series of accidental circumstances, she opened herself to a voice inside her that she had, until then, mainly ignored because it lay inside her precisely as a voice that was almost non-existent, almost unfelt, and largely unnoticed. But once touched, it gushed up as the deepest and most real thing inside her and set the direction of her life forever afterwards. Like C.S. Lewis, she too, once she had opened herself to it, felt it as an unyielding moral compulsion opening her to ultimate liberation.

Why doesn't God show himself to us more directly and more powerfully so as to make faith easier? That's a fair question for which, partly, there is no fully satisfying answer. But the answer we do have lies in understanding the manner in which God manifests himself in our lives and in our world. Unlike most everything else that's trying to get our attention, God never tries to overwhelm us. God, more than anyone else, respects our freedom. For this reason, God lies everywhere, inside us and around us, almost unfelt, largely unnoticed, and easily ignored, a quiet, gentle nudge; but, if drawn upon, the ultimate stream of love and energy.

—*In Exile,* April 21, 2014

WHY DARK NIGHTS OF THE SOUL?

Atheism is a parasite that feeds on bad religion. That's why, in the end, atheistic critics are our friends. They hold our feet to the fire.

Friedrich Nietzsche, Ludwig Feuerbach, and Karl Marx, for example, submit that all religious experience is ultimately psychological projection. For them, the God we believe in and who undergirds our churches is, at the end of the day, simply a fantasy we have created for ourselves to serve our own needs. We have created God as opium for comfort and to give ourselves divine permission to do what we want to do.

They're largely correct, but partially wrong, and it's in where they're wrong that true religion takes it root. Admittedly, they're right in that a lot of religious experience and church life is far from pure, as is evident in our lives. It's hard to deny that we are forever getting our own ambitions and energies mixed up with what we call religious experience. That's why, so often, we, you and I, sincere religious people, don't look like Jesus at all: We're arrogant where we should be humble, judgmental where we should be forgiving, hateful where we should be loving, self-concerned where we should be altruistic, and, not least, spiteful and vicious where we should be understanding and merciful. Our lives and our churches often don't radiate Jesus. Atheism is a needed challenge because far too often we have our own life force confused with God and our own ideologies confused with the Gospel.

Fortunately, God doesn't let us get away with it for long. Rather, as the mystics teach, God inflicts us with a confusing, painful grace called, a *dark night of the soul*. What happens in a dark night of the soul is that we run out of gas religiously in that the religious experiences that once sustained us and gave us fervor dry up or get crucified in a way that leaves us with no imaginative, affective, or emotional sense of either God love or of God's existence. No effort on our part can again conjure up the feelings and images we once had about God and the security we once felt within ourselves about our faith and religious beliefs. The heavens empty and inside of ourselves we feel agnostic, as if God didn't exist, and we are no longer able to create an image of God that feels real to us. We become helpless inside of ourselves to generate a sense of God.

But that's precisely the beginning of real faith. In that darkness, when we have nothing left, when we feel there is no God, God can begin to flow into us a pure way. Because our interior religious faculties are paralyzed we can no longer manipulate our experience of God, fudge it, project ourselves into it, or use it to rationalize divine permission for our own actions. Real faith begins at the exact point where our atheistic critics think it ends, in darkness and emptiness, in religious impotence, in our powerlessness to influence how God flows into us.

Even Jesus, in his humanity, had to undergo this darkness, as is evident in Gethsemane and his cry of abandonment on the cross. After his agony in the Garden of Gethsemane, we are told that an angel came and strengthened him. Why, we might ask, didn't the angel come earlier when seemingly he most needed the help? God's assistance couldn't come until he was completely spent in terms of his own strength; his humanity wouldn't have let the divine flow in purely but would have inserted itself into the experience. He had to be completely spent of his own strength before the divine could truly and purely flow in. So too for us.

Dark nights of faith are needed to wash us clean because only then can the angel come to help us. —*In Exile,* November 14, 2016

TO WHOM CAN WE GO?

"To whom else shall we go? You have the message of eternal life." Peter says these words to Jesus. But they are spoken in a very conflicted context: Jesus had just said something that upset and offended his audience and the Gospels tell us that everyone walked away grumbling that what Jesus was teaching was "intolerable." Jesus then turns to his apostles and asks them: "Do you want to walk away too?" Peter answers: "To whom

else can we go?" But that's more a statement of stoic resignation than an actual question.

His words function at two levels. On the surface, they express an unwanted humility and helplessness that sometimes beset us all: "I have no alternative! I'm so invested in this relationship that now I have no other options. I'm stuck with this!" That's a humble place to stand and anyone who has ever given himself or herself over in an authentic commitment will eventually stand on that place, knowing that he or she no longer has another practical choice.

But those words also express a much deeper quandary, namely, where can I find meaning if I cannot find it in faith in God? All of us have at some point asked ourselves that question. If I didn't believe in God and had no faith or religion, what would give meaning to my life?

Where can we go if we no longer have an explicit faith in God? A lot of places, it seems. I think immediately of so many attractive stoics who have wrestled with this question and found solace in various forms of what Albert Camus would call "metaphysical rebellion" or in the kind of Epicureanism that Nikos Kazantzakis advocates in *Zorba, the Greek*. There's a stoicism which offers its own kind of salvation by drawing life and meaning simply from fighting chaos and disease for no other reason than that these cause suffering and are an affront to life, just as there is an Epicureanism that meaningfully grounds life in elemental pleasure. There are, it would seem, different kinds of saints.

There are also different kinds of immortality. For some, meaning outside of an explicit faith, is found in leaving a lasting legacy on this earth, having children, achieving something monumental, or becoming a household name. We're all familiar with the axiom: *Plant a tree; write a book; have a child!*

Poets, writers, artists, and artisans often have their own place to find meaning outside of explicit faith. For them, creativity and beauty can be ends in themselves. Art for art's sake. Creativity itself can seem enough.

And there are still others for whom deep meaning is found simply in being good for its own sake and in being honest for its own sake. There's also virtue for virtue's sake and virtue is indeed its own reward. Simply living an honest and generous life can provide sufficient meaning with which to walk through life.

So, it appears that there are places to go outside of explicit faith where one can find deep meaning. But is this really so? Don't we believe that true meaning can only be found in God? Can anything other than faith and God really quiet the restless fires within us?

Yes, there are things that can do that, but all of them—fighting chaos, curing diseases, having children, living for others, building things, inventing things, achieving goals, or simply living honest and generous lives—leave us, in an inchoate way, radiating the transcendental properties of God and working alongside God to bring life and order to the world. How so?

Christian theology tells us that God is *One, True, Good*, and *Beautiful*. And so, when an artist gives herself over to creating beauty, when a couple has a child, when scientists work to find cures for various diseases, when artisans make an artifact, when builders build, when teachers teach, when parents parent, when athletes play a game, when manual laborers labor, when administrators administrate, when people just for the sake integrity itself live in honesty and generosity, and, yes, even when hedonists drink deeply of earthily pleasure, they are, all of them, whether they have explicit faith or not, acting in some faith because they are putting their trust in either the *Oneness, Truth, Goodness*, or *Beauty* of God.

Lord, to whom else can we go? You have the message of eternal life. Well, it seems that there are places to go and many go there. But these aren't necessarily, as is sometimes suggested by misguided spiritual literature, empty places that are wrong and self-destructive. There are, of course, such places, spiritual dead-ends; but, more generally, as we can see simply by looking at the amount of positive energy, love, creativity, generosity, and honesty that still fill our world, those places where people who are seeking God outside of explicit faith still has them meeting God. —*In Exile,* June 26, 2017

SELF-ABANDONMENT AND OBEDIENCE UNTO DEATH

There is a contemporary parable told about a Cretan peasant. He was a man who deeply loved his life and his work. He enjoyed tilling the soil, feeling the warm sun on his naked back as he worked in the fields, and feeling the soil under his feet. He loved the planting, the harvesting, the very smell of nature. He loved especially his wife and his children and his friends, and he enjoyed being with them, eating together, drinking wine, talking, making love, and simply being united in a shared life. And he loved Crete, his tiny country. The earth, the sky, the sea, it was his! This was his home.

One day he sensed that death was near. What frightened him, however was not fear of the beyond, for he had lived a good life. No. What he feared was leaving Crete, leaving his wife, his children, his friends, his home, and his land. Thus, as he prepared to die, he grasped in his hand a few grams of soil from his beloved Crete and told his loved ones to bury him with it.

He died, awoke, and found himself at heaven's gate, the soil still in his hand, and heaven's gate firmly barred against him. Eventually St. Peter emerged through the heavy gates and addressed him: "You've lived a good life, and we have a place for you inside, but you cannot enter unless you drop that handful of soil. You cannot enter as you are now." The man, however, was reluctant to drop the soil and protested: "Why? Why must I let go of this soil? Indeed, I will not! What's inside those gates I don't know. But this soil I know—it's my life, my wife, my works my family, it's all that I know and love, it's Crete! I will not let it go!"

Silent, seemingly defeated, Peter left him and closed the large gates behind him. There seemed little point in arguing with the peasant. Several minutes later, the gates opened a second time and this time, from them, emerged a very young child. She did not try to reason with the man, nor did she try to coax him into letting go of the soil in his hand. She simply took his hand and, as she did, it opened and the soil of Crete spilled to the ground. She then led him through the gates of heaven. A shock awaited the man as he entered heaven . . . there, before him, lay all of Crete.

This parable illustrates what Jesus meant when he said that one of the dictates inherent in love itself is that it demands "obedience unto death." Love demands, by its very nature, that we continually let go of what we cling to instinctually and pragmatically so as to be open to receive that very thing in its reality and fullness. To be obedient to love, to give oneself over to its inherent dynamics, means, always, hearing the call to self-sacrifice, to self-abandonment, to let oneself be "broken."

All three of the contemplative traditions that we outlined previously make this point. The mystics tell us that we come to purity of heart by moving beyond ourselves; the Protestant tradition on holiness assures us that purity of heart lies in submission to the Holy; and the tradition of philosophical theism highlights the point that we are in fact always acting under obedience to some God. Thus, for all of them, purity of heart will only come when we give ourselves over to something above us.

Jesus expresses this in his own way at the end of John's Gospel. After having asked Peter three times: "Do you love me?" and being assured by Peter that he does, Jesus says to him: "When you were younger, you girded your belt and walked wherever you wished; but when you grow old, you will stretch out your hands, and someone else will gird you, and bring you to where you would rather not go." What Jesus is telling Peter is that part of the essence of love, of any life of true self-giving, is a certain conscriptive obedience—being led, by something and Somebody outside oneself, to where one would rather not go. Dag Hammarskjöld, in a famous entry in his diaries, put it this way: "I don't know who—or what—put the question, I don't know when it was put. I don't even remember answering. But at some moment I did answer yes to someone—or something—and from that hour I was certain that existence is meaningful and that, therefore, my life, in self-surrender, had a goal."

The road beyond the practical atheism of our everyday consciousness lies in obedience and self-abandonment. If John of the Cross were your spiritual director and you went to him with the complaint that God did not seem very alive or real to you in your everyday life, he would, among other things, prescribe this exercise: "As unpopular as this advice might be in a world that tells you, above all, to do your own thing, bend your will according to the beatitudes of Jesus. Stand before your loved ones and before your God and practice saying what Jesus said to his Father in the garden: 'Not my will, but yours, be done.' Then come back in a few years and tell me whether or not God still seems absent within your experience."

Revirginization and Second Naïveté

If you ask a naïve child: "Do you believe in Santa Claus?" he or she will say yes. If you ask a bright child the same question, he or she will say no. However, if you ask yet an even brighter child that question, he or she will reply yes . . . , though now for a different reason.

This little vignette is a prescriptive counsel for the restoration of wonder within our lives. A truly contemplative consciousness, one that is truly attuned to the full depth and mystery within reality, not only *wonders-how* but it especially *wonders-at*, and one wonders-at things when one has the eyes, the mind, and the heart of a child and a virgin.

Simply put, the principle here can be expressed as follows: to perceive what is most primitive and primordial in reality, we need something akin to a primitive spirit; to perceive virginal truth, we need a virginal spirit; and to consistently see the truth about the childhood of the world, we need to see the world with a certain childlike directness. To come to purity of heart we must strive constantly to live in a second naïveté and to, daily, revirginize.

What is involved in this process?

Revirginization refers to a process of continually recapturing the posture of a child before reality, while second naïveté describes that posture as it exists in an adult who has already moved beyond the natural naïveté of a child but who is not fixated in the deserts of cynicism, criticism, and false sophistication. Second naïveté refers to a condition of being post-critical, post-adult, post-sophisticated. But this calls for explanation.

As children we are natural contemplatives. We spontaneously wonder at things and we see things with a certain directness. Reality, for a child, is naturally mysterious. As well, for a child, reality is all too full of the aesthetic and the supernatural. Little children, prior to the critical judgments that come with sophistication, perceive the world as laden with beauty and spirits. It is easy for children to believe in angels, ghosts, and other supernatural and mythical things; only as we mature and grow more critical, and thus approach reality with more *a priori* filters, do we grow skeptical and begin to despoil the world of its full aesthetic, mysterious, romantic, and supernatural dimensions.

But this is a necessary and a good process. A child's natural contemplative faculties are based upon, among other things, a certain naïveté that would hardly be an ideal quality within an adult. As we grow to maturity, it is for our own good that our critical and practical faculties sharpen. Our naïveté should disappear. However, as we hinted earlier, this growth in being critical and practical is itself not an end, but simply part of a process of further development. Beyond the loss of natural naïveté and natural contemplativeness lies another kind of naïveté and another kind of awareness, second naïveté, the awareness which returns us to the posture of a child, which sees again with the directness of a child, but has now integrated into that posture the critical and practical concerns of an adult. In natural naïveté we are childish; In second naïveté we are childlike.

Unfortunately, and this is especially true today in a postmodern and very sophisticated culture, the criticalness which destroys our initial naïveté is taken, all too often, as an end in itself. Childishness is destroyed but there is no movement towards childlikeness. Virginity is lost but there is no movement towards revirginization. When that happens, there sets in a certain fatigue within human perception. As Chesterton puts it, we then fall in "the greatest of all illusions, the illusion of familiarity." This familiarity manifests itself as a tiredness of soul, which Allan Bloom, the American philosopher of education, rightly calls "eros gone lame."

Moreover, with that familiarity, almost always, there occurs a certain loss of innocence, a loss of virginity. We become progressively less childlike, losing the sense of awe that is characteristic of being a child. We grow rather in experience, knowledge, and sophistication which militate against naïveté. We become life-smart, and proud of it. Like Adam and Eve, after the fall, our eyes are opened. With that comes the proclivity for cynicism since life now holds few surprises, few taboos, and few sacred dimensions. In metaphorical terms, we now stand before the burning bush with our shoes on. It is not surprising that it is children, not adults, who like to go barefoot.

It is when this loss of our childish naïveté and the attendant increase in criticalness, sophistication, and knowledge are not seen as part of a further development, namely, growth towards second naïveté, second innocence, and second virginity, that distorted awareness and practical atheism occur in our lives. Why? Because when this happens, true agnosticism ceases and, with it, true wonder. There is an unhealthy fixation at a certain level of questioning and experiencing and there is a refusal to contemplate. Atheism and idolatry take their basis there.

Thus, if we want a more real sense of God within our lives we must move towards second naïveté. We must constantly revirginize. What specifically does this entail? It entails touching the nerve of novelty, purging ourselves of the illusion of familiarity, and learning to see things as if seeing them for the first time. The answer to atheism and agnosticism is not a closed mind, but a higher agnosticism, wonder. And we move towards this higher agnosticism when we, deliberately and consciously, make the attempt to purge ourselves of all traces of cynicism, contempt, and of every attitude, however subtle and unconscious, which would identify mystery with ignorance. . . .

What type of *praxis* leads us towards an awareness which allows us to see reality in this way? Again, let me resort to metaphor. Two metaphors are particularly helpful here.

The image of weather revirginizing a geographical terrain. Imagine a geographical terrain that has been ravaged by natural disaster and despoiled by human beings. Its waters are dirty and polluted, its vegetation is dead, and its natural beauty is destroyed. However, given time and weather—sun, rains, winds, storms, frost and snow—it, in time, will revirginize. Its waters will again grow clear and pure, its vegetation will return, and eventually its natural beauty too returns. It again becomes virgin territory. So too our hearts, our minds, our souls, and our bodies: as soon as we stop despoiling them through the illusion of familiarity, the attitude which thinks it has already understood, they too will regain, gradually, their virginity and begin again to blush in the very wonder of knowing and loving. A chastity in perceiving will return.

The image of fetal darkness. Imagine the gestation process within a womb. The process begins with a microscopic egg, a cellular speck, which is being gestated, formed, cared for, shaped by things around it, and which is nourished by a reality that is infinitely larger than itself. The process takes place in darkness, in a dark place. Eventually the child has grown sufficiently and emerges from the darkness, opens his or her eyes to the light, and sees this world for the first time. The sheer overwhelmingness of what it sees so overpowers the child that it takes a long time, years of time, for the child's senses and mind to harden sufficiently so that it can begin to understand. Initially the child just looks and wonders. So too the process of being reborn, to second naïveté, to new virginity. To revirginize we must, metaphorically speaking, make a recessive journey, a voyage to the sources, to the fetal darkness of the womb, and be reduced again to a mere egg so that we can be gestated anew in a dark understanding that, in the words of John of the Cross, understands more by not understanding than by understanding, so that we can again open our eyes and see a reality which is so wild, so startling, so agnostic, and so overpowering that we are reduced to silence, unable to name and number, able only to ponder and to wonder.

A few qualifications are called for here, however: as we said before, childlikeness should not be confused with childishness and second naïveté is not to be identified with simply being naïve. Second naïveté is not a posture that willfully blinds itself to hard reality and refuses to ask the tough questions. It is not a sticking of one's head in the sand or a false optimism, nor is it anti-intellectual and anti-critical. It is postcritical, post-sophisticate, post-taboo breaking. It is genuinely agnostic, fully open to wonder, believing that it knows so little and reality is so rich and multifarious that perhaps there might be a Santa Claus and an Easter Bunny after all.

And there, too, might be a God after all! Atheism is not, as is so popularly purported, the result of us, the human race, coming of age, of finally asking the hard questions with nerve and having the courage to rid ourselves of fairy tales and superstitions. Atheism, for the most part, is rooted in the opposite. It questions too little, it examines too narrowly, it is a fixation at a certain level of wonder and agnosticism. In the end, as the mystical tradition asserts, it arises out of a certain lack of chastity in perception. Jesus tells us that it is children and virgins that intuit the kingdom and see God. It is not surprising that atheism, both of the theoretical and the practical variety, has never been big on either childlikeness or virginity.

Thus, to exercise again our contemplative muscles so as to regain the ancient instinct for astonishment, we must work at revirginization, at regaining the wonder, the awe, and the openness of a child. If Jesus was my spiritual director and I came to him complaining that the sense of God was habitually absent within my everyday experience, I suspect that, among other things, he would challenge me to try to get into a more vital contact with the little boy and the virgin within me.

—*The Shattered Lantern*, 187–195

THE DESERT—THE PLACE OF GOD'S CLOSENESS

In her biography, *The Long Loneliness*, Dorothy Day shares how, shortly after her conversion to Catholicism, she went through a painful, desert time. She had just given birth to her daughter and her decision to have the child baptized, coupled with her profession of faith, meant the end of her relationship with a man she deeply loved. She suddenly found herself alone. All her old supports had been cut off and she was left with no money, no job, few friends, no practical dream, and no companionship from the person she loved the most deeply in this world. For a while she just stumbled on, trusting that things would soon get better. They didn't. She remained in this desert.

One day, she traveled to Washington, D.C. to write about a "hunger march" of the unemployed, organized by the Communists. Finding herself wishing that Catholics could be leading such a march, she visited the National Shrine of the Immaculate Conception, and there offered a prayer "with tears and anguish" that she might find her vocation. Her prayer there was wrenching, naked. She describes how she laid bare her helplessness, spilling out her confusion, her doubts, her fears, and her temptations to bitterness and despair. In essence, she said to God: "I have given up everything that ever supported me, in trust, to you. I have nothing left to hold on to. You need to do something for me, soon. I can't keep this up much longer!" She was, biblically speaking, in the desert—alone, without support, helpless before a chaos that threatened to overwhelm her—and, as was the case with Jesus, both in the desert and in Gethsemane, God "sent angels to minister to her." God steadied her in the chaos. She caught a train back to New York and, that very night, as she walked up to her apartment she saw a man sitting there. His name was Peter Maurin and the rest is history. Together they started the Catholic Worker. We should not be surprised that her prayer had such a tangible result. The desert, scripture assures us, is the place where God is specially near.

Martin Luther King shares a similar story. In *Stride Towards Freedom*, he relates how one night a hate-filled phone call shook him to his depths and plunged him into a desert of fear. Here are his words:

> *An angry voice said: "Listen, nigger, we've taken all we want from you; before next week you'll be sorry you ever came to Montgomery." I hung up, but I couldn't sleep. It seemed that all of my fears had come down on me at once. I had reached the saturation point. I got out of bed and began to walk the floor. Finally I went to the kitchen and heated a pot of coffee. I was ready to give up. With my coffee sitting untouched before me I tried to think of a way to move out of the picture without appearing a coward. In this state of exhaustion, when my courage had all but gone, I decided to take my problem to God. With my head in my hand, I bowed over the kitchen table and prayed aloud. The words I spoke to God that midnight are still vivid in my memory.*
>
> *"I am here taking a stand for what I believe is right. But now I am afraid. The people are looking to me for leadership and if I stand before them without strength and courage, they too will falter. I am at the end of my powers. I have nothing left. I've come to the point where I can't take it alone." At that moment I experienced the presence of the Divine as I had never experienced Him before.*

God sends his angels to minister to us when we are in the desert and in the garden of Gethsemane. This incident in Martin Luther King's life demonstrates how.

The desert, as we know, is the place where, stripped of all that normally nourishes and supports us, we are exposed to chaos, raw fear, and demons of every kind. In the desert we are exposed, body and soul, made vulnerable to be overwhelmed by chaos and temptations of every kind. But, precisely because we are so stripped of everything we normally rely on, this is also a privileged moment for grace. Why? Because all the defense mechanisms, support systems, and distractions that we normally surround ourselves with so as to keep chaos and fear at bay work at the same time to keep much of God's grace at bay. What we use to buoy us upwards off both chaos and grace, demons and the divine alike. Conversely, when we are helpless we are open. That is why the desert is both the place of chaos and the place of God's closeness. It is no accident that Dorothy Day and Martin Luther King felt God's presence so unmistakably just at that point in their lives where they had lost everything that could support them. They were in the desert. Scripture assures us that it is there that God can send angels to minister to us.

—*In Exile,* April 2, 2000

GOD'S MERCY AND PEACE

We must give up the mistaken notion that in committing suicide, a person puts himself or herself outside of God's mercy.

After the resurrection, we see Christ, time and again, going through locked doors to breathe forgiveness, love, and peace into hearts that are unable to open up because of fear and hurt. God's mercy and peace can reach through when we can't. This side of eternity, sometimes all the love, stretched-out hands, and professional help in the world can no longer reach through to a heart locked inside a prison of pain and illness. We try to reach through but our efforts are for naught and suicide claims our loved one anyway.

God's compassion however can reach through where ours can't. God's love can descend into hell, where it can breathe peace and reconciliation right into the middle of wound, anger, and fear. God's hands are gentler than our own, God's understanding infinitely surpasses ours, and God is not, as scripture assures us, stymied by locked doors in the same way as we are.

When our loved ones die of suicide and awake on the other side, Christ is standing inside their huddled fear, gently saying: "Peace be with you." Jesus told us that God does not promise to eliminate pain, death, and suicide in this world. These remain. What God does promise is to redeem these, to write straight with their crooked lines, and to rescue us even beyond suicide.

Then too there is the myth about suicide that expresses itself this way: This could have been prevented if only I had done more, been more attentive, and been there at the right time. Rarely is this the issue. Most of the time, we weren't there for the very reason that the person who fell victim to this disease did not want us to be there. He or she picked the moment, the spot, and the means precisely so that we wouldn't be there. Perhaps, more accurately, it could be said that suicide is a disease that picks its victim precisely in such a way so as to exclude others and their attentiveness.

Of course, this may never be an excuse for insensitivity to the needs of others, especially those suffering from dangerous depression, but it is a healthy check against false guilt and neurotic second-guessing. I have stood at the bedside of a number of people who were dying and there wasn't anything I could do to stop the process. They died, despite my attentiveness, presence, and prayers. So too, generally, with those who have died of suicide. We were present in their lives to the end, though not (as we found out after the fact) in a way that could stop them from dying.

The Christian response to suicide should not be horror, fear for the victim's eternal salvation, and guilty self-examination about what we didn't do. Suicide is indeed a horrible way to die, but we must understand it for what it is, a sickness, and then stop second-guessing and worrying about the eternal salvation of its victim. In the pain of losing a loved one to suicide, we must affirm the bottom line of our faith, God redeems everything and, in the end, all will be well and every manner of being will be well—even beyond suicide. —*In Exile,* July 30, 2000

ON THE ROAD TO EMMAUS

Nearly 2,000 years ago, two disillusioned youths consoled each other as they walked that seven-mile stretch of road separating Jerusalem from Emmaus. They moved slowly, depression having taken the spring from their steps. A double feeling clung to their hearts that day. They were hurting and there was reason. Their messiah and their dreams had just been crucified. A deep dark disappointment dampened their spirits. And there was fear. Most of all, there was fear. Not fear that they themselves might be crucified. That prospect loomed more welcome than the thought of going on. Theirs was that more horrible fear, the fear that comes from the realization that perhaps nothing makes a difference after all, maybe our dreams and our hopes point to nothing more real than Santa and the Easter Bunny. Maybe hope is only for children and the naïve? They had been so excited, so full of hope. The uncrucified Christ had filled them with a dream. With that dream had come a new innocence, a freshness, an energy, a feeling absent since they had been children and which, prior to meeting Jesus, they had, long ago, unconsciously despaired of ever feeling again.

One weekend, one black Friday, had changed it all. They walked now, realistic again, more than 48 hours older, their dreams, like their messiah, dead, entombed. They had grown up a lot in one weekend. Their naïveté had died as it hung exposed, mocked and ridiculed by the wise. There was a lesson hard learned, but it brought a hurt and a disappointment beyond words. But another feeling clung to them too, like a demon refusing to be exorcised. The dream still burned holes in their hearts. Mocked and dead—maybe it didn't matter? Maybe something was more real than even death! Hurt beyond words, confused beyond doubts, they searched for words, grasped for trust. Then a stranger caught their step and caught their mood. They didn't recognize him. How could they? In their loss of trust, their messiah had died.

But the stranger begins to find the words: "Do they not yet understand the ways of God? Isn't it always when they don't understand, and have to trust, that they understand the most deeply? Wasn't it necessary for naïveté to be so exposed and ridiculed? Is that not its glory?" His words burned in them, touching and soothing that same deep part of the heart where the dream had lain. But they were only words, a balm, a momentary salve, nothing more. The doubt, the hurt, the fear, these lingered on. Emmaus and twilight appeared at the same time. The stranger had been a consolation. Why not ask him to stay? They continued to share, bread and consolation. Suddenly their eyes were opened. Their minds and hearts were opened even further. They understood. Jesus was with them again. The dream exploded anew like an atom split. They split, immediately, for the ends of the earth, hanging their naïveté and their dreams on crosses everywhere. The dream never died again. Easter Sunday had eclipsed a godless Friday. Christianity goes through multiple moods and feelings. Each age must struggle with its own emotions. Today, in terms of feeling, we live in that time between Good Friday and Easter Sunday. We are trudging along the road to Emmaus. Like the two disciples, we live with crucified dreams. Aesthetically, romantically, ethically, and religiously, we are surrounded by despair and its child, cynicism.

Dreams are giving way before the caveat of the cynic; faith is daily being displaced by doubt; and perseverance and long-suffering are all but extinct in a culture and church of release and enjoyment. Worst of all, there is fear, an unconscious fear whose tentacles are beginning to color every facet of life. It is the fear that perhaps our Christian hopes and dreams point to nothing beyond our own hopes and dreams. Perhaps faith is, after all, only a naïveté. Isn't Christ as dead as he was on Good Friday? Who, save perhaps for a few good thieves, is still turning to a cross for salvation? Yet there is something else: The dream still clings to us, refusing to let us go. It burns holes in us still, hanging on to us, even when in infidelity and despair we can no longer hang on to it. Hope is still more real than death. In our hurt, we are struggling for words and grasping for trust. We need to remain on the road to Emmaus. The stranger still stalks that same road. In his company we need to discuss our doubts, discuss the scriptures and continually offer each other bread and consolation. At some moment too, our eyes will be opened. We will understand and we will recognize the risen Lord. Then the dream will explode anew like a flower bursting in bloom after a long winter. We will be full of a new innocence. Easter Sunday will happen again. —*In Exile,* April 1, 1984

8

The Prominent Place of Justice and Charity

Ron credits his professors in San Francisco with introducing him to the riches of Catholic social teaching. In The Holy Longing, *he names social justice as one of the four essential pillars undergirding any healthy Christian life. (The other three pillars are private prayer and private morality; mellowness of heart and spirit; and community as a constitutive element of true worship.)*

In this chapter, he begins by explaining the difference between social justice and private charity from the perspective of Christian discipleship. All Christians must be attuned to the issues of social justice. Private charity, while important, is not enough. "We can be wonderfully charitable, kind, moral, and generous," Ron writes, "and still be unfairly profiting from an historical, social, political, and economic system that is unduly rewarding us even as it is unfairly burdening and robbing others." God always stands on the side of the weak, Ron reminds us, and we must too. He closes this chapter with a bracing riff on a familiar prayer: "A Lord's Prayer for Justice."

SOCIAL JUSTICE—NEW KNOWLEDGE/NEW RESPONSIBILITY

Former Jesuit Superior General, Pedro Arrupe, was once asked why there is such an emphasis today on social justice when, in the past, many saintly persons and good spiritual writings appeared to almost entirely neglect this, at least in terms of an explicit development. He answered rather simply: "Today we know more!"

He's right. In the past, because we knew less, it was possible to be good and saintly and less involved in social justice, despite the fact that scripture and Christ's explicit teaching make the call to justice just as non-negotiable as the call to prayer and private morality. Today we know more, not just because modern communications daily shows us the victims of injustice on our television screens and in our newspapers, but also, and especially, because we are less sociologically naïve. Put positively, this lack of naïveté means that we understand better how social systems affect us, both for good and for bad . . . and social justice is really about how *systems* affect us, especially adversely.

It is very important that this be understood. Although they interpenetrate each other and depend upon each other, social justice and social morality are distinct from private charity and private morality. Private morality is something that, precisely, I do on my own. Other persons might guide me or inspire me, but, in the end, I am moral and charitable at this level on the basis of my own personal goodness and personal actions. Social justice, on the other hand, has to do with the social systems I am part of and participate in. I can be a good person in my private life, churchgoing, prayerful, kind, honest, gentle, and generous in my dealings with others, and still, at the same time, be part of a social, economic, political, and even ecclesial system that is unfair in that it works for the benefit of some at the cost of victimizing others. Issues such as war, poverty, violation of the ecology, feminism, native rights, abortion, and racism (to name just a few) are caused not just, nor indeed any longer primarily, by individual persons acting in bad conscience and doing bad things, but by huge impersonal systems which are inherently unfair and are, to an extent, beyond the control of the individuals who participate in them.

Let me try to illustrate the difference between social justice and private charity with a story, famous in social justice circles:

> *Once upon time there was a town which was built beyond the bend in a river. One day some of its children were playing by the river when they spotted 3 bodies floating in the water. They ran to get help and the towns-folk quickly pulled the bodies from the river. One body was dead so they buried it. One was alive, but quite ill, so they put it into the hospital. The third was a healthy child, so they placed it in a family who cared for it and took it to school. From that day on, each day a number of bodies came floating around the bend in the river and, each day, the good charitable townspeople pulled them out and tended to them—burying the dead, caring for the sick, finding homes for the children, and so on. This went on for years, and the townspeople came to expect that each day would bring its quota of bodies . . . but, during those years, nobody thought to walk up the river, beyond the bend, and check out why, daily, those bodies came floating down the river.*

The difference between private charity and social justice is, in one way, the difference between handling the bodies that have come down the river and doing preventive work up the river. It's more complex than that, especially when one sees the web of intertwined social, political, historical, and economic factors responsible for those bodies, but the analogy at least helps show a key distinction. Private morality has more to do with personal charity and personal goodness and honesty. Social justice has to do more with changing systems which, although often managed by persons in good conscience, are of themselves evil in that they, knowingly or unknowingly, victimize certain people. Thus, for instance, a man may be very sincere and, in his private life, very charitable, gentle, prayerful, and moral. Yet, he might, blindly, unknowingly, participate in and help sustain (through his work, his political affiliations, his economic ideology and investments, and simply by a consumeristic lifestyle) systems which are far from charitable, gentle, prayerful, and moral. While good for him they might be horrible for others.

When Pedro Arrupe said: "Today we know more!" he was referring precisely to the fact that current sociological and economic analysis has shown us, with a clarity that we cannot rationalize any distance from, how our political, economic, social, and ecclesial systems, irrespective of how individually sincere we might be in our support of them, are unfair and wounding to so many others. Given this, daily, our ignorance is less inculpable and the imperative to "walk justly" becomes less escapable.

—*In Exile,* April 15, 1991

WHAT IS LOVE ASKING OF US NOW?

> *You can safely assume you've created God in your own image when it turns out that God hates all the same people you do.* —Anne Lamott

Those are words worth contemplating, on all sides of the political and religious divide today. We live in a time of bitter division. From our government offices down to our kitchen tables, there are tensions and divisions about politics, religion, and versions of truth that seem irreparable. Sadly, these divisions have brought out the worst in us, in all of us. Common civility has broken down and brought with it something that effectively illustrates the biblical definition of the "diabolic"—widespread lack of common courtesy, disrespect, demonization and hatred of each other. All of us now smugly assume that God hates all the same people we do. The polarization around the recent U.S. elections, the storming of the U.S. Capitol buildings by a riotous mob, the bitter ethical and religious debates about abortion, and the loss of a common notion of truth, have made clear that incivility, hatred, disrespect, and different notions of truth rule the day.

Where do we go with that? I am a theologian and not a politician or social analyst so what I say here has more to do with living out Christian discipleship and basic human maturity than with any political response. Where do we go religiously with this?

Perhaps a helpful way to probe for a Christian response is to pose the question this way: What does it mean to love in a time like this? What does it mean to love in a time when people can no longer agree on what is true? How do we remain civil and respectful when it feels impossible to respect those who disagree with us?

In struggling for clarity with an issue so complex, sometimes it can be good to proceed via the *Via Negativa*, that is, by first asking what should we avoid doing. What should we not do today?

First, we should not bracket civility and legitimize disrespect and demonization; but we should also not be unhealthily passive, fearful that speaking our truth will upset others. We may not disregard truth and let lies and injustices lie comfortable and unexposed. It is too simple to say that there are good people on both sides in order to avoid having to make real adjudications vis-à-vis the truth. There are sincere people on both sides, but sincerity can also be very misguided. Lies and injustice need to be named. Finally, we must resist the subtle (almost impossible to resist) temptation to allow our righteousness to morph into self-righteousness, one of pride's most divisive modalities.

What do we need to do in the name of love? Fyodor Dostoevsky famously wrote that love in action is a harsh and fearful thing, and our first response should be to accept that. Love is a harsh thing and that harshness is not just the discomfort we feel when we confront others or find ourselves confronted by them. Love's harshness is felt most acutely in the (almost indigestible) self-righteousness we have to swallow in order to rise to a higher level of maturity where we can accept that God loves those we hate just as much as God loves us—and those we hate are just as precious and important in God's eyes as we are.

Once we accept this, then we can speak for truth and justice. Then truth can speak to power, to "alternative truth," and to the denial of truth. That is the task. Lies must be exposed, and this needs to occur inside our political debates, inside our churches, and at our dinner tables. That struggle will sometimes call us beyond niceness (which can be its own mammoth struggle for sensitive persons). However, while we cannot always be nice, we can always be civil and respectful.

One of our contemporary prophetic figures, Daniel Berrigan, despite numerous arrests for civil disobedience, steadfastly affirmed that *a prophet makes a vow of love, not of alienation.* Hence, in our every attempt to defend truth, to speak for justice, and to speak truth to power, our dominant tone must be one of love, not anger or hatred. Moreover, the evidence that we are acting in love or alienation will always be manifest—in our civility or lack of it. No matter our anger, love still has some non-negotiables: civility and respect. Whenever we find ourselves descending to adolescent name-calling, we can be sure we have fallen out of discipleship, out of prophecy, and out of what is best inside us.

Finally, how we will respond to the times remains a deeply personal thing. Not all of us are called to do the same thing. God has given each of us unique gifts and a unique calling; some are called to loud protest, others to quiet prophecy. However, we are all called to ask ourselves the same question: *Given what is happening, what is love asking of me now?*

—*In Exile,* January 11, 2021

THE IMPORTANCE OF THE INTERIOR AND PRIVATE

We can never be challenged too strongly with regards to being committed to social justice. A key, non-negotiable, summons that comes from Jesus himself is precisely the challenge to reach out to the poor, to the excluded, to those whom society deems expendable.

Therefore the huge, global issues of justice should preoccupy us. Can we be good Christians or even decent human beings without letting the daily news baptize us? The majority of the world still lives in hunger, thousands are dying of Ebola and other such illnesses, countless lives are torn apart by war and violence, and we are still, as a world, a long ways from dealing realistically with racism, sexism, abortion, and the integrity of physical creation. These are major moral issues and we may not escape into our own private world and simply ignore them.

However, precisely because they are so mammoth and important, we can get the impression that the other moral issues we have to deal with, issues of private morality, are not as important. It's all too easy to conclude that, given the mega-problems in our world, it doesn't matter much how we live in the deeper recesses of our private worlds.

Our private, little moral concerns can look pretty petty when weighed against the problems of the world as a whole. Do we really believe that God cares much whether or not we say our morning prayers, gossip about a colleague, nurse a grudge or two, or are less than fully honest in our sexual lives? Does God really care about these things?

Yes. God cares because we care. Large, global issues notwithstanding, issues of personal integrity are generally what make or break our happiness, not to mention our character and our intimate relationships. In the end, they aren't petty concerns at all. They shape the big things. Social morality is simply a reflection of private morality. What we see in the global picture is simply a magnification of the human heart.

When ego, greed, lust, and selfishness are not dealt with inside the private recesses of the heart, it's naïve to think that they will be dealt with at a global level. How are we to build a just, loving world, if we cannot, first of all, tame selfishness inside us? There will be no transparency at a global level as long as we continue to think it's okay to not be transparent in our private lives. The global simply reflects the private. The failure to recognize this is, to my mind, the elephant in the room in terms of our inability to bring justice to the earth.

Social action that does not have private morality as its base is not spirituality, but simple political action, power dealing with power, important in itself, but the not to be confused with real transformation. The kingdom of God doesn't work that way. It works by conversion and real conversion is an eminently personal act. Carlos Castaneda, the Native American mystic, writes: "I come from Latin America where intellectuals are always talking about political and social revolution and where a lot of bombs are being thrown. But nothing has changed much. It takes little daring to bomb a building, but in order to stop being jealous or to come to internal silence, you have to remake yourself. This is where real reform begins."

Thomas Merton makes the same point. During the 1960s, when so many intellectuals were involved in various social struggles, Merton was tucked away in a monastery, far (it would seem) from the real battlefronts. Stung by outside criticism of his monastic seclusion, he admitted that to most outsiders it "must seem like small potatoes" to be engaged mainly in a war against one's private demons. However, he still believed that he was fighting the real battle: that of changing hearts. When you change a heart, he says, you have helped bring about some permanent structural, moral change on this planet. Everything else is simply one power attempting to displace another.

Private morality and all that comes with it—private prayer and the attempt to be honest and transparent in even the smallest and most secret of things—is the core from which all morality takes its root. John of the Cross, in teaching about the vital importance of honesty in small things, says: "It makes no difference whether a bird is tied down by a heavy rope or by the slenderest of cords, it can't fly in either case."

—*In Exile,* January 12, 2015

BUT WHERE ARE THE OTHERS?

Most of us have been raised to believe that we have a right to possess whatever comes to us honestly, either through our own work or through legitimate inheritance. No matter how large that wealth might be, it's ours, as long as we didn't cheat anyone along the way. By and large, this belief has been enshrined in the laws of our democratic countries and we generally believe that it is morally sanctioned by Christianity. That's partially true, but a lot needs to be nuanced here.

This is not really the view of our Christian scriptures, nor of the social teachings of the Catholic Church. Not everything we acquire honestly through our own hard work is simply ours to have. We're not islands and we don't walk through life alone, as if being solicitous for the welfare of others is something that's morally optional. The French poet and essayist, Charles Péguy, once suggested that when we come to the gates of heaven we will all be asked: "*Mais où sont les autres?*" ("But where are the others?") That question issues forth both from our humanity and our faith. *But what about the others?* It's an illusion and a fault in our discipleship to think that everything we can possess by our own hard work is ours by right. To think this way is to live the partially examined life.

Bill Gates Sr., writing in *Sojourners* in the 2003 January/February issue, challenges not only his famous son but the rest of us too with these words:

> Society has an enormous claim upon the fortunes of the wealthy. This is rooted not only in most religious traditions, but also in an honest accounting of society's substantial investment in creating fertile ground for wealth-creation. Judaism, Christianity, and Islam all affirm the right of individual ownership and private property, but there are moral limits imposed on absolute private ownership of wealth and property. Each tradition affirms that we are not individuals alone but exist in community—a community that makes claims on us. The notion that "it is all mine" is a violation of these teachings and traditions.

Society's claim on individual accumulated wealth "is rooted in the recognition of society's direct and indirect investment in the individual's success. In other words, we didn't get there on our own."

Nobody gets there on his own and so, once there, he needs to recognize that what he has accumulated is the result not just of his own work but also of the infrastructure of the whole society within which he lives.

Scripture and the Catholic social teaching would summarize it this way: God intended the earth and everything in it for the sake of all human beings. Thus, in justice, created goods should flow fairly to all. All other rights are subordinated to this principle. We do have a right to private ownership and no one may ever deny us of this right but that right is subordinated to the common good, to the fact that goods are intended for everyone. Wealth and possessions must be understood as ours to steward rather than to possess absolutely. Finally, perhaps most challenging of all, no person may have surplus if others do not have the basic necessities. In any accumulation of wealth and possessions we have to perennially face the question: *"Mais où sont les autres?"*

—*In Exile,* March 25, 2019

PROPHETIC BALANCE

A couple of years ago, while serving on a board seeking to hire a fulltime social justice director, we were discerning the pros and cons of hiring a particular person we had just interviewed. He was a man with a fierce passion for justice. Sadly, however, that passion, whatever its full motives, lacked balance, making him one-sided and unable to really hear or see anything that did not fit his vision. One of my colleagues, however, pushed strongly for hiring him: "He has the passion for it—that's what's important!"

At the time, I agreed with him, ardent passion seemed enough. I no longer agree. Prophecy is more, considerably more, than fiery passion. Anyone can be angry. Anyone can be one-sided. Anyone can be in somebody else's face. Prophecy requires more. It requires the capacity to listen, to respect, to have critical balance, to carry complexity, to walk in unresolved tension, and to empathize with those who do not agree with us. Unfortunately, that is not the current vision.

Today we pride ourselves on, precisely, being one-sided, on being so on fire about something that we refuse all balance. This is equally true for both the left and the right. Everyone, it seems, is a warrior for truth and few, it seems, remember that one man's freedom fighter is another man's fanatic. The line between prophecy, as it is currently understood, and fundamentalism is thinly drawn.

Hence, if we move in conservative circles, we tend to identify prophecy with a one-sided passion for prolife causes, family values, sexual purity, and dogmatic orthodoxy. If we move in liberal circles, prophecy then becomes an equally one-sided passion for social justice, feminism, freedom of expression, and individual rights. Good as all of these are in themselves, they may never be taken one-sidedly, but are all part of a larger truth. Curiously, both circles have some glaring ideological inconsistencies. One would think that the left would be defending communal rights and the rights of government to govern and the right would be the champion of individual rights, but passion, all on its own, makes for strange anomalies.

Thus, when passion is everything and balance is nothing you get that curious situation wherein the religious right thinks that to be religious you have to be extremist and fundamentalistic—and the religious left agrees!

What is needed today is prophecy that is more than just one-sided passion. We need, curious as this may sound, prophets who can model balance and carry the tensions of the time. Hence we need persons who can be equally passionate about both individual rights and the laws that protect those rights; about both the value of institutions that foster community and about individual expression and charism; about both private morality and social justice; about both sexual purity and sexual passion; and about both feminism and family. We need persons who can speak for sexual responsibility even as they respect the rights of gays and lesbians.

Ernst Käsemann once said that the problem in the world is that the liberals aren't pious and the pious aren't liberal. That is both true and tragic. We tend to be one or the other and yet there are prophetic qualities in both. Just imagine, if you will, a world within which the pious would be socially committed and social activists would properly value private prayer and private morality. Imagine a world within which prolife and pro-family groups would value feminism and feminists would be prolife and pro-family. Imagine someone who could be critical of church authority and ecclesial institution even as he or she could deeply love and respect the tradition that grounds him or her. Imagine someone liberal and pious both at the same time, who can, in Jesus' words, pull out of the sack the old as well as the new.

Impossible to do? Indicative of being wishy-washy and non-committed? This is someone who wants it both ways? No. This is prophecy. To be prophetic religiously is precisely to have this balance, this complexity, this capacity to carry unresolved tension, this ability to be both liberal and pious.

—*In Exile,* August 28, 1997

THE IMPORTANCE OF MELLOWNESS OF HEART

In the summer of 1985, I attended a church conference that brought together persons from every continent on earth. In the group within which I was the recording secretary, there was a young nun from the third world who was very much in the mode of Mother Teresa. She wore a traditional religious habit, had a deep life of prayer, went to Eucharist every day, and nobody could have had the slightest doubt concerning private moral life.

She was no stranger to the church's social teachings either. In sharing her story, she described how, she and her whole community, had made a decision to try to be in radical solidarity with the poor. Hence, they had abandoned many of the comforts they had formerly enjoyed. Now she lived in a convent where the nuns slept on beds with straw mattresses, had only two sets of clothing each (a Sunday habit and a work habit), fasted regularly, avoided luxuries of all kinds, and, as a ministry, worked full-time with the poor.

But that is not the end of what she would share with us.

Our conference was being held in a retreat center, near Bruges, Belgium, and the accommodations, while comfortable, were not palatial. Hence no one was scandalized that we were living too high, even as we talked about poverty in the third world.

On the fifth day, at the noon meal, Christiane Brusselmans, who had organized the conference, stood up and announced that we had been working too hard and deserved a break. Accordingly she decreed a free afternoon. Our sole challenge for the rest of the day was to go into the beautiful city of Bruges, spend the afternoon shopping, taking strolls, having drinks, and then, at 7:00 o'clock, meet at a restaurant for a gourmet dinner. A general cheer went up . . . but not everyone, as we found out the next day, was so enthusiastic.

A number of the participants later complained that it was wrong that we, while talking about the poor, should spend time and money so frivolously.

The conference ended with a Eucharist at which there was an open microphone. People were invited to come forward and share if they had experienced some deep grace. Many people spoke, especially people from the first world, who shared what a grace it was for them to meet and share with their brothers and sisters from the third world. Near the end of this, the young nun also approached the microphone and shared in words to this effect:

> *I too had a graced-experience these past days—and I was converted in a way that I never dreamed I needed to be converted. It began with the announcement of the free afternoon. From the second it was announced, something inside of me froze and I was angry. I kept thinking: What an insult to the poor! This is a waste of time and money. We are here with the money and time of the poor, and what do we do with it? We walk around terraces and drink alcohol and have a gourmet meal! I only went along because I wanted to stay with the group, but*

> *I was miserable all afternoon. We walked and looked at shops loaded with luxuries and then I was offered a drink on a cafe terrace. I was so miserable that I didn't even refuse—I drank my first gin and tonic. Everything culminated when we got to the restaurant for the dinner. I walked in, saw all the silver knives, forks, and the linen serviettes, and I felt nauseated and couldn't go through with it. I went out and sat on the bus and waited while everyone ate.*
>
> *But I had to sit there a long time. Many thoughts ran through my head and I asked myself the question: Would Jesus be in there eating and drinking and having a good time? And l had the horrible realization that he would be! I realized that there was something wrong with me. There was coldness inside me. I had become like the older brother of the prodigal son, doing all the right things, but having no celebration in my heart.*

A most revealing story. Here is a young woman who is seemingly living out Jesus' full praxis. She is praying, fasting, and giving alms, combining private prayer and a good moral life with a healthy concern for social justice. So what is missing in her life? Where is her spirituality inadequate? She, herself, gives the answer: "l was becoming too much like the older brother of the prodigal son."

Fasting, as Jesus prescribes it, also includes fasting from bitterness of heart. Mellowness of heart is a non-negotiable within the spiritual life.

—*In Exile,* April 19, 1998

SYSTEMIC INJUSTICE

Social justice has to do with changing the way the world is organized so as to make a level playing field for everyone. In simple terms this means that social justice is about trying to organize the economic, political, and social structure of the world in such a way so that it values equally each individual and more properly values the environment. Accomplishing this will take more than private charity. Present injustices exist not so much because simple individuals are acting in bad faith or lacking in charity but because huge, impersonal systems (that seem beyond the control of the individuals acting within them) disprivilege some even as they unduly privilege others. This is what social justice language terms systemic injustice and systemic violence.

To offer just one example of this, we might look at the issue of abortion. Despite the bitter rhetoric that often exists between those who favour legalized abortion and those who oppose it, nobody, ultimately, wants abortion and everyone on both sides recognizes that whenever an abortion happens something is far from ideal. Too often, though, neither side acknowledges the deeper, systemic, issues that underlie the problem. Ultimately abortion takes place because there is something wrong within the culture, within the system, and not simply because this or that particular woman is seeking to end an unwanted pregnancy. When a particular woman enters a hospital or a clinic seeking an abortion she is more than a simple individual making a private decision. She is the tip of a cultural pine-cone. Behind her, helping push her into that clinic and that decision, stands an entire system (economic, political, cultural, mythical, and sexual). Her problem is as much political as it is personal. How so?

First of all there is our political structure, democracy itself, at least in how it is presently understood and lived out. We know of course no better way to organize ourselves politically than through the democratic process, but democracy is far from perfect. At one level, it works by the free bartering of rights and skills. Capital, labour, management, workers, business corporations, elected governments, entrepreneurs, and the down-and-out all bargain and jostle with each other for resources, privileges, and power. In the ideal it is a fair system, but in practice it is not. Those who enter the arena with historical privileges, with stronger voices, and with more valued skills reap more benefits than the others. Conversely, those who have not been historically privileged, who have weaker voices, or possess less valued skills end up being disprivileged and find themselves at the bottom of the chain. It is no accident that laissez-faire democracy has rarely been kind to the poor.

In such a system, to be entirely voiceless, as are the unborn, is to be exceedingly vulnerable and in the ever-present danger of being decertified right out of existence. That is one of the systemic issues underlying abortion. There is another, more important, one.

We live in system, a cultural one, within which it is acceptable for men and women to have sex with each other even though they are in no way committed to each other and who do not wish to have children with each other. In such a system, abortion is inevitable and no laws and no law enforcement can stop it because the system will continually keep producing someone (who could be anyone) who finds herself pregnant and isolated in a way that would make the birth of this child from this man at this time an existential impossibility for her. In such a climate you will always have abortion and the particular woman who is seeking the abortion is dealing as much with a political issue as she is with a personal one. She is the tip of a pine-cone behind which stands a whole culture that has chosen to dissociate sex from marriage and procreation. In such a system, wherein sex is an extension of dating, abortion will always happen. Abortion can only stop if the system changes. This does not excuse abortion, but it does explain it.

It is the same for every other social justice issue: war, poverty, racism, sexism, the ecology. There can be no peace, universal prosperity, equality, harmony between the sexes, and proper respect for the environment until there is universal justice, that is, until the systems we live within are made to be fair to and respectful of everyone and everything. —*The Holy Longing,* 170–172

OUR NEED TO SHARE OUR RICHES WITH THE POOR

We need to give away some of our own possessions in order to be healthy. Wealth that is hoarded always corrupts those who possess it. Any gift that is not shared turns sour. If we are not generous with our gifts we will be bitterly envied and will eventually turn bitter and envious ourselves.

These are all axioms with the same warning, we can only be healthy if we are giving away some of our riches to others. Among other things, this should remind us that we need to give to the poor, not simply because they need it, though they do, but because unless we give to the poor we cannot be healthy ourselves. When we give to the poor both charity and justice are served, but some healthy self-interest is served as well, namely, we cannot be healthy or happy unless we share our riches, of every kind, with the poor. That truth is written inside human experience and inside every authentic ethical and faith tradition.

For example: We know from experience that when we give of ourselves to others we experience a certain joy in our lives, just as when we selfishly hoard or protect what is ours we grow anxious and paranoid. Native American cultures have forever enshrined this in their concept of Potlatch, namely, their belief that, while everyone has a right to private property, there are real limits to how much someone may own. Once our wealth reaches a certain point we need to begin to give some of it away—not because others need it but because our own health and happiness will begin to deteriorate if we hoard all of those possessions for ourselves.

Jewish spirituality shares the same idea: Again and again in the Jewish scriptures, we see that when a religious leader or prophet tells the Jewish community that they are the chosen people, a nation specially blessed, that affirmation comes with the admonition that this blessing is not for them alone, but that, through them, all the nations of the earth might be blessed. In Jewish spirituality, blessing is always intended to flow through the person receiving it so as to enrich others. Hindu, Buddhist, and Islamic spiritualities, each in their own way, also affirms this, namely that it is only in giving away some of our gifts that we ourselves can remain healthy.

Jesus and the Gospels, of course, teach this repeatedly and without compromise: For instance, the Gospel of Luke, a Gospel within which Jesus warns us that it is easier for a camel to pass through the eye of a needle than for a rich person to enter the Kingdom of Heaven, nevertheless praises the rich who are generous, condemning only the rich who are stingy. For Luke, generosity is the key to health and heaven. In the Gospel of Matthew, when Jesus reveals what will be great test for the final judgment, his single set of criteria have entirely to do with how we gave to the poor: Did you feed the hungry? Give drink to the thirsty? Cloth the naked? Finally, even more strongly, in the story of the widow who gives her last two pennies away, Jesus challenges us to not only give of our surplus to the poor, but to also give away some of what we need to live on. The Gospels, and the rest of the Christian scriptures, strongly challenge us to give to the poor—not because they need our charity, though they do, but because our giving to them is the only way we can stay healthy.

We see the same message, consistent and repeated, in the social doctrine of the Catholic Church.

From Pope Leo XIII's *Rerum Novarum* in 1891 to Pope Francis' recent, *Evangelii Gaudium*, we hear the same refrain: While we have a moral right to own private property, that right is not absolute and is mitigated by a number of things, namely, we only have a right to surplus when everyone else has the necessities for life. Hence, we must always be looking towards the poor in terms of dealing with our surplus. Moreover, Catholic social doctrine tells us too that the earth was given by God for everyone and that truth too limits how we define what is really ours as a possession. Properly speaking, we are stewards of our possessions rather than owners of them. Implicit in all of this, of course, is the implication that we can be moral and healthy only when we view private ownership in a larger picture that includes the poor.

We need, always, to be giving some of our possessions away in order to be healthy. The poor do need us, but we also need them. They are, as Jesus puts it so clearly when he tells us we will be judged by how we gave to the poor, our passports to heaven. And they are also our passports to health. Our health depends upon sharing our riches. —*In Exile,* March 31, 2014

PROPHETIC MANTRA ABOUT THE POOR

Nobody gets to heaven without a letter of reference from the poor! That's a quote attributed to James Forbes, an interdenominational pastor in New York City, and it wonderfully captures something that the ancient prophets of Israel underlined many centuries ago.

The great prophets of Israel had coined this mantra: The quality of your faith will be judged by the quality of justice in the land. And the quality of justice in the land will always be judged by how "widows, orphans, and strangers" are faring while you are alive. That phrase, "widows, orphans, and strangers," was code for the three weakest, most-vulnerable, groups in society at the time. For the great prophets of Israel, ultimately we will be judged religiously and morally on the basis of how the poorest of the poor fared while we were alive.

That's a scary thought which becomes scarier when we see how Jesus strongly endorsed that view. While this needs to be contextualized within Jesus' message as a whole, we have in Matthew's Gospel the famous text about the Last Judgment where Jesus tells us that, at the end of day, when we stand before the great King on the day of judgment, we will be asked only one set of questions and they all will have to do with how we treated the poor: Did you feed the hungry? Give drink to the thirsty? Welcome the stranger? Clothe the naked? Visit the sick? Visit prisoners? I doubt that any of us would have the raw courage to preach this, just as it is written in the Gospels, from any pulpit today. And yet Jesus meant it. Nobody gets to heaven without a letter of reference from the poor.

Now there's a whole series of challenges in this.

First: The demand to live lives that reflect justice and real concern for the poor is an integral and non-negotiable part of Christian discipleship. It's not something that is grounded in some particular ideology which I can buy into or neglect, as long as I am living honestly and prayerfully in my private life. It's an essential part of the Gospel, equal in demand to praying, going to church, and keeping my private moral-life in order. For a Christian, it is not enough just to be pious, good, and church-going. We need too a concrete letter of reference from the poor.

Next: What that mantra of the prophets and Jesus' teaching on the Last Judgment also teaches is that charity alone is not enough. Charity is a great virtue, integrally part of the greatest virtue of all, love. It may never be downplayed. But charity isn't necessarily justice. I can be a wonderfully charitable, kind, moral, and generous person in my own life and still be unfairly profiting from an historical, social, political, and economic system that is unduly rewarding me even as it is unfairly burdening and robbing others. The things that I attain honestly through my own hard work and which I am very generous with in terms of sharing with others, can at the same time be the product of a system which is unfair to others. Taking care of "widows, orphans, and strangers" requires not just personal goodness and charity, but requires too that I have the courage to look at how my honest wealth may also be partially the product of a dishonest system. Who loses while I gain?

Finally: The mantra of the prophets and the teachings of Jesus about the Last Judgment should be a challenge to perennially scrutinize myself with the question: Am I actually reaching out to the poor? Do I have real "orphans, widows, and strangers" in my life? Is my commitment to the poor something only in theory, an ideal that I uphold but something that never actually impacts the poor? It is easy to pay lip-service to this ideal and it is even easier to write it into my curriculum vitae so that I look good to others and feel good about myself. However, as Ruth Burrows asks: Does our rhetoric about the poor actually help them or does it just help us feel better about ourselves?

I concede that these are not easy questions and we should be slow to answer them. Sometimes all we can do is admit our helplessness. I was once at a talk given by Gustavo Gutiérrez where, after the presentation, a man stood up and, with pained honesty, shared about his own helplessness in reaching out to the poor: What can one person do in the face of all the global issues of injustice that beset us?

Gutiérrez acknowledged the complexity of the question and sympathized with the man's helplessness, but then added: "Minimally, make sure that you always have at least one concrete poor person in your life to who you are specially attending. This will ensure that your commitment will always at least have some concrete flesh!"

A single letter of reference from the poor is better than no letter at all. —*In Exile*, August 7, 2011

KISSING THE LEPER

There is a story told about Francis of Assisi, perhaps more mythical than factual, which illustrates how touching the poor is the cure for a mediocre and dying faith:

> *One night prior to his conversion, Francis, then a rich and pampered young man, donned his flashiest clothes, mounted his horse, and set off for a night of drinking and carousing. God, social justice and the poor were not on his mind. Riding down a narrow road, he found his path blocked by a leper. He was particularly repulsed by lepers, their deformities and smell revolted him, and so he tried to steer his horse around the leper, but the path was too narrow. Frustrated, angry, but with his path clearly blocked before him, Francis eventually had no other choice but to get down off his horse and try to move the leper out of his path. When he put out his hand to take the leper's arm, as he touched the leper, something inside of him snapped. Suddenly irrational, unashamed and undeterred by the smell of rotting flesh,*

he kissed that leper. His life was never the same again. In that kiss, Francis found the reality of God and of love in a way that would change his life forever.

Today many of us struggle with the same issues as did the pre-converted Francis—a pampered life and a mediocre and dying faith. We know that our faith calls us to work for social justice and that this demand is non-negotiable.

We know too, as somebody once put it with a succinctness that is praiseworthy, that strength without compassion is violence; that compassion without justice is weakness; that justice without love is Marxism; and that love without justice is baloney!

What we often don't know is that the preferential option of the poor is the cure for our mediocre and dying faith. We must kiss the leper.

Simply put, if we touch the poor, we will touch Christ. In this way, touching the poor can be a functional substitute for prayer . . . and given the power of Western culture today, we often need this substitute. Let me try to explain: Western culture today is so powerful and alluring that it often swallows us whole. Its beauty, power and promise generally takes away both our breath and our perspective. The lure of present salvation—money, sex, creativity, the good life—has, for the most part, entertained, amused, distracted and numbed us into a state where we no longer have a perspective beyond that of our culture and its short-range soteriology.

One way out of this, of course, is through prayer. A life of prayer can cure a dying faith. The problem here, however, is that what our culture erodes in us is, precisely, our life of prayer. The hardest thing to sustain within our lives today is prayer. Everything militates against it.

Given this, perhaps the only way we have of not letting ourselves be swallowed whole by our culture is to kiss the leper, to place our lot with those who have no place within the culture, namely, the poor with their many faces: the aged, the sick, the dying, the unborn, the handicapped, the unattractive, the displaced and all those others who are not valued by the culture.

To touch those who have no place within our culture is to give ourselves a perspective beyond our culture.

Daniel Berrigan, who writes eloquently on this, describes in his memoirs how much his perspective changed when he began to work fulltime in a cancer ward, ministering to the terminally ill.

When you walk home from work after a day of being with those who are dying, he says, your vision clears pretty well and what your culture offers to you no longer seems so overpowering and irresistible. Concrete contact with the poor is Christian contemplation. It knocks the scales off one's eyes!

"Whatsoever you do to the least of my people, that you do unto to me," Christ assures us. In the poor, God is ever-present in our world, waiting to be met. In the powerless, one can find the power of God; in the voiceless, one can hear the voice of God; in the economically poor, one can find God's treasures; in the weak, one can find God's strength; and in the unattractive, one can find God's beauty.

The glory of God might indeed be humanity fully alive, but the privileged presence of God lies especially in and with the poor.

Thus, like Francis, we need to get off our horses and kiss the leper. If we do, something will snap, we will see our pampered lives for what they are, and God and love will break into our lives in such a way that we will never be the same again.

—*In Exile,* September 20, 1993

CAN THE GROUND CRY OUT?

Does the earth feel pain? Can it groan and cry out to God? Can the earth curse us for our crimes?

It would seem so, and not just because ecologists, moralists, and Pope Francis are saying so. Scripture itself seems to say so.

There are some very revealing lines in the exchange between Cain and God, after Cain had murdered his brother Abel. Asked where his brother was, Cain tells God that he doesn't know and that he's not responsible for his brother. But God says to him: *Your brother's blood cries out to me from the ground. Now you are cursed from the ground which has opened its mouth to receive your brother's blood from your hand. When you will till the ground, it will no longer yield to you its strength.*

Your brother's blood cries out to me from the ground . . . and from now on the ground will curse you! Is this a metaphor or a literal truth? Is the ground we walk on, till and plant seeds in, build highways and parking lots over, and call "Mother Earth," nothing other than simple dumb, lifeless, speechless, brute matter which is totally immune to the suffering and pain that humans and other sentient beings feel or indeed to the violence we sometimes inflict on it? Can the earth cry out to God in frustration and pain? Can it curse us?

A recent, wonderfully provocative book by Mark L. Wallace entitled *When God was a Bird—Christianity, Animism, and the Re-Enchantment of the Word* would say, yes, the world can and does feel pain and it can and does curse us for causing that pain. For Wallace, what God says to Cain about the earth crying out because it is soaked in murderous blood is more than a metaphor, more than just a spiritual teaching. It also expresses an ontological truth in that there is a real causal link between moral degeneration and ecological degeneration. We're not the only ones who bear the consequences of sin, so too does the earth.

Here's how Wallace puts it:

> The earth is not dumb matter, an inanimate object with no capacity of feeling and sentiment, but a spirited and vulnerable living being who experiences the terrible and catastrophic loss of Abel's death. Its heart is broken and its mouth agape, Earth "swallows," in the text's startling imagery, mouthfuls of Abel's blood. . . . Bubbling up from the red earth, Abel's cries signal not only that Cain had murdered his brother but that he has done lasting, perhaps irreparable, violence to the earth as well. . . .

> [Now] wounded and bloodied, Earth strikes back. Earth has its revenge. Earth does not passively acquiesce to Cain's attacks and stand by and watch his gory rampage proceed with impunity. On the contrary, Earth retaliates and "inflicts a curse" on Cain by "withholding its bounty" from this farmer-killer who now must roam the land unprotected and without security.

The earth now refuses to give its bounty to Cain.

What Wallace affirms here is predicated on two beliefs, both true. First, everyone and everything on this planet, sentient and non-sentient being alike, are all part of one and the same supreme living organism within which every part ultimately affects all the other parts in a real way. Second, whenever we treat the earth (or each other) badly, the earth retaliates and withholds its strength and bounty from us, not just metaphorically but in a very real way.

Perhaps no one puts this more poignantly than John Steinbeck did some eighty years ago in *The Grapes of Wrath*. Describing how the soil which produces our food is now worked over by massive steel tractors and huge impersonal machines that, in effect, are the very antithesis of a woman or man lovingly coaxing a garden into growth, he writes: *And when that crop grew, and was harvested, no man had crumpled a hot clod in his fingers and let the earth sift past his fingertips. No man had touched the seed, or lusted for the growth. And men ate when they had not raised, had no connection with the bread. The land bore under iron, and under iron gradually died; for it was not loved or hated, it had not prayers or curses.*

When Jesus says that the measure we measure out is the measure that will be measured back to us, he's not just speaking of a certain law of karma within human relationships where kindness will be met with kindness, generosity with generosity, pettiness with pettiness, and violence with violence. He's also speaking about our relationship to Mother Earth. The more our houses, cars, and factories continue to breathe out carbon monoxide, the more we will inhale carbon monoxide. And the more we continue to do violence to the earth and to each other, the more the earth will withhold its bounty and strength from us and we will feel the curse of Cain in violent storms, deadly viruses, and cataclysmic upheavals. —*In Exile,* November 16, 2020

EVERYTHING IS INTERCONNECTED

Everything is of one piece. Whenever we don't take that seriously, we pay a price.

There's a delightful little African tale that highlights the interconnectedness of everything and illustrates how, if we separate a thing from its sisters, we soon pay a price. The tale goes this way:

> *Once upon a time, when animals still talked, the mice on a farm called a summit of all the other animals. They were worried, they lamented, because they had seen the mistress of the house buy a mousetrap. They were now in danger. But the other animals scoffed at their anxiety. The cow said that she had nothing to worry about. A tiny little contraption couldn't harm her. She could crush it with her foot. The pig reacted in a similar way. What did he have to worry about in the face of a tiny trap? The chicken also announced that it had no fear of this gadget. "It's your concern. No worry for me!" it told the mice.*
>
> *But all things are interconnected and that soon became evident. The mistress set the mousetrap and, on the very first night, heard it snap. Getting out of her bed to look what it had caught and she saw that it had trapped a snake by its tail. In trying to free the snake she was bitten and the poison soon had her feeling sick and running a fever. She went to the doctor who gave her medicines to combat the poison and advised her: "What you need now to get better is chicken broth." (You can guess where the rest of this is going.) They slaughtered*

> *the chicken, but her fever lingered. Relatives and neighbors came to visit. More food was needed. They slaughtered the pig. Eventually the poison killed her. A huge funeral ensued. A lot of food was needed. They slaughtered the cow.*

The moral of the story is clear. Everything is interconnected and our failure to see that leaves us in peril. Blindness to our interdependence, willful or not, is dangerous. We are inextricably tied to each other and to everything in the world. We can protest to the contrary but reality will hold its ground. And so, we cannot truly value one thing while we disdain something else. We cannot really love one person while we hate someone else. And we cannot give ourselves an exemption in one moral area and hope to be morally healthy as a whole. Everything is of one piece. There are no exceptions. When we ignore that truth we are eventually snake-bitten by it.

I emphasize this because today, virtually everywhere, a dangerous tribalism is setting in. Everywhere, not unlike the animals in that African tale, we see families, communities, churches, and whole countries focusing more or less exclusively on their own needs without concern for other families, communities, churches, and countries. Other people's problems, we believe, are not our concern. From the narrowness in our churches, to identity politics, to whole nations setting their own needs first, we hear echoes of the cow, pig, and chicken saying: "Not my concern! I'll take care of myself. You take care of yourself!" This will come back to snake-bite us.

We will eventually pay the price for our blindness and non-concern and we will pay that price politically, socially, and economically. But we will even pay a higher price personally. What that snake-bite will do is captured in Von Balthasar's warning: Whoever ignores or denigrates beauty will, he asserts, eventually be unable to pray or to love. That's true too in all cases when we ignore our interconnectedness with others. By ignoring the needs of others we eventually corrupt our own wholeness so that we are no longer able to treat ourselves with respect and empathy and, when that happens, we lose respect and empathy for life itself—and for God—because whenever reality isn't respected it bites back with a mysterious vengeance.

—*In Exile,* January 21, 2019

A LORD'S PRAYER FOR JUSTICE

In the world's schema of things, survival of the fittest is the rule. In God's schema, survival of the weakest is the rule. God always stands on the side of the weak and it is there, among the weak, that we find God.

Given the truth of that, let me risk a commentary on the Lord's Prayer:

> ***Our Father*** *. . . who always stands with the weak, the powerless, the poor, the abandoned, the sick, the aged, the very young, the unborn, and those who, by victim of circumstance, bear the heat of the day.*
>
> ***Who art in heaven*** *. . . where everything will be reversed, where the first will be last and the last will be first, but where all will be well and every manner of being will be well.*
>
> ***Hallowed be thy name*** *. . . may we always acknowledge your holiness, respecting that your ways are not our ways, your standards are not our standards. May the reverence we give your name pull us out of the narcissism, selfishness, and paranoia that prevents us from seeing the pain of our neighbor.*
>
> ***Your kingdom come*** *. . . help us to create a world where, beyond our own needs and hurts, we will do justice, love tenderly, and walk humbly with you and each other.*
>
> ***Your will be done*** *. . . open our freedom to let you in so that the complete mutuality that characterizes your life might flow through our veins and thus the life that we*

help generate may radiate your equal love for all and your special love for the poor.

On earth as in heaven *. . . may the work of our hands, the temples and structures we build in this world, reflect the temple and the structure of your glory so that the joy, graciousness, tenderness, and justice of heaven will show forth within all of our structures on earth.*

Give *. . . life and love to us and help us to see always everything as gift. Help us to know that nothing comes to us by right and that we must give because we have been given to. Help us realize that we must give to the poor, not because they need it, but because our own health depends upon our giving to them.*

Us *. . . the truly plural us. Give not just to our own but to everyone, including those who are very different than the narrow us. Give your gifts to all of us equally.*

This day *. . . not tomorrow. Do not let us push things off into some indefinite future so that we can continue to live justified lives in the face of injustice because we can use present philosophical, political, economic, logistic, and practical difficulties as an excuse for inactivity.*

Our daily bread *. . . so that each person in the world may have enough food, enough clean water, enough clean air, adequate health care, and sufficient access to education so as to have the sustenance for a healthy life. Teach us to give from our sustenance and not just from our surplus.*

And forgive us our trespasses *. . . forgive us our blindness towards our neighbor, our obsessive self-preoccupation, our racism, our sexism, and our incurable propensity to worry only about ourselves and our own. Forgive us our capacity to watch the evening news and do nothing about it.*

***As we forgive those who trespass against us** . . . help us to forgive those who victimize us. Help us to mellow out in spirit, to not grow bitter with age, to forgive the imperfect parents and systems that wounded, cursed, and ignored us.*

***And do not put us to the test** . . . do not judge us only by whether we have fed the hungry, given clothing to the naked, visited the sick, or tried to mend the systems that victimized the poor. Spare us this test for none of us can stand before this Gospel scrutiny. Give us, instead, more days to mend our ways, our selfishness, and our systems.*

***But deliver us from evil** . . . that is, from the blindness that lets us continue to participate in anonymous systems within which we need not see who gets less as we get more.*

Amen.

—*In Exile*, May 22, 1996

9

The Passion and the Cross

In his final chapter, Ron helps us understand the many layers of meaning in the universal symbol of the cross. He describes it as "perhaps the ultimate symbol, for death, love, fidelity, and faith." The crucifixion shows us the inner workings of a nonviolent, vulnerable God. In God's vulnerability lies the secret to our coming to love and community.

Ron's perspective on what it means that Jesus "takes away the sin of the world" is as intriguing as it is challenging. We are all called to do as Jesus did, to help carry tension and remove sin in the world. His insights lead to one of his most memorable analogies, the water purifier, presented in the final column of this book.

If we choose to step forward and follow Jesus' example, Ron concludes, we too will sweat blood. But God will help sustain us in love and faith, "right inside the madness and the fire."

THE CROSS OF JESUS

Among all the religious symbols in the world none is more universal than the cross. You see crosses everywhere, on walls, on hillsides, in churches, in houses, in bedrooms, on chains around peoples' necks, on rings, on ear-rings, on old people, on young people, on believers, and on people who aren't sure in what they believe. Not everyone can explain what the cross means or why they choose to wear one, but most everyone has an inchoate sense that it is a symbol, perhaps the ultimate symbol, for depth, love, fidelity, and faith.

And the cross is exactly that, the ultimate symbol of depth, love, fidelity, and faith. René Girard, an anthropologist, once commented that "the cross of Jesus is the single most revolutionary moral event in all of history." The world measures time by it.

What is so morally revolutionary in the cross?

Precisely because it is such a deep mystery, the cross is not easy to grasp intellectually. The deeper things in life, love, fidelity, morality, and faith are not mathematics, but mysteries whose unfathomable depths always leave room for more still to be understood. We never quite arrive at an adequate understanding of them.

But that doesn't mean that we don't know them. Knowing is different than understanding and we intuit a lot more than we can intellectually imagine or express.

For example, *TIME* magazine did a cover story some years ago on the meaning of the cross and interviewed a large number of people asking what the cross of Jesus meant to them. One woman admitted that she couldn't really explain what the cross of Jesus meant to her, but stated that she had a sense of its meaning: When she was young girl, her mother was murdered by a jealous boyfriend. When she saw the blood-soaked mattress and her mother's bloody hand-print on the wall, she realized that she had to find a connection between her mother's story (and her blood on that mattress) and Jesus' story (and his blood on the cross). Sometimes the heart intuits where the head needs to go.

Beyond this gut-knowledge, what can we intellectually grasp about the meaning of the cross? What is its revolutionary moral character?

Theologians, classically, have tried to come to grips with this mystery by dividing the meaning of the cross (and of Jesus' death) into two parts: First, the cross gives us our deepest understanding of the nature of God. Second, the cross is redemptive, it saves us. All Christians believe that somehow we are washed clean in the blood of Jesus, the Lamb of God.

Neither of these concepts is easy to explain, though theologians do better with the first, the cross as revelation, than with the second, the cross as redemptive. But both concepts, even to the limited extent that we can intellectually understand them, are thoroughly morally revolutionary.

Christianity is 2000 years old, but it took us nearly 1900 years to fully grasp the fact that slavery is wrong, that it goes against the heart of Jesus' teaching. The same can be said about the equality of women. Much of what Jesus revealed to us is like a time-released medicine capsule. Throughout the centuries, slowly, gradually, incrementally, Jesus' message is dissolving more deeply into our consciousness.

And this is particularly true about our understanding of the cross and what it teaches. For example: There have been popes for 2000 years, beginning with Peter, but it was only Pope John Paul II, in our own generation, who stood up and said with clarity that capital punishment is wrong (independent of any arguments about whether or not it is a deterrent, brings closure to the victims' families or not, or can be argued in terms of justice). Capital punishment is wrong because it goes against the heart of the Gospel as revealed in the cross, namely, that we should forgive murderers, not kill them.

That is just one of the morally revolutionary features inside of the cross. There are countless more. Rene Girard, speaking as an anthropologist, puts it one way when he says that the cross is the most revolutionary moral event in the history of the planet. Mark, the Evangelist, speaking as a disciple of Jesus, puts it another way: For him, the cross of Jesus is the deep secret to everything.

In Mark's Gospel, to the extent that we understand the cross of Jesus, we grasp life's deepest secret. And the reverse is just as true: To the extent that we don't grasp the meaning of the cross, we miss the key that opens up life's deepest secrets. When we don't grasp the cross, life deep mysteries become a riddle.

—*In Exile,* April 1, 2007

THE TEARING OF THE TEMPLE VEIL

There are so many haunting lines in the passion narratives. Who of us, for instance, is not stirred in the soul when the passion story is read in church and we come to the part where Jesus takes his last breath and there is that minute of silence, where we all drop to our knees? No Good Friday homily is ever as effective as that single line ("he gave up his spirit") and the moving silence that ensues.

Another such line that has always haunted me is the one that follows immediately after. Jesus dies and we are told that, at the very second of his death, "the veil of the temple was torn in two, from top to bottom." My imagination, even when I was very little, has always been able to picture that. I have this picture in my mind of it growing dark in the middle of the day and then at the second of Jesus' death, almost as if by lightening, the temple veil is ripped from top to bottom while everyone looks on stunned, convinced now, too late, that the person they've just mocked and crucified is the Christ. It's a great picture. But, my imagination aside, what is really meant by that phrase that the veil of the temple ripped open at the moment of Jesus' death?

Biblical scholars tell us that the veil of the temple was precisely a curtain. It hid the holy of holies. The ordinary worshipper in the temple could not see what was behind it. It shielded a person from the great mystery. Thus, when the Gospel writers say that at the precise moment of Jesus' death the temple veil was ripped apart from top to bottom, the point they are making is not, as my imagination would want it, that God shredded what was most precious to the those who crucified Jesus to show them how wrong they were. No. The point is rather this: The temple-veil was understood to hide the mystery of God from the people. In the crucifixion that mystery is laid open for everyone to see. Jesus' death, understood properly, shows the inner workings of God. It rips away our false understandings of God and shows us what God really looks like. And what do we see behind the veil? Among other things, we see a God who spills his own blood to reach through to us rather than want us to spill ours to reach through to Him/Her. What is meant by this?

There is a centuries-old question that asks why Jesus had to die in so horrible a manner. Why all this blood? What kind of cosmic and divine game is being played out here? Is Christ's blood, the blood of the lamb, somehow paying someone off for the sin of Adam and Eve and for our own sins? Why does blood need to be spilled?

This is a complex question and every answer that can be given is only a very partial one. We are dealing with the greatest of all mysteries here. However even mysteries can be partially understood. One of the reasons why Jesus dies in this way—one of the reasons for all the blood—is clear and its implications are profound. It has precisely to do with blood.

From the beginning of time right up until the crucifixion of Jesus, all cultures sacrificed blood to their gods. Why blood? Because blood is so identified with the life-principle. Blood carries life, is life, and its loss is death. Thus it shouldn't be surprising to us that everywhere in ancient cultures the idea was present that what we owe to God is blood, that God needs blood. In their view of things, blood was the only language that God really understood. So they felt that they should be offering blood to God. And they did. For a long time, this included human blood. Humans were killed on altars everywhere. Eventually however many cultures eliminated explicit human sacrifice and used animals instead. By the time of Jesus, the temple had become a giant butchery with priests killing animals nearly non-stop. Some scholars suggest that when Jesus upset the money changers' tables in the temple about 90% of commerce in Jerusalem was in one way or the other connected with animal sacrifice. No small wonder Jesus' action was perceived as a threat!

So why all that blood at Jesus' death? Because, as Richard Rohr so aptly put it, for all these centuries we have been spilling blood to try to get to God and, in the crucifixion, things get reversed: God spills his own blood to try to get to us. It's this reversal that rips open the old veil of fear, the false belief that God wants blood. God does not want us to spill blood to get to Him/Her. We are not meant to live in fear of God. All the blood in the crucifixion of Jesus is meant to tell us that.

—*In Exile,* April 16, 2000

THE MEANING OF JESUS' DEATH

Jesus' death washes everything clean, including our ignorance and sin. That's the clear message from Luke's account of his death.

As we know, we have four Gospels, each with its own take on the passion and death of Jesus. As we know too these Gospel accounts are not journalistic reports of what happened on Good Friday but more theological interpretations of what happened then. They're paintings of Jesus' death more so than news reports about it and, like good art, they take liberties to highlight certain forms so as to bring out essence. Each Gospel writer has his own interpretation of what happened on Calvary.

For Luke, what happened in the death of Jesus is the clearest revelation, ever, of the incredible scope of God's understanding, forgiveness, and healing. For him, Jesus' death washes everything clean through an understanding, forgiveness, and healing that belies every notion suggesting anything to the contrary. To make this clear, Luke highlights a number of elements in his narrative.

First, in his account of Jesus' arrest in the Garden of Gethsemane, he tells us that immediately after one of his disciples struck the servant of the high priest and cut off his ear, Jesus touched the man's ear and healed him. God's healing, Luke intimates, reaches into all situations, even situations of bitterness, betrayal, and violence. God's grace will ultimately heal even what's wounded in hatred.

Then, after Peter denied him three times and Jesus is being led away after his interrogation by the Sanhedrin, Luke tells us that Jesus turned and looked straight at Peter in a look that made Peter weep bitterly. Everything in this text and everything that comes after it suggests that the look from Jesus that caused Peter to weep bitterly was not one of disappointment and accusation, a look that would have caused Peter to weep in shame. No, rather it was a look of such understanding and empathy as

Peter had never before seen, causing him to weep in relief, knowing that everything was all right and he was all right.

And when Luke records Jesus' trial before Pilate, he recounts something that's not recorded in the other Gospel accounts of Jesus' trial, namely, Pilate sending Jesus to Herod and how the two of them, bitter enemies until that day, "became friends that same day." As Ray Brown, commenting on this text puts it, "Jesus has a healing effect even on those who mistreat him."

Finally, in Luke's narrative, we arrive at the place where Jesus is crucified and as they are crucifying him, he utters the famous words: Father, forgive them for they know not what they do. Those words, which Christians forever afterwards have taken as the ultimate criterion as to how we should treat our enemies and those who do us ill, encapsulate the deep revelation contained in Jesus' death. Uttered in that context as God is about to be crucified by human beings, these words reveal how God sees and understands even our worst actions: Not as ill-will, not as something that ultimately turns us against God or God against us, but as ignorance—simple, non-culpable, invincible, understandable, forgivable, akin to the self-destructive actions of an innocent child.

In that context too, Luke narrates Jesus' forgiveness of the "good thief." What Luke wants to highlight here, beyond the obvious, are a number of things: First, that the man is forgiven not because he didn't sin, but in spite of his sin; second, that he is given infinitely more than he actually requests of Jesus; and finally, that Jesus will not die with any unfinished business, this man's sin must first be wiped clean.

Finally, in Luke's narrative, unlike the narratives of Mark and Matthew, Jesus does not die expressing abandonment, but rather dies expressing complete trust: "Father, into your hands I commit my spirit." Luke wants us to see in these words a template for how we can face our own deaths, given our weaknesses. What's the lesson? Léon Bloy once wrote that there is only one true sadness in life, that of not being a saint. At the end of the day when each of us face our own death this will be our biggest regret, that we're not saints. But, as Jesus shows in his death, we can die in (even in weakness) knowing we are dying into safe hands.

Luke's account of the passion and death of Jesus, unlike much of Christian tradition, does not focus on the atoning value of Jesus' death. What it emphasizes instead is this: Jesus' death washes everything clean, each of us and the whole world. It heals everything, understands everything, and forgives everything—despite every ignorance, weakness, infidelity, and betrayal on our part. In John's passion narrative, Jesus' dead body is pierced with a lance and immediately "blood and water" (life and cleansing) flow out. In Luke's account, Jesus' body is not pierced. It doesn't need to be. By the time he breathes his last he has forgiven everyone and everything has been washed clean.

—*In Exile,* April 6, 2020

THE CROSS AS REVEALING THE NON-VIOLENCE OF CHRIST

The cross of Christ is like a carefully-cut diamond. Every time you turn it in the light you get a different sparkle. It means so many things and its depths can never be fully fathomed, always more meaning spills over. We can never get our minds around it, but, and we sense this, ultimately the cross is the deepest word that can ever be spoken about love. No wonder it is perhaps the most universally-cherished symbol on earth.

How can one begin to unravel the multifarious levels of meaning carried by a cross? The best place to start is with God. What the cross tells us, more clearly than any other revelation, is that God is absolutely and utterly non-violent and that God's vulnerability, which the cross invites us into, is a power for community with God and with each other. What's being said here? How does the cross reveal God as non-violent?

We are forever connecting God to coercion, threat, guilt, reckoning, and to the idea that a power should somehow rise up and crush by force all that's evil. That concept is the main reason why so many of us either fear God, hate God, try to avoid God, or are disappointed in God ("Why doesn't God do something about the world?"). But what scripture reveals about God, and this is seen full-bloom on the cross, is that God is neither coercion, threat, guilt, nor the great avenger of evil and sin.

Rather God is love, light, truth, and beauty; a gentle, though persistent, invitation, that's never a threat. God is like a mother, gently trying to coax another step out of a young child learning to walk ("Come on, try, just another step!"). God exists as an infinite patience that endures all things, not as a great avenger, Rambo and John Wayne, who kills all the bad guys when he has finally had enough. The cross of Christ reveals that God works far differently than do our movies and our imaginations. God never overpowers anyone.

Radically, of course, God could. God has all the power. However God's power to create love and community, paradoxically, works precisely by refusing to ever overpower. It works instead through vulnerability, through something the Gospels call *exousia*. What is this?

The Gospels tell us that when people witnessed Jesus' life and ministry they saw something that sharply differentiated him from others. "He spoke with great power, unlike the scribes and pharisees." However they use a curious word to name that power. They never say that Jesus spoke with great *energia* ("Wow, is he energetic!") or *dynamis* ("What dynamism!"). Instead they use the (Greek) word, *exousia*, a word with no English equivalent, but whose meaning can be conveyed in an image:

If you would put the strongest man in the world into a room with a new-born baby which of these two would be more powerful? Obviously at one level, the man is more powerful, he could kill the baby if he wanted. But, the baby possesses a different kind of power, a far deeper one, one that can move things muscles can't. A baby has *exousia*, its vulnerability is a great power. It doesn't need to out-muscle anyone. A baby invites, beckons, and all that's moral and deep in the conscience simply cannot walk away. It's no accident that God chose to be incarnated into this world as a baby.

It's no accident either that Jesus died as he did on Good Friday. The cross reveals the power of God in this world, a power that is never the power of a muscle, a speed, a brilliance, a physical attractiveness, or a grace which simply leaves you no other choice but to acknowledge its superiority and bend your knee in obeisance. The world's power works this way, movies end that way. God's power is the power of *exousia*, a baby that lies helpless, muted, patient, beckoning for someone to take care of it. It's this power that lies at the deepest base of things and will in the end, gently, have the final say. It's also the only power upon which love and community can be created because it, and it alone, ultimately softens rather than breaks the heart.

And it's a power that invites us in. It's good to know this so that we don't give into bitterness and grow vicious ourselves when we are slighted and can't defend ourselves, when our dreams get crushed and there's nothing we can do about it, when we so desperately want to do something that stands out but haven't the talent to do so, or when we find ourselves a minority of one before a jeering crowd.

The cross of Christ tells us that, at those moments of painful helplessness, when we can't impress or overpower anyone, we are acting in a divine way, non-violently, and in that vulnerability lies the secret to our coming to love and community.

—*In Exile,* February 10, 2002

GOD AS REDEEMER, NOT AS RESCUER

Before you get serious about Jesus, first consider how good you are going to look on wood!

That's a line from Daniel Berrigan that rightly warns us that faith in Jesus and the resurrection won't save us from humiliation, pain, and death in this life. Faith isn't meant to do that. Jesus doesn't grant special exemptions to his friends, no more than God granted special exemptions to Jesus. We see this everywhere in the Gospels, though most clearly in Jesus' resurrection. To understand this, it's helpful to compare Jesus' resurrection to what Jesus himself does in raising Lazarus from the dead.

The Lazarus story begs a lot of questions. John, the evangelist, tells us the story: He begins by pointing out that Lazarus and his sisters, Martha and Mary, were very close friends of Jesus. Hence, we are understandably taken aback by Jesus' seeming lack of response to Lazarus' illness and the request to come and heal him. Here's the story:

Lazarus' sisters, Martha and Mary, sent word to Jesus that "the man you love is ill" with the implied request that Jesus should come and heal him. But Jesus' reaction is curious. He doesn't rush off immediately to try to heal his close friend. Instead he remains where he is for two days longer while his friend dies. Then, after Lazarus has died, he sets off to visit him. As he approaches the village where Lazarus has died, he is met by Martha and then, later, by Mary. Each, in turn, asks him the question: "Why?" Why, since you loved this man, did you not come to save him from death? Indeed, Mary's question implies even more: "Why?" Why is it that God invariably seems absent when bad things happen to good people? Why doesn't God rescue his loved ones and save them from pain and death?

Jesus doesn't offer any theoretical apologia in response. Instead he asks where they have laid the body, lets them take him there, sees the burial site, weeps in sorrow, and then raises his dead friend back to life. So why did he let him die in the first place? The story begs that question: Why? Why didn't Jesus rush down to save Lazarus since he loved him?

The answer to that question teaches a very important lesson about Jesus, God, and faith, namely, that God is not a God who ordinarily rescues us, but is rather a God who redeems us. God doesn't ordinarily intervene to save us from humiliation, pain, and death; rather he redeems humiliation, pain, and death after the fact.

Simply put, Jesus treats Lazarus exactly the same way as God, the Father, treats Jesus: Jesus is deeply and intimately loved by his Father and yet his Father doesn't rescue him from humiliation, pain, and death. In his lowest hour, when he is humiliated, suffering, and dying on the cross, Jesus is jeered by the crowd with the challenge: "If God is your father, let him rescue you!" But there's no rescue. Instead Jesus dies inside the humiliation and pain. God raises him up only after his death.

This is one of the key revelations inside the resurrection: We have a redeeming, not a rescuing, God.

Indeed, the story of the raising of Lazarus in John's Gospel was meant to answer a burning question inside the first generation of Christians: They had known Jesus in the flesh, had been intimate friends with him, had seen him heal people and raise people from the dead, so why was he letting them die? Why wasn't Jesus rescuing them?

It took the early Christians some time to grasp that Jesus doesn't ordinarily give special exemptions to his friends, no more than God gave special exemptions to Jesus. So, like us, they struggled with the fact that someone can have a deep, genuine faith, be deeply loved by God, and still have to suffer humiliation, pain, and death like everyone else. God didn't spare Jesus from suffering and death, and Jesus doesn't spare us from them.

That is one of the key revelations inside of the resurrection and is the one we perhaps most misunderstand. We are forever predicating our faith on, and preaching, a rescuing God, a God who promises special exemptions to those of genuine faith: Have a genuine faith in Jesus, and you will be spared from life's humiliations and pains! Have a genuine faith in Jesus, and prosperity will come your way! Believe in the resurrection, and rainbows will surround your life!

Would it were so! But Jesus never promised us rescue, exemptions, immunity from cancer, or escape from death. He promised rather that, in the end, there will be redemption, vindication, immunity from suffering, and eternal life. But that's in the end; meantime, in the early and intermediate chapters of our lives, there will be the same kinds of humiliation, pain, and death that everyone else suffers.

The death and resurrection of Jesus reveal a redeeming, not a rescuing, God.

—*In Exile,* March 24, 2013

THE CROSS AS REVEALING GOD'S PRESENCE IN THE POOR

Several years ago, in Canada's prairies, not far from where I was born and raised, a man named Robert Latimer killed his severely-handicapped daughter, Tracy. He put her into the family truck, hooked a tube to the exhaust-emission, sealed the windows and doors, and let her fall asleep. He wasn't malicious in intent. He loved his daughter. In his mind, this was an act of mercy. He couldn't bear to see her suffer any longer. Nobody doubted his sincerity. His daughter was almost totally disabled physically and mentally, lived in constant pain, and there was no favorable prognosis in terms of her ever getting better or of her pain ever lessening. So he, in as humane a way as possible, ended her life.

Her death became a huge national story, a drawn-out court-battle that lasted for years, ending up in the Supreme Court of Canada, and a country-wide moral and religious debate that has bitterly divided families and communities. The death of this young girl, Tracy Latimer, raises an issue we can't agree on today: What's the value of a human life that is severely disabled?

What's the value of a life such as Tracy Latimer's? Biblically, the answer is clear: When someone is deemed expendable, for whatever reason, at that moment she or he becomes the most important person, spiritually, in the community: The stone that is rejected by the builders is the cornerstone for the building. This means that the Tracy Latimers within our lives are a privileged place where the rest of us can experience God.

One of the central revelations of the cross is that there is a very privileged presence of God in the one who is excluded, in the one of whom society says: "better that she should die for the people." Scripture is clear on this: Already in the Jewish scriptures, we see that the prophets emphasize the idea that God has special sympathy for "orphans, widows, and strangers." At that time, these particular groups had the least status, the least power, and were deemed the most expendable. They could be left to die so that society could get on with its more urgent business. The prophets' message was revolutionary: God has a special sympathy for those whom society deems least important and how we treat those persons is the litmus test of our faith, morals, and religiosity.

Jesus takes this a notch further: In his teaching, not only does God have special sympathy for those whom society deems least important and most expendable, but God's very presence is identified with them: "Whatsoever you do to the least of these, you do to me!" Jesus identifies God's presence with the outcasts, with the excluded ones, and he tells us that we have a privileged experience of God in our contact with them.

Nowhere is this stated more clearly than in Jesus' death on the cross: The crucified one is the stone rejected by the builders, the one deemed expendable so that normal life will not be disrupted. But the crucified one is also God and there is a special intimacy with God that can be had only in standing, as did Mary and John, near the cross, in solidarity with the crucified one, the one who is being excluded.

Many of us are familiar with an incident recorded by Elie Wiesel. In one of the Nazi death camps, a prisoner had escaped and, in retaliation, the Nazis took a young boy, hanged him publicly, and forced everyone to watch this horrific spectacle. As the young boy dangled on a rope in front of them, one man cursed bitterly: "Where is God now?" Another man answered: "There, on that rope. That's God!"

One of the revelations of the cross is precisely that, in the crucified one is the presence of God. —*In Exile,* March 10, 2002

HOW JESUS TAKES AWAY THE SIN OF THE WORLD

Jesus is the lamb of God who takes away the sin of the world! That formula, expressed in various ways, lies at the center of what we believe about Jesus. What is meant by it? How does his sacrificial giving of himself take away our sins? How can one person take sin out of the world?

In trying to answer that, we should be careful not to fall into a common misunderstanding. Because of certain biblical and doctrinal ways of expressing this, the impression can be given that Jesus' suffering and death took away the sins of the world by somehow paying off a debt to God, namely, that God took Jesus' suffering as compensation for our sin—implying that God had lived in anger since Adam's sin, waiting for someone to adequately pay the debt before that sin could be forgiven. The images and metaphors used to express Jesus' expiation for sin can, if taken literally, give that impression, but that is not what they mean. What do they mean?

There is a rich background to this concept: Many pre-Christian cultures had rituals involving a scapegoat. It was not enacted the same way in every place, but in essence it went something like this: At regular intervals, a community would try to purge itself of the evils that were besetting it (divisions, rivalries, jealousies, violence, warfare, theft, anger, murder, and the like) by a ritual designed to take these things out of the community. The ritual went like this: They would take a goat and would, through some symbol (which often included draping the goat in purple and putting a crown of thorns on its head), figuratively load on its back all that they felt was wrong inside of their community. The goat was then driven out into the desert to die. The idea was that the goat was taking the sin of the community away with it. Curiously, this generally had a certain effectiveness. For a time afterward, there would more unity within the group.

Of course no real transformation took place. Nothing really changed. Jealousies and anger remained as before, even if for a time people were able to live together more harmoniously. A goat, driven into the desert to die, does not take sin out of a community. How then does Jesus, as the lamb slain, take sin out of a community?

Jesus, as the lamb of God, does not take away the sin of the world by somehow carrying it off so that it is no longer present inside of the community. He takes it away by transforming it, by changing it, by taking it inside of himself and transmuting it. We see examples of this throughout his entire life, although it is most manifest in the love and forgiveness he shows at the time of his death. In simple language, Jesus took away the sin of the community by taking in hatred and giving back love; by taking in anger and giving out graciousness; by taking in envy and giving back blessing; by taking in bitterness and giving out warmth; by taking in pettiness and giving back compassion; by taking in chaos and giving back peace; and by taking in sin and giving back forgiveness.

This is not an easy thing to do. What comes naturally is to give back in kind: hatred for hatred, anger for anger, coldness for coldness, revenge for hurt. Someone hits us so we hit back. But then sin stays inside of the community and no amount of scapegoating, ritualized in liturgy or otherwise, is of any real value in changing things because we are not transforming anything but are simply acting as conduits, passing on the identical energy that is pressed on to us. Jesus did otherwise. He did not simply pass on what was done to him. Rather he took it in, held it, carried it, transformed it, and eventually gave it back as something else. This is what constitutes the sacrificial part of his love, namely, the excruciatingly pain (*ex cruce*, from the cross) that he had to undergo in order to take in hatred and give back love. But that is the only way that sin can ever leave a community, someone has to take it in, hold it, carry it, and, through a certain excruciating sacrifice of self, transform it into something else. For this reason Christianity, among all the religions and philosophies of the world, is the only one that worships the scapegoat.

Moreover this dynamic is not just something we are asked to admire in Jesus. The incarnation is meant to be ongoing. We are asked to continue to give flesh to God, to continue to do what

Jesus did. Thus our task too is to help take away the sin of the world. We do this whenever we take in hatred, anger, envy, pettiness, and bitterness, hold them, transmute them, and eventually give them back as love, graciousness, blessing, compassion, warmth, and forgiveness. —*In Exile,* May 23, 1999

JESUS' LAST WORDS

Just before he dies on the cross, Jesus utters these words: "It is finished!" What's "finished"?

These words can be spoken in different ways: They can be words of defeat and despair ("It's over, hopeless, I give in!) or they can be words of accomplishment and triumph ("I've done it, succeeded, I've held out!").

Obviously, for Jesus, these are not words of defeat. He has triumphed, succeeded, run the toughest race of all to its finish. When he speaks these words, he's like the winner in the Olympic marathon throwing up his arms in triumph at the finish-line; except in this case both his exuberance of spirit and his arms are nailed down so that his utterance of triumph is not like the pumped-fist of an Olympic winner, but like the cry of an new-born baby that's finally succeeded in pushing itself through the birth-canal; a startling triumph, but one that, for a time, has you lying in blood, tears, and helplessness.

And his triumph here left him precisely in blood, tears, and helplessness. He's won, but it's cost him his life, tested his faith to the limit, lost him his popularity, scattered his friends, shrouded his life in misunderstanding, left him looking compromised, and isolated him in an unspeakable loneliness.

It's not easy then to pump your fist in triumph, even when you've won, especially since your victory isn't evident to anyone who isn't journeying inside of this with you. To everyone else, this looks like defeat, the worst kind of defeat.

So what's "finished"?

At one level, what's finished is Jesus' own struggle with doubt, fear, and loneliness. What was that struggle? The painful, lonely, crushing discrepancy he habitually felt between the warmth and ideals inside his heart and the coldness and despair he met in the world.

Everything inside of him believed that, in the end, always, it is better to give yourself over to love than to hatred, to affirmation than to jealousy, to gentleness of heart than to bitterness, to honesty than to lying, to fidelity than to compromise, to forgiveness than to revenge. Everything about him too was a testimony that the reality of God, immaterial and fanciful though it can seem, is in the end more real than the undeniable reality of our physical bodies and our physical world. And finally, everything about him pointed uncompromisingly towards the "road-less-taken" and revealed that real love means carrying your solitude and chastity at a high level.

But, for him, as for us, it wasn't easy to live that out. As scripture says, sometimes it gets dark in the middle of the day, we find ourselves very much alone in what we believe in, and God seems far away and dead. Faith and love aren't easy because they feel empty and fanciful whenever they're betrayed and they only work and prove that they're real when they're persevered in.

Jesus, though, did persevere in them and when he utters those famous words: "It is finished!", it's a statement of triumph, not just of his own faith, but of love, truth, and God. He's taken God as his word, risked everything on faith, and, despite the pain it's brought, is dying with no regrets. The struggle for faith, for him, is finished. He's crossed its finish line, successfully.

But there's a second level of meaning to his words. "It is finished" also means that the reign of sin and death is finished. An order of things (wherein we live our lives believing that, eventually, everyday joys give way to darkness and the underworld; that paranoia and sin unmask trust and goodness as naïve; that the reality of the physical world and this life is all there is; that compromise and infidelity trump everything else, and that death is more real than hope) is also finished. It is exposed as unreal, as a lie, by love, fidelity, gentleness, trust, childlikeness, vulnerability, and the paradoxical power of a God who, in the deeper recesses of things, works more by underwhelming than by overpowering.

"It is finished!" Jesus uttered those words when he realized that, despite all the pain and sin in the world, the center does hold, love can be trusted, God is real, and, because of that, in the end, "every manner of being will indeed be well." The forces of sin and death are finished because we can, in full maturity and utter realism, believe in the sun even when it isn't shining, in love even when we don't feel it, and in God, even when God is silent. Faith and God deliver on their promise.

Mohandas Gandhi, in a remarkable passage, once wrote: "When I despair, I remember that all through history, the way of truth and love has always won. There have been murderers and tyrants, and for a time they can seem invincible. But in the end they always fall. Think of it, always." Many things were finished on the cross, including rule of tyranny and murder.

—*In Exile,* April 9, 2006

STANDING WITH MARY UNDER THE CROSS

One of the most popular images in all of scripture (an icon that's been endlessly painted, sung, put into litanies, written up into poetry, and used to trigger every kind of pious feeling) is the image of Mary, the mother of Jesus, standing silently under the cross as her son dies.

As Jesus was dying, the Gospels tell us that Mary, his mother, stood under the cross. What's in that image? What's in this picture that invites us to more than simple admiration, piety, or sympathy?

This is a mystical image and it is anything but pious. In the Gospels, after Jesus, Mary is the most important person to watch. She's the model of discipleship, the only one who gets it right. And she gets it very right under the cross. What's she doing while standing there?

On the surface, it seems she isn't doing anything at all: She doesn't speak, doesn't try to stop the crucifixion, and she doesn't even protest its unfairness or plead Jesus' innocence. She is mute, seemingly passive, overtly doing nothing. But at a deeper level, she is doing all that can be done when one is standing under the weight of the cross, she's holding the tension, standing in strength, refusing to give back in kind, and resisting in a deeper way.

What's meant by this?

Sometimes well-intentioned artists have painted Mary as lying prostrate under the cross, the wounded mother, helplessly distraught, paralyzed in grief, an object for sympathy. But that doesn't honor what happened there nor teach its lesson. Prostration, in this situation, is weakness, collapse, hysteria, resignation. In the Gospels, "standing" is the opposite, a position of strength. Mary "stood" under the cross.

Still, why the silence and why her seeming unwillingness to act or protest?

In essence, what Mary was doing under the cross was this: She couldn't stop the crucifixion (there are times when darkness has its hour) but she could stop some of the hatred, bitterness, jealousy, heartlessness, and anger that caused it and surrounded it. And she helped stop bitterness by refusing to give it back in kind, by transforming rather than transmitting it, by swallowing hard and (literally) eating bitterness rather than giving it back, as everyone else was doing.

Had Mary, in moral outrage, begun to scream hysterically, shout angrily at those crucifying Jesus, or physically tried to attack someone as he was driving the nails into Jesus' hands, she would have been caught up in the same kind of energy as everyone else, replicating the very anger and bitterness that caused the crucifixion to begin with. What Mary was doing under the cross, her silence and seeming unwillingness to protest notwithstanding, was radiating all that is antithetical to the crucifixion: gentleness, understanding, forgiveness, peace, light.

And that's not easy to do. Everything inside us demands justice, screams for it, and refuses to remain silent in the presence of injustice. That's a healthy instinct and sometimes acting on it is good. We need, at times, to protest, to shout, to literally throw ourselves into the face of injustice and do everything in our power to stop the crucifixion.

But there are times too when things have gone so far that shouts and protests are no longer helpful, darkness is going to have its hour come what may and all we can do is to stand under the cross and help eat its bitterness by refusing to participate in its energy. In those situations, like Mary, we have to say: "I can't stop this crucifixion, but I can stop some of the hatred, bitterness, jealousy, brute-heartlessness, and darkness that surround it. I can't stop this, but I will not conduct its hatred."

And that's not the same thing as despair. Our muted helplessness is not a passive resignation but the opposite. It's a movement towards the only rays of light, love, and faith that still exist in that darkness and hatred. And, at that moment, it's the only thing that faith and love can do.

As the Book of Lamentations says, there are times when the best we can do is "put our mouths to the dust and wait!" Sometimes too, as Rainer Maria Rilke says, the only helpful thing is to absorb the heaviness: "Do not be afraid to suffer, give the heaviness back to the weight of the earth; mountains are heavy, seas are heavy."

That's not passivity, resignation, or weakness; it's genuine, rare strength. It's "standing under the cross" so as to help take away some of its hatred, chaos, bitterness, and violence.

So this is the image: Sometimes darkness has its hour and there is nothing we can do to stop it. Sometimes the blind, wounded forces of jealousy, bitterness, violence, and sin cannot, for that moment, be stopped. But, like Mary under the cross, we are asked to "stand" under them, not in passivity and weakness, but in strength, knowing that we can't stop the crucifixion but we can help stop some of the hatred, anger, and bitterness that surrounds it.

—*In Exile,* April 2, 2006

DYING INTO SAFE HANDS

Few images are as primal, and as tender, as that of a mother holding and cradling her newborn baby. Indeed the words of the most-renowned Christmas carol of all time, "Silent Night," were inspired by precisely this image.

Joseph Mohr, a young priest in Germany, had gone out to a cottage in the woods on the afternoon of Christmas Eve to baptize a newborn baby. As he left the cottage, the baby was asleep in its mother's lap. He was so taken with that image, with the depth and peace it incarnated, that, immediately upon returning to his rectory, he penned the famous lines of "Silent Night." His choir director, Franz Gruber, put some guitar chords to those words and froze them in our minds forever. The ultimate archetypal image of peace, safety, and security is that of a newborn sleeping in its mother's arms. Moreover, when a baby is born, it's not just the mother who's eager to hold and cradle it. Most everyone else is too.

Perhaps no image then is as apt, as powerful, as consoling, and as accurate in terms of picturing what happens to us when we die and awake to eternal life as is the image of a mother holding and cradling her newborn child. When we die, we die into the arms of God and surely we're received with as much love, gentleness, and tenderness as we were received in the arms of our mothers at birth. Moreover, surely we are even safer there than we were when we were born here on earth. I suspect too that more than a few of the saints will be hovering around, wanting their chance to cuddle the new baby. And so it's okay if we die before we're ready, still in need of nurturing, still needing someone to help take care of us, still needing a mother. We're in safe, nurturing, gentle hands.

That can be deeply consoling because death renders every one of us an orphan and, daily, there are people dying young, unexpectedly, less-than-fully-ready, still in need of care themselves. All of us die, still needing a mother. But we have the assurance of our faith that we will be born into safer and more nurturing hands than our own. —*In Exile,* November 3, 2013

FACING OUR TOUGH HOURS

When we find ourselves in a situation that's causing us deep interior anguish, do we walk away, assuming that the presence of such pain is an indication that this isn't the right place for us, that something's terminally wrong here? Or, like Jesus, do we accept to stay, saying to ourselves, our loved ones, and our God: "What shall I say, save me from this hour?"

At the very moment that Jesus was facing a humiliating death by crucifixion, the Gospel of John hints that he was offered an opportunity to escape. A delegation of Greeks, through the apostle Philip, offer Jesus an invitation to leave with them, to go to a group that would receive him and his message. So Jesus has a choice: Endure anguish, humiliation, and death inside his own community or abandon that community for one that will accept him. What does he do? He asks himself this question: "What shall I say, save me from this hour?"

Although this is phrased as a question, it's an answer. He is choosing to stay, to face the anguish, humiliation, and pain because he sees it as the precise fidelity he is called to within the very dynamic of the love he is preaching. He came to earth to incarnate and teach what real love is and now, when the cost of that is humiliation and interior anguish, he knows and accepts that this is what's now being asked of him. The pain is not telling him that he's doing something wrong, is at the wrong place, or that this community is not worth this suffering. To the contrary: The pain is understood to be calling him to a deeper fidelity at the very heart of his mission and vocation. Until this moment, only words were asked of him, now he is being asked to back them up in reality; he needs to swallow hard to do it.

What shall I say, save me from this hour? Do we have the wisdom and the generosity to say those words when, inside our own commitments, we are challenged to endure searing interior anguish? When Jesus asks himself this question, what he is facing is a near-perfect mirror for situations we will all find ourselves in sometimes. In most every commitment we make, if we are faithful, an hour will come when we are suffering interior anguish (and often times exterior misunderstanding as well) and are faced with a tough decision: Is this pain and misunderstanding (and even my own immaturity as I stand inside it) an indication that I'm in the wrong place, should leave, and find someone or some other community that wants me? Or, inside this interior anguish, exterior misunderstanding, and personal immaturity, am I called to say: What shall I say, save me from this hour? This is what I'm called to! I was born for this!

I think the question is critical because often anguishing pain can shake our commitments and tempt us to walk away from them. Marriages, consecrated religious vocations, commitments to work for justice, commitments to our church communities, and commitments to family and friends, can be abandoned on the belief that nobody is called to live inside such anguish, desolation, and misunderstanding. Indeed, today the presence of pain, desolation, and misunderstanding is generally taken as a sign to abandon a commitment and find someone else or some other group that will affirm us rather than as an indication that now, just now, in this hour, inside this particular pain and misunderstanding, we have a chance to bring a life-giving grace into this commitment.

I have seen people leave marriages, leave family, leave priesthood, leave religious life, leave their church community, leave long-cherished friendships, and leave commitments to work for justice and peace because, at a point, they experienced a lot of pain and misunderstanding. And, in many of those cases, I also saw that it was in fact a good thing. The situation they were in was not life-giving for them or for others. They needed to be saved from that "hour." In some cases though the opposite was true. They were in excruciating pain, but that pain was an invitation to a deeper, more life-giving place inside their commitment. They left, just when they should have stayed.

Granted, discernment is difficult. It's not always for lack of generosity that people walk away from a commitment. Some of the most generous and unselfish people I know have left a marriage or the priesthood or religious life or their churches. But

I write this because, today, so much trusted psychological and spiritual literature does not sufficiently highlight the challenge to, like Jesus, stand inside excruciating pain and humiliating misunderstanding and instead of walking away to someone or some group that offers us the acceptance and understanding we crave, we instead accept that it is more life-giving to say: *What shall I say, save me from this hour?* —*In Exile,* May 18, 2020

CARRYING TENSION

One of the things we're asked to do as Christians is to help "take away the sins of the world" as Jesus did. How?

Jesus "took away the sins of the world" by holding, carrying, purifying, and transforming tension, that is, by taking in the bitterness, anger, jealousy, hatred, slander, and every other kind of thing that's cancerous within human community, and not giving it back in kind.

In essence, Jesus did this by acting like a purifier, a water filter of sorts: He took in hatred, held it, transformed it, and gave back love; he took in bitterness, held it, transformed it, and gave back graciousness; he took in curses, held them transformed them, and gave back blessing; and he took in murder, held it, transformed it, and gave back forgiveness. Jesus resisted the instinct to give back in kind, hatred for hatred, curses for curses, jealousy for jealousy, murder for murder. He held and transformed these things rather than simply re-transmit them.

And, in this, he wants imitation, not admiration. Christian discipleship invites us, like Jesus, to become a "lamb of God," a purifier, that helps take tension out of our families, communities, friendship circles, churches, and work-places by holding and transforming it rather than simply give it back in kind.

But that's not easy. Jesus did this, but the Gospels say that he had to "sweat blood" to achieve it. To carry tension is to fill with tension ourselves and, as we know, this can be unbearable. We don't have God's strength and we aren't made of steel. As we try to carry tension for others, what do we do with our own tensions? How do we carry tension without becoming resentful and bitter? How do we carry another's cross without, however subtly, sending him or her the bill?

This isn't easy, as every health professional can tell you. Tension wreaks havoc inside us, physically and emotionally. You can die of high blood pressure or of disappointment. But there are some rules that can help.

First, carrying tension for others does not mean putting up with abuse or not confronting pathologically or clinical dysfunction. To love someone, as we now know, does not mean accepting abuse in the name of love.

Second, we need to find healthy outlets to release our own tensions. However we should never download them on the same people for whom we are trying to carry them. For example, parents carry tension for their children, but, when frustrations build up, they should not angrily vent those frustrations back on the kids themselves. Rather they should deal with their own tensions away from the children, with each other and with friends, when the kids are in bed, over a bottle of wine. The same holds true for everyone: We should never vent our frustrations on the very person or persons for whom we are trying to carry tension.

Finally, in order to deal with the frustrations that build up in us, we need, in the midst of the tensions, to be connected to something (a person, a friendship, a hand, a God, a creed, a perspective) beyond ourselves and the situation we're in.

Scripture offers some wonderful images for this. It tells us, for example, that as Stephen was being stoned to death out of hatred and jealousy, he kept his "eyes raised to heaven." That's not so much a physical description of things, as every artist knows, but a commentary on how Stephen kept himself from drowning in the spinning chaos that was assaulting him. He stayed connected to a person, a hand, a friendship, an affirmation, a perspective, and a divine power outside of the madness.

We see the same thing, just a different metaphor, in the story of the three young men who are thrown into the blazing furnace in the Book of Daniel. We're told that they walked around, right in the midst of the flames, untouched by the fire because they were singing sacred songs. Like Stephen, they sustained their love and faith amidst bitter jealousy and hatred by staying connected to something outside of the fiery forces that were consuming everyone else.

We need to contemplate that lesson. Like Jesus, and like everyone else who's ever walked this planet, we all find ourselves forever inside families, communities, churches, friendships, and work-circles that are filled with tension of every kind. Our natural temptation, always, is to simply give back in kind, jealousy for jealousy, gossip for gossip, anger for anger. But what our world really needs is for some women and men, adults, to step forward and help carry and purify this tension, to help take it away by transforming it inside themselves.

But that's not easy. Like Jesus, it will involve "sweating blood." So, as we volunteer to step into the fire, it's wise not to go in alone, but to stay connected to some hand, some friend, some creed, and some God who will help sustain us in love and faith, right inside the madness and fire. —*In Exile,* October 31, 2004

MODERN SPIRITUAL MASTERS
Robert Ellsberg, Series Editor

Already published:
Modern Spiritual Masters (edited by Robert Ellsberg)
Swami Abhishiktananda (edited by Shirley du Boulay)
Metropolitan Anthony of Sourozh (edited by Gillian Crow)
Eberhard Arnold (edited by Johann Christoph Arnold)
Pedro Arrupe (edited by Kevin F. Burke, S.J.)
Daniel Berrigan (edited by John Dear)
Thomas Berry (edited by Mary EvelynTucker and John Grim)
Dietrich Bonhoeffer (edited by Robert Coles)
Robert McAfee Brown (edited by Paul Crowley)
Dom Helder Camara (edited by Francis McDonagh)
Carlo Carretto (edited by Robert Ellsberg)
G. K. Chesterton (edited by William Griffin)
Joan Chittister (edited by Mary Lou Kownacki and Mary Hembrow Snyder)
Yves Congar (edited by Paul Lakeland)
The Dalai Lama (edited by Thomas A. Forsthoefel)
Alfred Delp, S.J. (introduction by Thomas Merton)
Catherine de Hueck Dogerty (edited by David Meconi, S.J.)
Virgilio Elizondo (edited by Timothy Matovina)
Jacques Ellul (edited by Jacob E. Van Vleet)
Ralph Waldo Emerson (edited by Jon M. Sweeney)
Charles de Foucauld (edited by Robert Ellsberg)
Mohandas Gandhi (edited by John Dear)
Bede Griffiths (edited by Thomas Matus)
Romano Guardini (edited by Robert A. Krieg)
Gustavo Gutiérrez (edited by Daniel G. Groody)
Thich Nhat Hanh (edited by Robert Ellsberg)
Abraham Joshua Heschel (edited by Susannah Heschel)
Etty Hillesum (edited by Annemarie S. Kidder)
Caryll Houselander (edited by Wendy M. Wright)
Pope John XXIII (edited by Jean Maalouf)
Rufus Jones (edited by Kerry Walters)
Clarence Jordan (edited by Joyce Hollyday)
Walter Kasper (edited by Patricia C. Bellm and Robert A. Krieg)
John Main (edited by Laurence Freeman)
James Martin (edited by James T. Keane)

Anthony de Mello (edited by William Dych, S.J.)
Thomas Merton (edited by Christine M. Bochen)
John Muir (edited by Tim Flinders)
John Henry Newman (edited by John T. Ford, C.S.C.)
Henri Nouwen (edited by Robert A. Jonas)
Flannery O'Connor (edited by Robert Ellsberg)
Karl Rahner (edited by Philip Endean)
Walter Rauschenbusch (edited by Joseph J. Fahey)
Brother Roger of Taizé (edited by Marcello Fidanzio)
Richard Rohr (edited by Joelle Chase and Judy Traeger)
Ronald Rolheiser (edited by Alicia von Stamwitz)
Oscar Romero (by Marie Dennis, Rennie Golden, and Scott Wright)
Joyce Rupp (edited by Michael Leach)
Rabbi Zalman Schacter-Shalomi (edited by Or N. Rose and Netanel Miles-Yépez)
Albert Schweitzer (edited by James Brabazon)
Frank Sheed and Maisie Ward (edited by David Meconi)
Jon Sobrino (edited by Robert Lassalle-Klein)
Sadhu Sundar Singh (edited by Charles E. Moore)
Mother Maria Skobtsova (introduction by Jim Forest)
Dorothee Soelle (edited by Dianne L. Oliver)
Jon Sobrino (edited by Robert Lasalle-Klein)
Edith Stein (edited by John Sullivan, O.C.D.)
David Steindl-Rast (edited by Clare Hallward)
William Stringfellow (edited by Bill Wylie-Kellerman)
Pierre Teilhard de Chardin (edited by Ursula King)
Mother Teresa (edited by Jean Maalouf)
St. Thérèse of Lisieux (edited by Mary Frohlich)
Phyllis Tickle (edited by Jon M. Sweeney)
Henry David Thoreau (edited by Tim Flinders)
Howard Thurman (edited by Luther E. Smith)
Leo Tolstoy (edited by Charles E. Moore)
Evelyn Underhill (edited by Emilie Griffin)
Vincent Van Gogh (by Carol Berry)
Swami Vivekananda (edited by Victor M. Parachin)
Simone Weil (edited by Eric O. Springsted)
John Howard Yoder (edited by Paul Martens and Jenny Howells)

CPSIA information can be obtained
at www.ICGtesting.com
Printed in the USA
LVHW090257171121
703363LV00007B/337

9 781626 984400

Evolution

Edward Hoare

Alpha Editions

This edition published in 2021

ISBN : 9789355115232

Design and Setting By
Alpha Editions
www.alphaedis.com
Email - info@alphaedis.com

EVOLUTION.

IT may appear a very rash thing for any person who does not claim to be a man of science to presume to give an opinion on any of the theories of scientific men. But there is a vast difference between the facts of science and the theories suggested for their explanation. The facts are, as it were, the property of the investigators. The investigators have a power of investigation which we outsiders have not, and it would be folly for us who have not that power to presume to call in question their information. But it is a very different matter with the theories either founded on these facts or invented to explain them. When science has given us the facts common-sense can discuss the theories founded on them; and, without presuming to call in question the ascertained results of scientific investigation, any person of ordinary intelligence may form his own opinion as to the conclusions derived from the known facts. The scientific men know the facts, and we do not; but, when they have told us the facts, we can think as well as they. This point was exceedingly well put by Canon Garbett at the Norwich Church Congress in 1865. He said: "Beyond a certain point the conclusions and arguments of the man of science cease to be exclusively his own, and become the common property of all men. All argument rests on common principles, and when once the facts of the case are clearly ascertained, any man who is trained to reason correctly is competent to judge of them." Again: "Let the man of science," said Canon Garbett, "reign supreme within his own sphere, and let none but those trained in the same school and learned in the same craft venture to dispute with him as he gathers his facts and generalizes his rules. But when all this is done, and he proceeds to reason, then it is different. He steps out of his special department into a sphere open to all men alike. Tell me what your facts are, and if I sufficiently master them I am as competent to judge of the validity of the conclusions drawn from them as the man of science himself."

There is scarcely any subject to which this principle applies more completely than it does to Evolution; for what is called "the doctrine of Evolution" is only a theory. It is not a collection of facts, but a theory which some of its warmest advocates—as, *e.g.*, Professor Drummond—declare to be "still unproved." [3] While, therefore, we fully recognise that it would be the utmost folly "to debate a point of natural history with Darwin, or a question of comparative anatomy with Owen," we may, by the aid of common-sense, form an opinion possibly as sound at theirs on the unproved theory which has been founded on the ascertained facts which those great investigators have placed within our reach. This is all that I would attempt to do in the present paper. I do not propose to call in question a single fact ascertained by men of science. All that I would venture to do is to exercise the ordinary powers of thought in considering one of the theories which some scientific men have suggested as an explanation of those facts. I say "some scientific men," for there is a very great difference of opinion amongst scientific men, and no one can read the admirable papers produced by the Victoria Institute without perceiving now much accurate observation, how wide a scientific knowledge, and how great a force of Baconian philosophy is arrayed against the theory just now in the fashion.

Let us begin, then, with a few facts respecting which we are all agreed, and which as they are sometimes called by the name of Evolution, are supposed to supply evidence of the correctness of the theory.

(1) We all believe in *growth*. It is a matter of fact that the world is full of growth. And this growth is not limited to gradual, or continuous, enlargement or development; but consists sometimes in most remarkable sudden changes, as when the egg becomes a chicken, the caterpillar a chrysalis, and the chrysalis a butterfly. Every living creature, whether plant or animal, has its own mode of growth; and no living creature is born into the world in the fulness of its stature. The man was once in his cradle, the eagle in its egg, the oak in its acorn; and no one can point to any living thing, either in the animal or vegetable kingdom, that began life with the full development of all the powers or properties of its species. Whatever men may think of any theory, as a matter of fact there is invariably growth as the first, and most certain, accompaniment of life.

(2) Within certain limits we all believe in *variations*. Both plants and animals of the same species vary according to circumstances, and are all more or less affected by country, by climate, and by culture. Amongst dogs, *e.g.*, there are countless varieties of breed, to say nothing of all the mongrels. Just so amongst flowers; there are countless varieties of the rose, and these varieties may be multiplied to

any extent by culture. There is, moreover, a power of adaptation to climate and other circumstances. In colder climates animals of the same species have thicker coats than they have under the tropics. There cannot be a question that both plants and animals will begin at once, if placed in a new position, to adapt themselves to it; and, as a general rule, if they fail in such adaptation, they die. Beyond all doubt, as a matter of fact, there are variations resulting both from parentage and environment. We are told by naturalists that some of these variations are not of a permanent character, as, *e.g.*, in the case of pigeons, of which it is stated by Darwin that any number of breeds, if left to themselves, will in time revert to the common Rock. But still the fact remains, that within certain limits there are numberless variations, and that these variations may be transmitted to posterity. Some of these appear to have been produced in one way, and some in another; but, however produced, there they are; and no one, whether scientific or unscientific, can for one moment call in question the fact.

(3.) We all believe in *progression.* We see progression all around us. It appears to be a universal law that there should be perpetual movement. Sometimes there is advance, and sometimes retrogression—but always movement; for when there is no advance, there is invariably decline. Then, again, as far as observation is concerned, we find this progression gradual and continuous. Characters are gradually formed; learning is gradually acquired; power is gradually gained; and the whole world advances by the gradual attainment of increasing knowledge. Such progression is seen both in creation and revelation.

In Creation, for no one supposes that the world was created and peopled by one instantaneous act of the Creator. There may be difficulties in some of the commonly received interpretations of some of the statements of that most wonderful narrative contained in Gen. i.; but there can be no doubt whatever that it teaches progression. It begins with chaos, and leads us step by step to a perfected cosmos. At the outset; "the earth was waste, or without form, and void, and darkness was upon the face of the deep." And at the end we see a fertile world covered with vegetation, peopled by countless living creatures, with man, in the image of God, at their head, all enjoying the bright light of the sun in heaven; and all in so perfect a condition that "God saw everything that He had made, and behold it was very good." But this change did not take place by one solitary act. The world did not leap by one bound from one condition to the other. There were, according to Scripture no less than six successive steps in the process. Let people explain the six days as they please, and I fully acknowledge that there may be legitimate differences in their explanations. But no one can doubt that the narrative teaches progression; and that, according to that narrative, it pleased God by a series of successive acts to complete the work which He pronounced to be very good. No one, therefore, who believes in the Book of Genesis can for one moment doubt progression in the work of the creation.

Nor can there be the slightest doubt as to progression in Revelation. Some people seem to speak of this as if it were a new discovery connected with the theory of Evolution. Such persons ought to read an admirable book called "The Philosophy of the Plan of Salvation," written many years ago, and new published by the Religious Tract Society. It is perfectly impossible to read through the Old and New Testaments as a complete book without seeing progression. It is deeply to be deplored that such a man as Professor Drummond should have said, as he is reported to have said in his Sunday lectures, at Grosvenor House, [5a] "The Book of Genesis must be regarded as presenting truth to children's minds;" and should have illustrated this by George Macdonald's poem, "The Baby," adding, "not literally true, but true for the child. So Moses gave truth in the form of a poem. If you say it is a scientific book, I give it up; but if you regard it as a poem, then I can deal with it." This appears to teach that the Book of Genesis is regarded by him as something like a nursery rhyme. But the report [5b] is evidently abridged; and I hope it is incorrect. We know that there are sixty-six books in the Bible; but we also believe that it is "a Book" complete in itself, and with all its parts so beautifully proportioned that it forms one perfect whole for the gradual development of the whole counsel of God. Thus we believe that the one verse (Gen. iii 15), "I will put enmity between thee and the woman, and between thy seed and her seed; it shall bruise thy head, and thou shalt bruise his heel," is the seed, or germ, of the whole Gospel; and that just as the oak is in the acorn, so in these few words is contained the whole covenant of God. The first twelve chapters of the Book of Genesis trace the pedigree of that seed of the woman till the call of the chosen family in Abraham; the historical books record the varied history of that family, and show how sorely the heel of the woman's seed first bruised by the serpent; while the prophecies enlarge, and expand the blessed hope of final victory in the promised One. At length the Gospels reveal the long-expected Christ; and the Acts and the Epistles unfold the principles and progress of His kingdom, till the whole is complete in the Apocalypse, where we read of "the new heavens and the new earth," with the curse of sin gone for ever, with Satan cast into the lake of fire, and with the seed of the woman triumphant over death and hell. As the acorn to the oak, so is that first promise to the Apocalypse. It is no poem, no myth, no nursery rhyme, but the germ of the whole counsel of God—a germ containing the whole Gospel, and requiring no less than four thousand years for its development.

Let no one suppose, therefore, for a moment that we do not believe in progression, for we see it throughout nature; and we find it distinctly taught in Scripture as a matter of historical fact, both in creation and revelation. But the fact of progression is a totally different thing from the theory of Evolution; and it is extremely important that the distinction should be carefully borne in mind; for there are many, and some of them clear-headed men, who, because they see the three things—growth, variation, and progression, avow themselves believers in Evolution, though all the while they really reject what should be strictly termed "the Evolution theory."

What then is the theory of Evolution? What is it which Bishop Temple describes as "just at present the leading scientific doctrine," [6a] and for which he says the evidence "is enormously great, and increasing daily"? [6b] It is extremely difficult to answer the question; for evolutionists themselves, although they are perpetually trumpeting forth the superiority of their scientific accuracy, very seldom take the trouble to tell us what they mean. In a defence of Mr. Drummond's book, in the *Expositor*, the defender states, with reference to an article of my own in the CHURCHMAN of February last, that there are at least four theories of Evolution; and he also informs us which of the four it is that Mr. Drummond teaches. It is a pity that Mr. Drummond did not tell us this in his book, instead of leaving us to conclude, as some of us have concluded that it was the doctrine of Mr. Herbert Spencer that appeared to call forth his enthusiastic admiration.

Bishop Temple speaks of "*the* two theories of Evolution;" and what he does with the other two I do not know. He describes the one as that of La Place, and the other as that of Darwin; the former being a theory for the construction of the universe, and therefore by some called "Cosmical Evolution;" the other for the development of vegetable and animal life, and therefore termed "Biological Evolution."

To begin with the *Biological*. This is briefly stated by Bishop Temple [7a] in the words: "It cannot be denied that Darwin's investigations have made it extremely probable that the vast variety of plants and animals have sprung from a much smaller number of original forms." So Darwin, in his summary, [7b] writes: "The several classes of facts which have been considered in this chapter seem to me to proclaim so plainly that the innumerable species, genera, and families with which this world is peopled, are all descended, each within its own class or group, from common parents, and have all been modified in the course of descent, that I should without hesitation adopt this view, even if it were unsupported by other facts or arguments." I presume that there are very few amongst us who would differ materially from either of these statements; for both of them fully admit the original existence of a variety of common parents, which is, in fact, a complete surrender of the whole position; and Darwin limits the modifications in the course of descent to changes, "each within its own class or group." Now this is all for which the anti-evolutionist contends; for all admit most freely the existence of most marked variations within the circles of the various groups.

But, although in this passage there is this limitation, as a matter of fact there is a great deal more claimed by both writers for Evolution; for the title of Darwin's book, "The Origin of Species," shows very clearly that he applies his theory not merely to variations within species, but to the formation of the species within which these variations take place. I do not gather from his book that his theory goes so far as to suppose that either plants or animals have passed over from one species to another, both species being already in existence; but rather that through the power of "the struggle for existence," "natural selection," and "survival of the fittest," existing races have been so changed and modified that new species have been evolved out of them, and that in every such evolution there has been what evolutionists consider to be improvement.

The arguments which Bishop Temple adduces for this theory are—

(1) "The unity of plan which can be found pervading any great class of animals seems to point to unity of ancestry." [7c] He illustrates this by remarking that vertebrate animals are formed on a common plan.

(2) "Slight variations are perpetually being produced." [7d]

(3) "The frequent occurrence both in plants or animals of useless parts which still remain as indications of organs that once were useful, and have long become useless." [7e]

But is this scientific evidence? As to the 1st, the Bishop only claims for it that it "*seems* to point." As to the 2nd, it quietly assumes the whole point at issue, for no one denies that there are variations "within each class or group," and the fact that such variations exist within a certain class or group is no proof that they can extend beyond it. And as for the 3rd who knows that those that are called "useless parts" are really useless, though their use may not be known? And if they are useless now, what evidence is there that they were once useful, or were ever used? There is not the slightest scientific evidence in any one of these three points for the theory which they are adduced to support. There is not a single fact to prove the theory, and all that can be said by the most ardent advocate is that the conjecture seems to be probable. But how different is the evidence on the other side of the controversy! There we find certain clearly-defined and indisputable facts which cannot be doubted, and which cannot be reconciled with this new theory.

(1) *Biological Evolution.*

There cannot be a doubt that there are certain great classes of plants and animals found in the world, which have certain distinct characteristics, and which, as a matter of fact, do not merge into each other. There seems to be considerable variation in the names given to them, and they appear to be distinguished by the name sometimes of "species," sometimes of "genus," sometimes of "class or group," and sometimes of "kind." In the sentence quoted from Darwin on p. 6, he speaks of species, genera, and families; and describes them as being all descended each within its own class or group. This confusion of terms is difficult to reconcile with the boasted claim to scientific accuracy. That I may not be entangled by any questionable name I will distinguish these groups as A, B, C, D, etc., and our question is whether they have been evolved from each other or through each other, from a common stock; or whether they are separate creations. For the answer to this question let three facts be carefully considered.

(i.) There is the remarkable and clearly-established law of the sterility of all hybrids between any two of these great divisions. Both A and B may contain a great number of varieties, and all the varieties of A can breed freely with each other. In such case there is no failure of fertility in the progeny. The same is true of B and all the varieties that spring from it. If these varieties be expressed by the figures 1, 2, 3, etc., A1 may breed with A2, A3, or any other number, and so may introduce a fresh variety in the race A. But if A, or any variation of A, should breed with B, or any variation of B, there may be in the first instance a progeny; but there is a fixed and invariable law of nature that there should be no perpetuation of that progeny, for every individual so born is barren. Mules e.g., can never give birth to mules, and the mule race has no power of self-propagation. Now see how this bears on the subject of Evolution. If B were evolved out of A, there would, of course, be countless intermediate variations, and these variations would all have the power of perpetuating their kind. A would produce A1, A1 would produce A2, and so on, till A98 would produce A99, and, finally, to complete the series, A99 would produce A100, or B. But at this point, if the Evolution theory is to be reconciled with facts, a new and most strange law must be suddenly evolved; and the continuity of law must be broken. A98 may breed with A99, and their offspring may perpetuate their race; but if A99 should breed with A100, which is B, it is true there may be offspring, but that offspring will bare no power of self-perpetuation. How can evolutionism explain such a fracture in the continuity of law? And is not the scientific fact dead against the Evolution theory?

(ii.) As a matter of fact we do not find that continuous chain of intermediate links which the theory requires. The theory is, that as there are to be no sudden jumps in nature, the various numbers are evolved from each other in a vast series of almost imperceptible improvement; and it follows of necessity that, if the theory were true, instead of finding distinct classes, we should find various lines of progress stealing into each other in steps so minute that it would be very difficult to detect their differences. If, *e.g.*, man has been evolved from monkey there ought not to be a yawning chasm, as there now is, between the two, but there ought to be a vast series of connecting links bridging the chasm between monkeyism and manhood; and there ought to be a race of monkeys still existing so near to man in physical structure and mental power that the birth of man from such a parentage should be within the range of natural probability. Let A be monkey, and B man, then there ought to be a continuous line of intermediate numbers, and A99 ought to approximate so closely to B that it would be perfectly natural for B to be its child.

But where are these links to be found? and what naturalist can discover them? If the theory be true, the process must still be going on, and the world must be teeming with these intermediate races. But where are they? Bishop Temple as attempted to answer this question thus:

> If it be asked why this variety does not range by imperceptible degrees from extreme forms in one direction to extreme forms in the other, the answer is to be found in the enormous prodigality, and the equally enormous waste of life and living creatures . . . Eggs, and seeds, and germs are destroyed by millions, and so in a less but still enormous proportion are the young that come from those that have not been destroyed. There is no waste like the waste of life that is to be seen in nature . . . The inevitable operation of this waste, as Darwin's investigation showed, has been to destroy all those varieties which were not well fitted to their surroundings, and to keep those that were. (P. 165.)

But if this be the solution of the difficulty, how is it that those at the bottom of the scale remain? One of the great principle employed to explain the theory is "the survival of the fittest." The result therefore must be continuous progress, and the *raison d'être* of each successive formation is its superior fitness above the form from which it sprang. A1 survives because it is superior in fitness to A, and A2 because it is superior to A1, and so forth. The effect therefore of the Bishop's principle would be that the inferior forms at the bottom of the scale would perish, while the superior that have risen out of them, by reason of their greater adaptation to their environment, would survive. But this is not the fact. As a matter of fact, A, at the bottom of the scale, survives, though A99, at the top, is gone. The countless multitude of intermediate formations has disappeared, but the parent stock remains. If ever there was a race of animals so near man as to render it nothing more than natural that it should give birth to man, that race has wholly disappeared, while animals vastly inferior still exist in all their strength. Such a fact appears to me to be fatal to the theory.

(iii.) But the geological evidence is stronger still. If all these creatures have arisen in succession, and perished, we may well ask, "Where are their bones?" Each successive race, according to the theory, has been sufficiently powerful to overpower its predecessors, and to reproduce its own kind. It is clear, therefore, that we should naturally look for the geological remains of those once-powerful animals. But here we are met by the hard, stubborn, rocky fact, that there is no trace of them in the geological record. We find the remains of A, B, C, D, etc., but between them there is a complete hiatus; and if there were 1000 links between A and B, the geologist cannot show you one of them. He can show you A, and he can show you B; but as for A 20, 30, and 40, he can only tell you that they are not yet discovered. I know that some good Christian people are afraid of geology, and in that I believe they make a great mistake; for though I grant there may be danger in shallow, superficial, theoretical geology, I never can doubt that the real record of the rocks is in perfect harmony with the real record of Scripture. So, in this instance, it has furnished us with an unanswerable proof that the evolutionist theory is not founded in fact, and that nothing has yet been discovered in the geological record to shake our confidence in the grand, old, Scriptural statement, "God made the beast of the earth after its kind, and the cattle after their kind, and everything that creepeth upon the ground after its kind: and God saw that it was good." We all know that it is not the object of the Book of Genesis to teach science; and some, I grieve to think, are not afraid of calling it a myth, or even a poem for the childhood of the world; but I venture to affirm that the statement of the Inspired Book which describes each kind as a separate creation is more in accordance with well-known geological facts, and is therefore more scientifically accurate than the theories of those who adopt the conjecture that the various kinds, species, or groups evolved themselves either from each other or from a common stock.

(2) ***Cosmical Evolution.***

But if this be the case with Biological Evolution, how is it with Cosmical Evolution, or the evolution of inanimate matter? Bishop Temple describes it as "that which begins with Laplace, and explains the way in which the earth was fitted to be the habitation of living creatures;" [11a] and again he says: [11b]

> It cannot, then, be well denied that the astronomers and geologists here made it exceedingly probable that this earth on which we live has been brought to its present condition by passing through a succession of changes from an original state of great heat and fluidity, perhaps even from a mixture mainly consisting of gases; that such a body as the planet Jupiter represents one of the stages through which it has passed; that such a body as the moon represents a stage toward which it is tending; that it has shrank as it cooled, and as it shrank formed the elevations which we call mountains, and the depressions which contain the seas and oceans; that it has been worn by the action of heat from within and water from without, and in consequence of this action presents the appearance when examined below the surface of successive strata or layers; that different kinds of animal and vegetable life have followed one another on the surface, and that some of their remains are found in these strata now: and that all this has taken enormous periods of time. All this is exceedingly probable, because it is the way in which, as Laplace first pointed out, under well established scientific laws of matter, particularly the law of gravitation and the law of the radiation of heat, a great fluid mass would naturally change.

There is nothing in that explanation to militate against the Scriptural accounts of the formation of the present world; and it may have pleased God to make use of the laws of gravitation and radiation of heat in order to bring our world into its present form. But the structure of the earth is not all, or nearly all.

There is found on the earth, and within it, an infinite variety of substances. There are metals; such as gold, silver, lead, iron, etc. There are precious stones of gorgeous beauty, diamonds, rubies, etc., etc. There is vegetable matter of every description, from the tenderest blade of grass to the hard wood of the forest oak. And there are animals of all classes and all characters, from the lowest mollusk to the most perfect and elaborate vertebrate. And the question is, What made them? Were they produced by the cooling of the earth? Was it gravitation or radiation that made the gold, the ruby, the fern, the oak, the animal, and the water?

But in addition to these various substances, the world abounds with what we call "Laws." There are the laws of electricity, of heat, of chemistry, of force, of motion, etc.; besides those to which all these great changes are ascribed, the laws of heat and gravitation—and, What made them? Are they all the result of the cooling of the earth? Was one mass of fluid matter cooled into iron, one into gold, one into wood, and one into flesh? and did they all evolve from themselves by some mysterious power, those wonderful laws of nature to which they are all subject and which they all obey? In their case there was no "struggle for existence," no "survival of the fittest," and no "natural selection"—no thought, no mind, no design, and no plan in themselves; and it is indeed hard to suppose that they not only evolved themselves, but also evolved laws of such marvellous subtlety and power, that their discovery and use form the greatest achievement of modern science.

It may perhaps interest some to know how it is all supposed to have been done, and as Mr. Herbert Spencer appears to be the great apostle of the theory, I will give, in his own words, the conclusion of his elaborate argument. In "First Principles" (p. 396) he gives his great conclusion, and prints it in italics that there may be no mistake as to its vast importance: "Evolution," he says, "is an integration of matter and concomitant dissipation of motion, during which the matter passes from an indefinite, incoherent homogeneity to a definite, coherent heterogeneity, and during which the retained motion undergoes a parallel transformation." Is it for such as that that we are to give up our faith in the creation of God?

But this is not all, for not merely is the earth filled with various substances, and governed by various laws; but there is a third element for which even Mr. Spencer's definition fails to account, and that is life. There is life abounding everywhere; but what science can tell us either what it is or whence it came? Was it produced either by gravitation or radiation? Did the cooling of the earth produce life on its surface? I know no greater evidence of the utter failure of the evolutionist theory than the suggestion made on one occasion (I think in an inaugural address to the British Association), that life came in a meteoric stone from some already formed habitable world. With reference to such an idea it is enough to ask four questions. How did it get into that other world? How did it attach itself to the meteoric stone? How did it survive the awful blow which it must have experienced when it struck the earth? and how did it spread itself when it found itself alone in the utter loneliness of an uninhabited world? Such is the theory of those who would struggle to create a world without a God; and I venture to affirm that there is infinitely more true science in the words, "All things were made by Him, and without Him was not anything made that was made. In Him was life, and the life was the light of men."

But, though I have thus followed Bishop Temple in his twofold division of the theory of Evolution, there is another twofold division which I regard as of incomparably greater importance. I refer to the Theistic and Atheistic theory.

I. There is a Theistic theory, for there can be no doubt whatever that many of those who accept the Evolution theory hold it in the firm belief in the creative power of a self-existing Creator. Bishop Temple, *e.g.*, states the question thus:

> In the one case the Creator made the animals at once such as they now are; in the other case He impressed on certain particles of matter, which either at the beginning or at some point in the history of His creation He endowed with life, such inherent powers that in the ordinary course of time living creatures such as the present were developed. The creative power remains the same in either case. [13]

For my own part, I should be almost disposed to consider that the creative power was the greater on the theory of Evolution; for to make a germ which should evolve itself into all the countless varieties, both of animate and inanimate existence, is, if possible, a greater miracle than the creation of each separate species. There is great skill shown in the manufacture both of a railway train and a steamboat, but the skill would be of a much higher order if a person were to construct a train with its engine and all its carriages, and impart to it the remarkable property that when it arrived at the sea-coast it should of itself without the action of man, turn itself into a steamboat.

Thus a person may hold the Evolution theory to its fullest extent without entertaining the slightest doubt as to the creative power of our God. Indeed, Bishop Temple says:

> The doctrine of Evolution leaves the argument for an intelligent Creator and Governor of the world stronger than it was before. There is still as much as ever the proof of an intelligent purpose pervading all creation. The difference is that the execution of that purpose belongs more to the original act of creation, less to acts of government since. There is more Divine foresight, there is less Divine interposition; and whatever has been taken from the latter has been added to the former. (P. 122.)

There is such a joy in the blessed assurance of Divine interposition, and it seems so clearly taught in Scripture, that it is impossible to regard without the utmost jealousy the suggestion of even such a transfer as that described in these words. But still, however greatly we may regret the theory, we are bound in justice to recognise the fact that those who hold it may believe in a Creator God with a faith as firm and unshaken as that which brings peace to our own souls.

I cannot refrain from adding that this was the view of Darwin himself. He has been claimed as an ally by those who deny the creation of God; so that it is most satisfactory to read such a passage as that with which his book concludes:

> There is grandeur in this view of life, with its several powers, having been originally breathed BY THE CREATOR into a few forms or into one; and that whilst this planet has gone cycling on according to the fixed law of gravity, from so simple a beginning endless forms, most beautiful and most wonderful, have been and are being evolved. (P. 429.)

We may wholly differ from him in his theory of Evolution, but we rejoice to agree with him in the conviction that life, was originally breathed forth by the Creator.

2. But there is also an Atheistic theory of Evolution, which does, in fact, substitute Evolution for God. The doctrine of Evolution is used, according to Bishop Temple, "to prove that no intelligence planned the world." The theory seems to be that through the power of certain laws the original atoms have gradually evolved themselves into all the beauties and endless varieties of this thickly-peopled world. It is pitiable to see the hopeless shifts to which intelligent men are driven in order to maintain such a theory. They are compelled to face the questions, "Whence came the atoms? and now did the laws originate?" And Mr. Herbert Spencer for an answer to such questions is compelled to resort to what he terms "The Persistence of Force." We might push the inquiry one step farther, and inquire what was the origin of this Persistence of Force? and we cannot but wonder that a man who is considered one of the great thinkers of the age should not be compelled, when thus driven into a corner, to acknowledge with candour that his persistent force is nothing less than the omnipotence of God. But no, he cannot admit the existence of a God, and in a note on p. 192 of his "First Principles," he actually tells us that he and Professor Huxley invented the term "Persistence of Force," instead of what used to be the term employed, "Conservation of Force," because "Conservation implies a Conserver," and that he denies. Thus his theory of Evolution is employed to show how the world evolved itself without the interference of a Creator, or even a Conserver of Force. The whole thing is supposed to have been done without design, without plan, without intelligence, without skill, and in fact without any action of mind or intelligent power. The whole is supposed to be the result of certain unintelligent laws, not ordained by any Lawgiver, or carried out by any Conserver. In other words, the Evolution theory is the Atheist's substitute for God.

Now surely, if this be the case, those who write and speak in favour of the Evolution theory ought to be much more careful than some of them have been in defining what they are speaking of. Some of them speak of "the doctrine of Evolution," as if there was only one doctrine, and some speak in most rapturous terms of its most extraordinary value—as, *e.g.*, when Mr. Drummond said in Grosvenor House that "It was the Great thought of the century, perhaps the greatest the world has ever found out;" but surely when they do so they are bound to tell us what they mean. Do they mean simply growth? or progression? or variation within species? Or do they mean evolution from species to species? or the evolution of the inanimate world? On such points there ought to be a clear and unmistakable definition. Above all, do they mean an evolution by God, or without Him? An evolution by the design of a divine Person, or by "Persistence of Force," whatever that may be? "Evolution," in the vocabulary of Mr. Spencer and his followers, means nothing less than a theory for the formation of the world and all things therein, without the action or design of a personal Creator; and surely it is to be deeply deplored that Christian advocates should employ exactly the same term without the slightest caution or protest. I do not say that in their writings there are no passages which, if carefully collected and spliced together, may indicate what they mean. But what I maintain is, that as the word "Evolution" is employed by them to express the mode according to which our Heavenly Father has formed the whole creation, both animate and inanimate, and by Atheists to express the mode by which the world is supposed to have formed itself, they ought not to use the word without making it as clear as the sun in heaven in what sense they employ it. They may speak of "Evolution" as the great scientific theory of the day, or as the greatest achievement of the age, and unless they are much more careful than some have been, their authority may be quoted as endorsing the theory invented by Atheists and maintained by them in support of their Atheism. Men's minds are governed by words, and surely we have a right to ask of those who glory in scientific accuracy that they should clearly define what they mean, and not leave their unscientific readers to discover, as best they may, whether they wish us to believe in self-evolution or Divine formation; in a self-evolution by Persistence of Force, or in a marvellous creation by the design, the skill, and the omnipotence of God. If they write about Evolution in the loose way in which some have done lately while they appear to speak with admiration of Mr. Herbert Spencer's philosophy, they cannot be surprised if they are regarded as teaching his Evolution theory, and if the effect of their writing is to weaken faith and strengthen Atheism.

But let no one suppose for one moment that, because we deplore the loose, inaccurate, and unscientific manner in which some of those who glory in their scientific accuracy appear to confound fact and theory, on that account we undervalue scientific investigations, or think lightly of scientific facts. In proof of this I would conclude this paper by an extract from the writings of a truly scientific investigator, the late Mr. F. Buckland, who writes:

> Of late years, the doctrines of so-called Evolution and Development have seemingly gained ground among those interested in natural history; but to put matters very straight, I steadfastly believe that the Great Creator, as indeed we are directly told, made all things perfect and "very good" from the beginning; perfect and very good every created thing is now found to be, and will so continue to the end. I am very willing to prove my case, by holding a court at any time or place, before any number of people of any class. I would impanel a jury of the most eminent and skilful railway and mechanical engineers, while the only witnesses I should call would be the fish fresh from the deep-sea trawler, the city fish market, or the fishmonger's slab: I would adduce from them evidence of "design, beauty, and order," as evinced in such as the electric organs of the torpedo, the gun-lock spine of the file-fish, the water-reservoir and spectacles of the eel, the teeth of the gilt-head bream, the anchor of the lump-sucker and remora, the colouring of the perch and bleak, the ichthyophagous teeth of the pike, shark, and silvery hair-tail; the tail of the fox shark, the prehensile lips of the dory and sprat, the nose of the barbel and dogfish, the resplendence of the arctic gymnetrus and scabbard-fish, the dagger in the tail of the sting-ray, the nest of the stickleback, the armour-plates of the sturgeon, the nostril-breathing powers and store of fat in the salmon; migrations of the salmon, herring, pilchard, sprat, and mackerel; and, above all, the enormous fertility of fishes useful as food to the human race. I am satisfied that I should obtain a verdict in favour of my view of the case, namely, that in all these wonderful contrivances there exists evidence of design and forethought, and a wondrous adaptation of means to an end. (*Life*, p. 424.)

FOOTNOTES.

[3] Address in Grosvenor House, May 3, 1885.

[5a] May 3, 1885.

[5b] In the *Christian Commonwealth*.

[6a] "Bampton Lectures," p. 162.

[6b] *Ibid.* p. 167.

[7a] "Bampton Lectures," p. 164.

[7b] "Origin of Species," p. 403.

[7c] "Bampton Lectures," p. 164.

[7d] *Ibid.* p. 164.

[7e] *Ibid.*, p. 166.

[11a] P. 167.

[11b] P. 162.

[13] "Lectures," p. 114.

CPSIA information can be obtained
at www.ICGtesting.com
Printed in the USA
LVHW090257171121
703363LV00007B/429

9 789355 115232

The Doors of Death

Arthur B. Waltermire

Alpha Editions

This edition published in 2021

ISBN : 9789355114495

Design and Setting By
Alpha Editions
www.alphaedis.com
Email - info@alphaedis.com

The Doors of Death

A strange and curious story is this, about a banker whose only fear was that he might be buried alive, like his grandfather before him

A heavy stillness hung about the great halls and richly furnished rooms of Judson McMasters' residence, and even seemed to extend out over the velvet lawns, the shrub-lined walks and sun-blotched reaches under the lacy elms and somber maples.

Biggs glided about the sick-chamber like a specter, apparently striving to keep busy, while he cast countless furtive, uneasy glances at the heavy figure under the white sheets. An odor of drugs and fever tainted the air, and a small walnut table near the flushed sleeper was laden with the familiar prescription bottle, tumbler and box of powders. On the wall behind the table, near the head of the bed, hung a small oil-painting of Napoleon.

The sleeper stirred restlessly, raised himself painfully and slowly, and attempted to seek fleeting comfort in a new position. At the first movement Biggs was a shadow at the bedside, deftly manipulating the coverings and gently aiding the sick man with a tenderness born of long service and deep affection. As the massive gray head sank into the fluffed pillow the tired eyes opened, lighted by a faint glint of thankfulness. Then they closed again and the once powerful body relaxed.

With a pitiful, wistful expression on his aged face, the faithful Biggs stood helplessly peering at the sick man until hot tears began to course down his furrowed cheeks, and he turned hastily away.

"Biggs!"

The voice, still strong and commanding, cut the semi-gloom like a knife.

Biggs, who was about to tuck the heavy curtains still more securely over the windows, whirled as though he had touched a live wire, and in a flash was across the great room and beside the bed.

"Did you call, sir?" His voice quavered.

"No"—a faint twinkle lighted the sick man's eyes—"I just spoke."

"Ah, now sir," cried the overjoyed Biggs, "you are better, sir."

"Biggs, I want some air and sunshine."

"But the doctor, sir——"

"Drat the doctor! If I'm going to pass out I want to see where I'm going."

"Oh, but sir," expostulated the old servant, as he parted the curtains and partially opened a casement window, "I wish you wouldn't say that, sir."

"I believe in facing a situation squarely, Biggs. My father and grandfather died from this family malady, and I guess I'm headed over the same route."

"Please, sir," entreated Biggs.

"Biggs, I want to ask you a question."

"Yes, sir?"

"Are you a Christian?"

"I try to be, sir."

"Do you believe in death?"

Biggs was thoroughly startled and confused.

"Why—a—we all have to die, sometime, sir," he answered haltingly, not knowing what else to say.

"But do we actually die?" insisted the sufferer.

"Well, I hope—not yet," ventured the old servant. "The doctor said——"

"Forget the doctor," interposed McMasters. "Biggs, you have been in our service since I was a lad, haven't you?"

Tears welled into the servant's eyes, and his voice faltered.

"Fifty-six years, come next November," he answered.

"Well, let me tell you something, that even in those fifty-six years you never learned, Biggs. My grandfather was buried alive!"

"Oh, sir! Impossible!" cried Biggs, in horror.

"Absolutely," asserted the banker.

"Why—are you—how do you know, sir?" in a hoarse whisper.

"My father built a family mausoleum in the far corner of this estate, didn't he?"

"Yes, sir—he hated burial in the earth, sir, after reading a poem of Edgar Allan Poe's, sir!"

"What poem was that, Biggs?"

"I don't recall the name of it, but I remember the line," faltered Biggs.

"What was it?"

"Oh, sir," cried the old man, "let's talk about something cheerful."

"Not until we're through with this discussion, Hiram."

The sound of his given name restored Biggs somewhat, for the banker resorted to it only on occasions when he shared his deepest confidences with his old houseman.

"Well, the line goes, 'Soft may the worms about him creep,' sir."

A slight shudder seemed to run through McMasters' body. Then after a tomb-like silence, "Good reason for building the mausoleum."

"Yes, sir, I think so, sir."

"Well," with an apparent effort, "when they exhumed my grandfather's remains to place them in the new vault, the casket was opened, and——"

"Oh, sir," cried Biggs, throwing out a trembling, expostulating hand, but the banker went on, relentlessly.

"——the body was turned over, on its side, with the left knee drawn up part-way."

"That's the way he always slept—in life." Biggs' voice was a hollow whisper.

"And that's the reason my father, after building himself a mausoleum, insisted that his body be cremated," said McMasters. "He took no chances."

Biggs' horrified eyes traveled dully to the massive urn over the great fireplace and rested there, fascinated.

"Hiram, where is heaven?"

Biggs' eyes flitted back to rest in surprize upon the questioner.

"Why, up there, sir," pointing toward the ceiling.

"Do you believe that the earth rotates on its axis?"

"That's what I was taught in school, sir."

"If that hypothesis is true, we are rolling through space at the rate of about sixteen miles a minute," figured the banker. "Now you say heaven is up there."

"Yes, sir."

"Biggs, what time is it?"

The servant glanced at the great clock in the corner.

"Ah, it's twelve o'clock, sir, and time for your medicine," in a voice full of relief.

"Never mind the drugs," commanded McMasters, "until we finish our problem in higher mathematics. Now, if I ask you where heaven is at midnight, which will be twelve hours from now, where will you point," triumphantly.

"Why, up there," replied the bewildered servant, again indicating the ceiling.

"Then," cried McMasters, "you will be pointing directly opposite from the place you indicated a moment ago; for by midnight the earth will have turned approximately upside down. Do you get my point?"

"Yes, sir," replied poor Biggs, thoroughly befuddled.

"Then where will heaven be at six o'clock this evening?" fairly shouted the sick man.

"Out there," replied the servant, hopelessly, pointing toward the window.

"And where will heaven be at six o'clock in the morning?"

"Over there." And Biggs pointed a trembling finger at the fireplace. Then, "Oh, sir, let's not—the doctor——"

"Hang the doctor," interrupted McMasters testily. "I've been thinking this thing over, and I've got to talk about it to someone."

"But don't you believe in a hereafter?" queried Biggs, a horrible note of fear in his pitiful voice.

For a moment the banker was silent; the massive clock ticked solemnly on. A coal toppled with a sputter and flare in the fireplace.

"Yes, Hiram," in a thoughtful voice, "I suppose I do."

"I'm glad to hear you say that," cried Biggs in very evident relief.

"Ah, if you could but tell me," continued the banker, "from whence we come, and whither we go?"

"If I knew, sir, I'd be equal with the Creator," answered Biggs with reverence.

"That's well said, Hiram, but it doesn't satisfy me. I've made my place in the world by getting to the root of things. Ah, if I could only get a peek behind the curtain, before I go—back-stage, you know—mayhap I would not be afraid to die," and his voice fell almost to a whisper.

"The Great Director does not permit the audience behind the footlights, unless he calls them," answered Biggs whimsically, the ghost of a smile lighting up his troubled features.

"Another thing, Biggs, do you believe those stories about Jonah, and Lazarus, and the fellow they let down through a hole in the roof to be healed?"

"I do, sir," with conviction.

"Do you understand how it was done?" testily.

"Of course not, sir, being only a human."

"Then tell me, Hiram, when you cannot see through it, how can you swallow all this theology?"

"My faith, sir," answered Biggs, simply, raising his eyes with reverence.

At this, a quizzical smile came over the sick man's face.

"In looking up, Hiram, don't forget, since it is twelve-thirty, that we have swung around four hundred and eighty miles from the spot you originally designated as the location of the Pearly Gates."

"Oh, sir, I beg of you," remonstrated the servant, "I cannot bear to have you jest on such a—why, master!" he broke off with a little cry, rushing to his bedside.

The quizzical smile on the banker's face had suddenly faded, and his head had fallen feebly back upon the pillow.

"Oh, why did he waste his strength so?" cried Biggs, piteously, as with trembling hands and tear-blurred eyes he searched the little table for the smelling-salts.

After a few breaths, the patient sighed and opened his eyes wearily.

"My medicine, Hiram, and then I must rest."

At midnight, Biggs, dozing in a big chair by the fire, was aroused by a voice from the sick bed.

"Hiram."

"Yes, sir," scurrying to turn on a subdued light.

"Where is heaven now?"

Noting the wan flicker of a smile, the old servant pointed solemnly downward.

"You are a bright pupil," came in a scarcely audible voice.

"Thank you, sir."

"Do you know, Biggs, I wish I had led a different—a better life."

"You have been a good master, sir. You have been kind, you have given liberally to charity," Biggs defended him.

"Yes," cynically, "I have given liberally to charity. But it has been no sacrifice."

"You have been a pillar in the church," ventured Biggs.

"Yes," bitterly, "a stone pillar. I have paid handsomely for my pew, and slept peacefully through the sermons. I have bought baskets of food for the poor at Thanksgiving and Christmas time, only to let others reap the happiness of giving them away. I could have had so much joy out of Christmas, if I would. I could have been a jolly, rosy-cheeked Santa Claus and gone to a hundred homes, my arms loaded with gifts."

"True, sir, but you made that joy possible for others."

"When I should have known the thrill of it myself. I have not really lived, Hiram. To draw the sweets truly out of life, one must humble himself and serve his fellow men. Yes, the scales have fallen from my eyes, Hiram. But it is too late, 'the spirit is willing but the flesh is weak'."

"It doesn't seem right, sir," said Biggs after a pause.

"What's that, Hiram?"

"Why, sir, that you should be stricken down in the prime of life, just at a time when you could mean so much to others, while I, old and useless, am permitted to live on. But I am not finding fault with Providence, sir," Biggs hastened to say; "I just can't find the meaning of the riddle, sir."

"Probably I've had my chance and fumbled it, Biggs."

"Even so, sir, God is not vindictive, according to my ideas. There surely is some other solution. I'm still going to pray that He will take me in your stead, even if a miracle must be performed."

"So you have faith in your prayers, do you, Biggs?"

"Yes, sir, if they are unselfish prayers."

"That brand is rather scarce, I take it," answered McMasters, but his tone was reflective rather than sarcastic.

"Oh, sir, I wish you would pray as I do. God would surely understand."

"Rather a queer request, Hiram. If my life depends upon your death no prayer shall ever pass my lips."

"But, sir, I'm an old——"

"However," interrupted McMasters, "I shall pray that if my life is spared in any other fashion, I will make full amends for my years of indifference and neglect. And, Hiram, no one knows how much I truly seek this divine dispensation. But I have always scoffed at death-bed confessions, and so my heart grows cold, for I have no right to ask—now." Again, wearily, "No right—now."

"Ah, master, God is plenteous in mercy. If you but have the faith, sir, it shall make you whole."

"Very good, had I lived as you have lived, Biggs." Then, after a pause, "Still, the cause is worthy, my heart is right and I shall approach the Throne. May God be merciful unto me, a sinner."

"I hope it is not too late yet," faltered Biggs. "Oh, if God would only call me in your stead, that you might still do the good work that you find it in your heart to do, how gladly would I go."

A deep sigh was his only answer.

A long silence was finally broken by the sick man. But when he spoke, his voice was so strange and uncanny that the servant hastened close and peered anxiously into the fever-flushed face of the sufferer.

"Hiram—I must tell you—a secret," came in a laborious, almost sepulchral, whisper.

Biggs came closer.

"Bring a chair and sit down. I must talk to you."

As the old servant again leaned forward, the sufferer hesitated; then with an obvious effort he began.

"Hiram, I am going to give you some instructions which you must obey to the letter. Will you promise to keep them?"

"I swear it, sir," with great earnestness.

"Good! Now, if this fever seals my lips and the doctor pronounces me dead——"

"Please, sir," Biggs broke in, tears streaming down his furrowed cheeks, but his master continued in the same subdued voice, "Whatever happens, I am not to be embalmed—do you hear me?—not embalmed, but just laid away as I am now."

"Yes, sir," in a choked voice, which fully betrayed the breaking heart behind it.

"And now, Hiram, the rest of the secret." He paused and beckoned Biggs to lean closer.

"In my vault—in the mausoleum, I have had an electric button installed. That button connects with a silver bell. Lift up that small picture of Napoleon, there upon the wall."

His hands trembling as with the palsy, Biggs reached out and lifted aside the picture hanging near the head of the bed, and there revealed the silver bell, fitted into a small aperture in the wall. Then, with a sob, he fell back into his chair.

"Hiram"—in a whisper—"after they bury me, you are to sleep in this bed."

With a cry, the old man threw out a horrified, expostulating hand. Catching it feverishly, the banker half raised himself in bed.

"Don't you understand?" he cried fiercely. "I may not be dead after all. Remember grandfather! And Biggs—if that bell rings, get help—quick!"

Suddenly releasing his hold, McMasters fell back limply among the pillows.

All through the long night the faithful Biggs maintained a sleepless vigil, but the banker lay as immovable as a stone. When the rosy-cheeked dawn came peeping audaciously through the casements, Biggs drew the heavy curtains tightly shut once more.

Not until the doctor's motor whirled away did the patient rouse from his lethargy.

Apparently strengthened by his deep stupor he spoke, and Biggs stood instantly beside him.

"What did the doctor say?"

Biggs hesitated.

"Out with it, I'm no chicken-hearted weakling."

"Nothing much," admitted Biggs, sadly. "He only shook his head very gravely."

"He doesn't understand this family malady any more than the old quack who allowed my grandfather to be buried alive," said McMasters almost fiercely.

Biggs shuddered and put a trembling hand to his eyes.

"What ails me, Biggs?" almost plaintively. "No one knows. This fever has baffled the scientists for years. When you fall into a comatose condition they call it suspended animation. That's the best thing they do—find names for diseases. My family doctor doesn't have any more of an idea about this malady than you or I. The average physician is just a guesser. He guesses you have a fever and prescribes a remedy, hoping that it will hit the spot. If it doesn't he looks wise, wags his head—and tries something else on you. Maybe it works and maybe it doesn't. The only thing my guesser is absolutely sure of is that if I live or if I die, he will collect a princely fee for his services."

Biggs remained statuesque during the pause.

"Gad," McMasters broke out again testily, "if I fiddled around in my business like that I'd be a pauper in a month."

"But the doctor says you're coming on," ventured Biggs.

"Sure he does," answered the banker with a sneer. "That's his stock in trade. I know that line of palaver. Secretly, he knows I am as liable to be dead as alive when he comes again."

"Oh, sir, you aren't going to die!"

"That's what I'm afraid of, Biggs. But they'll call me dead and go ahead and embalm me and make sure of it."

"Oh, sir, I wish——"

"Now remember, Biggs," broke in the sick man, "shoot the first undertaker that tries to put that mummy stuff in my veins."

"I understand perfectly, sir," answered Biggs, fearful lest the other's excitement might again give him a turn for the worse.

"I know I'm apparently going to pass away. My father and grandfather both had this cussed virus in their veins, and I don't believe either of them was dead when he was pronounced so!"

"Well, if by any chance—that is, if you," began Biggs desperately, "if you are apparently—dead—why not have them keep your body here in the house for a time?"

"Convention, formality, custom, hide-bound law!" the banker fairly frothed. "The health authorities would come here with an army and see that I was buried. No, Biggs, I've got a fine crypt out there, all quiet and secure, good ventilation, electric lights, like a pullman berth—and a push-button. That precludes all notoriety. It's secret and safe. The electrician who installed the apparatus died four years ago. So you and I, alone, possess this knowledge."

"Don't you think someone else should know of it too? Your attorney, or——"

"No, Biggs. If I really am dead I don't want anyone to write up my eccentricities for some Sunday magazine sheet. And if I do come back, then it will be time to tell the gaping public about my cleverness."

"I wish you weren't so—so cold-blooded about it all, sir."

"I have always hit straight from the shoulder, Hiram, and I'm facing this death business as I'd face any other proposition. I'm not ready to cash in, and if I can cheat the doctors, undertakers, lawyers, heirs, and chief mourners for a few more years, I'm going to do it. And don't forget poor old granddad. He might have been up and about yet had he but used my scheme."

Biggs turned away, sick at heart. It was too terrible beyond words. To him his religion was as essential as daily bread. Death was the culmination of cherished belief and constant prayer. As his years declined he had faced the inevitable day with simple faith that when the summons came he would go gladly, like him "who wraps the drapery of his couch about him and lies down to pleasant dreams." With throbbing heart he listened for another torrent of words that would still further stab his sensitive soul; for he had loved and revered his master from his youth up.

But no words came. He wheeled about. The massive head had fallen limply among the pillows. Pallid lips were trying to form sentences without result. Then the great body seemed to subside immeasurably deeper into the covers and a death-like stillness fell upon the room.

Intuitively feeling that his master was worse than at any previous relapse, Biggs made every effort to revive him, gently at first, and then by vigorously shaking and calling to him in a heart-broken, piteous voice. But to no avail. The heavy figure looked pallid and corpse-like under the snowy sheets.

Long hours dragged by, and still the lonely old servant sat mutely beside the bed, only aroused, at last, by the peremptory, measured call of the telephone bell.

"Yes," said Biggs in a quavering voice. "Oh yes, Doctor Meredith, Master's resting easy. Don't think you'll need to come until tomorrow."

"I'll keep them away as long as I can," he muttered, as he slipped back to his vigil. "God grant—maybe he'll come back—and take up the work of the Master, so long delayed. Oh God! If Thou wouldst only take me in his stead!"

Sleeping fitfully, Biggs sat dumbly through an interminable night, but the new day brought no reassuring sign from the inert form. The stillness was appalling. The other servants were quartered in a distant part of the mansion and only came when summoned. Again Biggs assured the physician that he could gain nothing by calling, and another awful night found him, ashen and distraught, at the bedside. Sometime in the still watches he swooned and kindly nature patched up his shredded nerves, before consciousness once more aroused him. But the strain was more than he could bear. So when the anxious specialist came, unbidden, he found a shattered old watchman who broke down completely and babbled forth the whole mysterious tale, concealing nothing but the secret of the tomb.

In a coffin previously made to order, they laid the unembalmed remains of Judson McMasters in the family mausoleum, and the world which had felt his masterful presence for so many years paused long enough to lay a costly tribute on his bier and then went smoothly on its way.

Not so with the faithful Biggs. Ensconced in his master's bedroom, he nightly tossed in troubled sleep, filled with the jangling of innumerable electric bells. And when—on the tenth night, after he had been somewhat reassured that all was well—he was suddenly awakened by a mad, incessant ringing from the hidden alarm, a deathly weakness overcame him and it was some time before he was able to drag his palsied body from the bed. With fumbling, clumsy fingers he tried to hasten, but it was many minutes before he tottered, half dressed, out of the room. And as he did so, his heart almost stood still, then mounted to his throat as if to choke him.

"Biggs!"—a voice—McMaster's voice was calling.

He staggered to the head of the wide, massive stairway and looked down. There stood the banker, pale, emaciated, but smiling.

And then, as from an endless distance, came more words:

"I forgot to tell you that I had a trap-door in the end of the casket. When you didn't answer the bell, I found I could come alone."

With an inarticulate cry, Biggs stretched out his trembling arms.

"My Master, I am coming now."

Then he swayed, stumbled, clutched feebly at the rail and plunged headlong to the foot of the stairs, a crumpled, lifeless form.

CPSIA information can be obtained
at www.ICGtesting.com
Printed in the USA
LVHW090257171121
703363LV00007B/430

9 789355 114495